Kuria Cattle Raiders

"The dominating question with regard to the Tarime native administration is cattle theft and its farreaching consequences."

Hans Cory, 1945

Kuria Cattle Raiders

Violence and Vigilantism on the Tanzania/Kenya Frontier

Michael L. Fleisher

Ann Arbor

THE UNIVERSITY OF MICHIGAN PRESS

2003   2002   2001   2000   4   3   2   1

A CIP catalog record for this book is available from the British Library.

Fleisher, Michael L., 1942–
    Kuria cattle raiders : violence and vigilantism on the Tanzania/Kenya frontier
/ Michael L. Fleisher.
        p. cm.
    Includes bibliographical references and index.
    ISBN 0-472-11152-3 (cloth : alk. paper) — ISBN 0-472-08698-7
(pbk. : alk. paper)
    1. Kuria (African people)—Domestic animals.   2. Kuria (African people)—
Social conditions.   3. Kuria (African people)—Economic conditions.
4. Cattle herders—Kenya.   5. Cattle herders—Tanzania.   6. Cattle stealing—
Kenya.   7. Cattle stealing—Tanzania.   8. Kenya—Social conditions.
9. Tanzania—Social conditions.   I. Title.

DT433.545.K87 F54   2000
967.62'004'96395—dc21   00-031521

*For my mother and father
and the memory of my stepfather*

Contents

Illustrations

Maps

Tables

Acknowledgments

In common with every other person who has ever done this kind of work, I am indebted to a great many extraordinary people. It would be folly even to attempt to list them all. Nonetheless, and with profuse apologies to anyone I may unintentionally have neglected to include, I would like to dedicate this space to expressing my lasting gratitude to A. O. Anacleti, Brian Barrons, Andrea Bierstein, Boniface Byarufu, Russell Carley, Emmanuel Chacha, Lucas Chacha, Maswi Chacha, James Conard, Kim and Stephanie Crutchfield, Tinka Dalali, Julius Dionis, Martin Fleisher, Anne and Pat Fleuret, Francis Flynn, Thomas Fricke, Rohan Halfpenny, Dominique Hoppe, Robert Jalbert, Masanda Joram, Bwire Kaare, Magai Kaare, Timothy Kaare, Festo Kapere, Raymond Kelly, Conrad Kottak, Kimberly Lucas, Aloysius Magabe, Edward Marwa Makuri, David Michelinie, Nell Moskowitz, Gabriel Polo Mrema, Gabreli Mshanga, Evans Mugaka, Pascal F. Mujuni, Ahmad A. Ng'wala, Monica Ghati Nyambali, Elias Nyangi, C. K. Omari, Miroslava Prazak, Barbara Price, Diana Putman, Carroll Rajabu, Elijah Sere, John Sivalon, Michael Snyder, Lucine Taminian, Patrick West, Hudson Winani, Peter Winani, Tricia Woodbury, and Julius A. Zedekiah.

To the people of Nyaheiya, who filled my time among them with meaning, exhilaration, and wonder, my debt of gratitude is incalculable.

Grateful acknowledgment is also owing to the National Science Foundation, the Mellon Foundation, and CIESIN (Consortium for an International Earth Science Information Network), institutions that, through their generous support, made possible the field research on which this book is based. Portions of this text are revised from published articles. "Cattle Raiding and Its Correlates: The Cultural-Ecological Consequences of Market-Oriented Cattle Raiding Among the Kuria of Tanzania," *Human Ecology* 26 (4): 547–72, courtesy Plenum Press; and *Africa: Journal of the International African Institute* 69, no. 2 (1999): 238–55.

I would like also to express my warmest, profoundest thanks to the people and the government of Tanzania, and particularly to the Tanzania Commission for Science and Technology, for granting me permission to carry out this research and for extending me their unfailing hospitality and kindness during my stay in one of the world's most gloriously beautiful countries.

CHAPTER 1

Introduction

The book that you are about to read is about cattle raiding as practiced—both historically and in the present day—by the Kuria people, a tribe[1] of Bantu-language-speaking agropastoralists whose population straddles the border between Tanzania and Kenya. Based on field research carried out over a nineteen-month period—from August 1994 to March 1996—in a Kuria village of the Nyamongo clan in the Tarime District lowlands of northern Tanzania, it endeavors to document and analyze an extraordinary transformation in the nature of Kuria cattle raiding that has occurred over the course of the past century, from the raiding of other tribes and other Kuria clans for prestige and bridewealth cattle to the highly organized, cash-market-oriented cattle raiding, carried out by heavily armed multiclan and multiethnic gangs, that is taking place today—the consequence, it is argued here, of the penetration and evolution of the colonial economy in the region and of the administrative policies of the postcolonial Tanzanian state.

The reciprocal raiding of cattle by pastoralists has a long and venerable history in East Africa, and it is discussed, albeit usually briefly, in many ethnographies (e.g., Evans-Pritchard 1940; Huntingford 1953; Ruel 1959; Dyson-Hudson 1966; Turnbull 1972; Spencer 1973; Moore and Puritt 1977). But there has been no book-length treatment of East African cattle raiding and, more importantly, no detailed case study of the newer, "modern" form of cattle raiding described here, in which cattle stolen in Tanzania are sold to buyers, mainly butchers, inside Tanzania or else run across the border for sale to Kenyan buyers either for local slaughter and consumption or for shipment, both as live animals and as canned beef, to Europe and the Middle East.

This "new" illicit cattle trade—that is, cattle raiding motivated not by a desire to enlarge or replenish family herds, but as a cash-income-producing enterprise—in which many young Kuria men are engaged is carried out by multiethnic gangs, armed sometimes with crude homemade shotguns fashioned by craftsmen in the villages, at other times with sophisti-

---

1. The word *tribe,* in widespread use in both Tanzania and Kenya owing to British influence, is used in this volume with the meaning of "ethnic group," that is, a group of people who share a common language and many common customs and who view themselves as sharing a common identity as a people.

cated factory-manufactured firearms bought, stolen, or rented for the occasion from police posts, army barracks, or corrupt military men or police. These gangs are often better armed and invariably better organized than the police, and the toll of human life and property claimed by this trade has been high. "Thieves use guns to steal cattle and kill people pointlessly," remarked one elderly Kuria man ruefully. "They don't care about old people or young people. They kill everyone they meet in their houses to take the cows away."

Kuria cattle raiders do not operate in a vacuum, of course. Their success depends on a network of accomplices and receivers on both sides of the porous Tanzania/Kenya border; on the reluctance of witnesses to testify against them; on corrupt village leaders, police officers, military men, and magistrates; and on a never-ending cycle of interclan and intertribal enmity and warfare, which is itself fostered, sustained, and promoted by cattle raiding, and which serves both as a pretext for raiding and as a training ground for novice raiders.

The story of Kuria cattle raiding is an intriguing, exciting story, but the question remains: why should anyone here in the Western world be overly concerned with the antics, however violent, of a group of agropastoralist "entrepreneurs" half a world away?

"The Coming Anarchy"

In a widely read, highly disturbing article previewing what he termed "the coming anarchy" of the early twenty-first century, Robert D. Kaplan painted an indelible portrait of the coming decades as a brave new world of "worldwide demographic, environmental, and societal stress, in which criminal anarchy emerges as the real 'strategic' danger" to the wealthy countries of the developed world (1994:46). In this new era, its salient features already plainly evident, in Kaplan's dark view, in strife-torn West Africa, state control will be feeble and its interventions futile, violent crime and vigilantism will have become endemic (45–46), and conventional distinctions between criminality and warfare will have become irrelevant or will have ceased to exist (Kaplan 1994:74; see also Van Creveld 1991:197).

As distorted and overdrawn as this bleak picture is—a pastiche of negative imagery patched together uncritically from a handful of African countries—one may nonetheless find elements of confirmation of it in Tanzania Kurialand, although the "strategic threat" that they pose is not to the affluent West, but to the lives and livelihoods of the Kuria people and others who inhabit this region. There, state presence is minimal, and its attempts at exercising its power are sporadic and ineffectual. Because the state sees little profit for itself in protecting the lives and property (mainly livestock) of its citizens who live there, and because its police force is fearful and corrupt, the only safety or security it offers against the depredations of cattle thieves takes the form of cooperating village vigilante groups, called *Sungusungu,* that are encouraged and sponsored by the state yet operate largely beyond its purview.

Crime

Particularly over the last twenty-five years or so, anthropologists have devoted a fair amount of attention to unlawful activities, which fall under the rubric of what is loosely termed the informal economy—also referred to as the second, underground, parallel, unrecorded, unofficial, shadow, or alternative economy—a term that refers generally to "economic activities that are unmeasured, unrecorded and, in varying degrees, illegal" (MacGaffey 1991:12). Informal economies flourish in all countries, and indications are that their extent worldwide is growing (1991:1), which makes an understanding of how they function especially important in the context of worldwide capitalist expansion and globalized trade.

Moreover, the size and extent of informal economies—relative to those of official, formal economies—appear to be especially great in the developing world. For Tanzania, Maliyamkono and Bagachwa estimate that "on average 30 per cent of the economic activity is not accounted for in the official statistics" (1990:61), while Tripp estimates that at least 80 percent of Tanzanian household income derives from sources other than salaries and wages (1988:6, cited in MacGaffey 1991:16).

Students of the "informal sector," however, in Africa and elsewhere, have generally been far more successful in collecting quality data on food selling (e.g., Macharia 1997), metal artisanship (e.g., King 1996), and other nonthreatening activities than in studying the more violent informal "occupations," which, by their very nature, pose such an overt threat to the power of weak states. Yet it is precisely these sorts of activities, thriving, as they do, wherever state power is tentative and ineffectual, that would seem to present the severest obstacles to economic development, the rule of law, and the creation of viable civil societies in the developing world.

Cattle raiding, in particular, now represents the greatest single threat to their security for many East Africans. In May 1998, the Kenyan newspaper *Daily Nation* reported that more than ten thousand people from Kenya's Marakwet District had fled their homes to seek refuge in Keiyo District following a series of deadly cross-border cattle raids (Too and Ngetich 1998), the most recent of which had resulted in an estimated eight deaths and approximately two thousand head of cattle and small stock stolen (Too and Omonso 1998). More than seventy-two primary and secondary schools were ordered closed in the wake of the clashes, disrupting the schooling of between four thousand and five thousand students (*Nation on the Web* 16 May 1998).

Violence, Food Insecurity, and Societal Stress

A new awareness is dawning that the reciprocal form of livestock raiding described in classic ethnographies has given way to far more dangerous, profoundly destabilizing forms of raiding, which, acting in complex synergy with recurrent drought, intra- and interethnic warfare, livestock disease, and famine, are wreaking havoc on the lives and fortunes of many of the pastoral peoples of East Africa (Hendrickson et al. 1996; Fleisher 1998; see also Homer-Dixon 1991).

Although the links uniting cash-market-oriented cattle theft with declining food production in Tanzania's agriculturally bountiful Tarime District, delineated in chapter 8, are often subtle and largely indirect, this study demonstrates that the theft of cattle for market sale, in concert with clan warfare and other factors, has led both to a drastically reduced cattle population and to plummeting areal food production.

Globalization

Finally, the phenomenon of Kuria cattle raiding carries with it significant implications for our understanding of globalization processes, for an analysis of the theft of Tanzanian cattle for sale in local, regional, and foreign markets serves to illuminate the ways in which a local economy articulates with economies at the regional, national, and international levels and transforms itself in accordance with the pressure that these larger economies exert.

Livestock Raiding among East African Pastoralists

As described in the classic ethnographies of East African herders, men waged war and raided for livestock as members of socially sanctioned groups, and the activities they engaged in generally redounded to the benefit of society as a whole. In organizing for warfare and raiding, two organizational principles were paramount: the segmentary lineage and age organization.

Segmentary Lineages

Among the Nuer of the Sudan, the textbook case for segmentary-lineage organization ever since the publication of Evans-Pritchard's *The Nuer* (1940), the members of each Nuer tribe saw themselves as descended from a common ancestor, and their various clans, lineages, and other segments as together comprising a single, vast genealogy. These various segments, which were often opposed to and hostile toward one another, nonetheless came together in predictable ways, like building blocks, to form larger and larger structures of alliance in times of conflict (Evans-Pritchard 1940:122, 139–47, 192–203; Mair 1974:125). In the case of the Nuer and other East African pastoralists, for whom the need for mobility exerts a strong influence on political organization, lineage segmentation provides the flexibility and fluidity that enable group alliances to form and re-form in a state of continuous flux (Burnham 1979:351, cited in Smith 1992:20).

The Nuer raided cattle both to replace animals lost to rinderpest (Evans-Pritchard 1940:19–20, 69) and to acquire cattle for deployment as bridewealth (Howell 1954:98, cited in Kelly 1985:116). Kelly argues persuasively, in fact, that the nineteenth-century Nuer expansion against the Dinka "was the end product of systematic cattle raiding" (1985:168) driven by the Nuer's intrinsically unbounded bridewealth requirements (231–35, 246–47).

Age Organization

Organization by age is also an extremely important feature among East African pastoralists because these societies capitalize on the values and constructions of manhood inculcated by age-set systems as a means of maximizing intragroup identity and enhancing the effectiveness of warfare and raiding (Fukui and Turton 1979:5; Smith 1992:20).

A key feature of age-set organization is that

> it immediately allocates to any individual in a collection of persons, however transient, a niche in a universal ranking system. Every individual has, accordingly, a pattern of response already roughly created, and needing only application to the context in which he finds himself. (Dyson-Hudson 1966:174)

Different territorial groups within the same tribe, sharing common values and, generally speaking, much the same political outlook and interests, can thus combine fairly easily with one another whenever coordinated action becomes essential (Dyson-Hudson 1966:252).

As described by Huntingford, organization for warfare among the Nandi was provided by an interlocking system of age-sets in conjunction with the *pororiet* system (1953:76). Originally denoting a "regiment" of warriors, all of whom had equal status as members of the same age-set, the term *pororiet* was later extended to embrace the territory in which the members lived, and, as the tribe expanded, these "regimental areas" became spread over the countryside, with some of them developing more than one branch (8).

The Nandi *pororiet* was thus a fighting force comprised of the warriors and the various sections, or *siritaiik,* into which they were divided, as well as a territorial unit that included all the people who lived in its area. The age-set system ensured a permanent and defined source of military manpower, but men fought as members of a *pororiet* (Huntingford 1953:12–13, 36, 79).

The Maasai were capable of organizing themselves on a much wider territorial basis than the Nandi, notes Huntingford, and thereby of dominating a much wider territory, by means of "integrated divisions or districts" that enabled them to concentrate large numbers of warriors into a formidable "tribal army" (1953:37). Fratkin argues that this powerful form of military organization is made possible by favorable ecological conditions, which, by liberating the Maasai *moran* from day-to-day herding tasks, enables them to congregate in their own sedentary "warrior villages"—the *manyata*—which facilitates the carrying-out of large, well-organized raids (1979:53, 66).

Berntsen and Jacobs disagree strongly over the basic impetus for Maasai cattle raiding, with Jacobs arguing that it "lacked any great economic importance and was little more than a 'sport'" (1975:130–31), and Berntsen holding that it was motivated by economic needs deeply rooted in their pastoral economy. Although most raiding merely enhanced the wealth and prestige of a clan-cluster, he writes, "certain series of raids . . . resulted in major political changes" (1979b:223). And when the herds were all but destroyed by rinderpest in the 1890s, raiding became crucial to the survival of Maasai society (224).

Among the Karamojong, of Uganda, large family cattle herds are constantly being divided up by inheritance as well as being steadily reduced by disease and slaughter. As a consequence, the formation of large herds usually depended on the activities of skillful raiders (Dyson-Hudson 1966:51).

With Karamojong men frequently away from their permanent settlements, a potentially serious organizational problem arises that age-set affiliation—because it is society-wide and overrules territorial and kinship affiliation—conveniently resolves, for it enables men to participate in a cattle raid or other activity being organized in a Karamojong settlement far from home, with their role in that activity dictated by their ranking in the age-set system (Dyson-Hudson 1966:174).

The Karamojong have only two age-sets, a senior and a junior (Dyson-Hudson 1966:157). It is the elders who "exhort the junior generation-set to raid the stock and kill the members of foreign groups" and the young initiates, acting as a group, who respond by carrying out the actual raids (185, 198).

In a revealing illustration of one of the many ways in which the modern state becomes implicated in what is often problematized as a "traditional," or even "primitive," activity, Schneider links increased raiding by the Karamojong of their Kenyan neighbors the Pokot to livestock losses suffered by the Karamojong as a consequence of the pressure exerted on them by Uganda's colonial and postindependence governments to increase beef exports from their area to help the country—despite its being detrimental to the Karamojong's pastoral economy for them to sell off more than 10 percent of their herds (1981:236–37). Karamojong raiding capacity was considerably enhanced, moreover, by their acquisition of military weaponry plundered from the Ugandan army during the Tanzania-Uganda War of 1978–79 (Avirgan and Honey 1982:77).

This technological advance notwithstanding, however, livestock raiding among the Karamojong, at least as it is described by Schneider, is still being carried out in pursuit of "traditional" raiding objectives, that is, the acquisition of cattle for subsistence uses, while among the Kuria, as this study will show, cattle raiding has been an informal-sector capitalist enterprise since the early decades of the twentieth century.

Motivation

Throughout the ethnographic record, motivations for raiding generally attributed to East African pastoralists include the desire for prestige, retaliation, loot, young girls, and trophies; the desire to claim victims in association with the death of favorite oxen; and the desire to acquire, or reacquire, cattle for the purposes of expanding herds, repairing stock losses, and amassing the stock needed for bridewealth payments (Fukui and Turton 1979:9–10; see also Almagor 1979; Baxter 1979; Fukui 1979; Jacobs 1979; Tornay 1979). Huntingford describes Nandi cattle raiding as "a form of sport . . . which gave them something real and exciting to live for" (1953:77), and, as we have seen, Jacobs has made a similar claim for the Maasai (1975:130–31).

Kuria cattle raiders, however, are in it for the money, and have been for approximately the past eighty years. Although, in precolonial and early colonial times, Kuria raiding parties were made up of warriors of a single clan or circumcision set (Ruel 1959:53), the contemporary, individualized pattern had become well-established by the 1920s, with the raiders' loyalties to their fellow clansmen being supplanted by new loyalties to multiclan and multiethnic gangs whose members are in the business of raiding for themselves.

This newer, "modern" form of Kuria cattle raiding, oriented toward
the cash market—in which cattle stolen in Tanzania are sold to buyers,
mainly butchers, inside Tanzania or else run across the border for sale to
Kenyan buyers either for local slaughter and consumption or for shipment, both as live animals and as canned beef, to foreign countries—has
the effect of rendering earlier theoretical formulations regarding cattle
raiding inadequate as well as of situating cattle raiding in a new, much
wider context of not merely local but also regional, national, and international trade.

Given this new context, it is argued here, whatever explanatory power
may once have been accorded the meaning and symbolic value of cattle in
attempts to illuminate the phenomenon of cattle raiding must now yield
pride of place to the more nakedly economic, which does not rule out the
use of some or all of the cash proceeds from raiding in striving to attain
such "traditional" objectives as amassing bridewealth with which to
acquire wives. Whichever way the money is spent, however, Kuria cattle
raiding today is most productively viewed as one item in a desperately
brief menu of cash-generating economic options available to the Kuria
people of rural Tanzania, options that they evaluate and exploit with the
rationality and opportunism of the most avid bean counter.

Presumed Functions

Similarly, earlier discussions of pastoralist livestock raiding, in East Africa
and elsewhere, that have focused on its presumed human-ecological functions of redistribution and herd management (e.g., Sweet 1965a,b; Vayda
1968:86; Turnbull 1972; Mair 1974:33; Lancaster 1981:121–23, 139–45)
are simply inapplicable and irrelevant to the market-oriented phenomenon described in this book. In the standard ecological-functionalist formulation, the "institutionalized" raiding of livestock serves to distribute
livestock over a wide area, sustaining a general balance of pastoral
economies through an extended region; circulating animals to where they
are most needed in times of famine or drought; functioning as "a continuously operating system of . . . exchange"; and supporting "the whole network of social and ideological relations" (Sweet 1965a:1146, 1149). "So
important has raiding been," argues Smith, "that in most cases it should
be viewed as a cohesive force among pastoral peoples" (1992:20).

Whatever merits these analyses may once have had in facilitating
understanding of how these systems operated under "traditional" conditions, they simply do not address—and cannot be said to address—the
supraregional issues of world-system articulation raised by the theft of cattle for sale in local, regional, and foreign markets that is taking place in
northern Tanzania today. For whatever may have been the case in former

times, the livestock that are taken in cattle raids carried out by Kuria raiders today do *not* circulate around a local or regional area in "a continuously operating system of . . . exchange" (Sweet 1965a:1146). Rather, they "circulate" as far as a butcher shop or slaughterhouse, and then through the alimentary canals of the people who eat them—not only in Tanzania and Kenya, but reportedly also in Somalia, Scandinavian countries, Israel, and the countries of the Persian Gulf—never to return to their traditional grazing grounds.[2]

Indeed, this book will argue that, far from supporting "the whole network of social and ideological relations" (Sweet 1965a:1149), market-oriented cattle raiding is tearing apart the social fabric of Kuria communities; that it has led to an ongoing, catastrophic decline of the cattle population in the study area; and that it is the driving force behind declining food production in the agriculturally bountiful Tarime District of Tanzania.

The Commoditization of Cattle

The phenomenon of large-scale cattle theft for market sale in East Africa is also both part and consequence of the commoditization of cattle, a process, or congeries of processes, set in motion by the protracted introduction of merchant capital and usurpation of land for settler agriculture instigated in the colonial era (Murmann 1974; Kitching 1980:200–240; Smith 1992:2).

In the standard commoditization scenario, based on the Kenya model, the following sequence occurs: (1) land that was formerly communally held becomes privatized; (2) as population grows and the land becomes divided by inheritance into smaller and smaller plots, agriculture intensifies, and land, which now has market value, becomes increasingly scarce and therefore valuable; (3) large family cattle herds, which require plentiful grazing land for their sustenance, are squeezed out, sometimes in favor of one or two exotic dairy, or "grade," cows that can be housed and fed in small cowsheds under conditions referred to as "zero grazing"; (4) as the area's cattle population declines, the economic utility and social importance of cattle also declines, and the continuing penetration and expanding influence of the market economy makes it possible to invest

---

2. In analyzing the links between contemporary livestock raiding and famine among the Turkana of Kenya, Hendrickson et al. (1996) distinguish between traditional, or "redistributive," raiding, which benefits "the entire pastoral system . . . due to the internal reallocation of resources which occurs between richer and poorer households" (1996:21), and wholly contemporary, "predatory" raiding, which is "systemically destabilizing" (1996:22), "driven by a criminal and acquisitive logic" (1996:18), and "both fuels and is fuelled by regional armed conflicts and illicit markets in cattle and light weapons" (1996:22).

income—whether from the sale of cash crops or wage labor—in invest-
ments other than cattle, for example, in small shops, bars, and transport
services; (5) the decline of the cattle population is mirrored in the decline
in the size of bridewealth payments, which become monetized; (6) people
now buy their meat at butcher shops, by the kilogram, as opposed to
slaughtering their own animals; and (7) cattle, now routinely bought and
sold for cash, as commodities, have become fully commoditized.

This is *not,* however, what is happening in Nyaheiya (not its real
name), the Kuria village in northern Tanzania that served as the primary
field site for the research on which this book is based—although few would
deny that the cattle there have become, in some significant sense, commoditized. Quite apart from the fact that quite a few young men in Nyaheiya habitually steal cattle and sell them for money—which is in turn
used to buy beer, clothing, and other commodities, including cattle—it is
abundantly clear that Nyaheiya villagers generally conceptualize cattle in
a way that at least includes their having commodity status.

In responding to questions posed to them on the homestead survey
(Fleisher 1997:334–48) conducted as one component of this research, for
example, 58 respondents out of a total of 190 respondents (30.5 percent of
the total) claimed to have sold cattle for cash within the previous twelve
months. These 58 respondents are equivalent to 56.9 percent of the number of respondents, of whom there were 102 in the survey, who claimed to
possess a cattle herd, of whatever size, at the time they were surveyed.

Similarly, 73 respondents (38.4 percent of the total) claimed to have
bought cattle for cash within the previous twelve months, a number
equivalent to 71.6 percent of the number of respondents who claimed
possession of a cattle herd at the time they were surveyed. Out of 190
respondents, 65 (34.2 percent of the total) claimed to derive cash income
through the sale of cow's milk. Of the homesteads that reported actually
having cattle in their own cattle corrals at the time they were surveyed (a
number that excludes those claiming to have no cattle in their own corral
but to possessing a "herd" anyway by virtue of their having "put out" cattle with stock associates), 78.3 percent reported earning income from the
sale of milk.

Notwithstanding all this buying and selling of cattle and cow's milk
for cash, however, the pat commoditization scenario laid out above is simply not—or at least not yet—playing itself out in Nyaheiya. Land is *not*
privately owned in Nyaheiya; it is owned by the village and is in plentiful
supply. The village cattle population *is* declining—alarmingly—and
declining village bridewealth payments mirror that decline, but the cause
of the decline is cattle raiding, not land shortage, as this book will show.
Moreover, bridewealth has *not* become monetized, and cattle have *not*
been supplanted by alternative forms of investment or alternative repositories of value, although there are a few villagers, a very few, who own vil-

lage shops, or a grinding mill, and have bank accounts. All of this argues strongly for the view that there are alternative routes to commoditization other than the one described for Kenya. Indeed, this book will argue that although land scarcity can serve as the engine of rising beef prices, it is access to the market economy alone that brings about commoditization.

Another view expressed in the literature regarding commoditization is that although cattle keeping is becoming increasingly market-oriented throughout this region, different herding peoples are differentially articulated with the commoditization process (Smith 1992:228), depending on local "ecological conditions, economic and socio-cultural features and variations in the influences brought about by colonization" (Murmann 1974:104; see also Rigby 1985:162).

In his historical-materialist analysis of Tanzania's Ilparakuyo Maasai, Rigby distinguishes between those pastoral peoples for whom "the herd is still largely conceived of as a means of production, and not as a product," and those for whom cattle have become fully commoditized (1985:129), his underlying theoretical assumption being that "increasing contact with capitalist formations and outside influences generally will require a shift towards commoditisation" (Smith 1992:225).

In "traditional" East African pastoralist systems, where engagement with cash markets was absent, family-herd management was oriented toward subsistence (i.e., toward the production of milk, blood, and meat) combined with offtake for social uses (i.e., bridewealth, ritual sacrifice, stock associateship) and, in systems lacking agriculture, occasional barter with horticulturalists for grain and/or other horticultural products. There exists a voluminous and valuable anthropological literature describing these systems.

At first blush, the Ilparakuyo studied by Rigby appear to represent an initial phase of market engagement and commoditization: among these people, a minority of the herd is set aside by the elders for sale in the market, with the proceeds then used to purchase carefully chosen animals "which are taken home to rebuild the herds and ensure the means of production necessary for the reproduction of the pastoral community" (1985:160). Thus:

> Articulation with commodity relations leads to a reconceptualization of the herd into its basic part (female cattle, heifers, productive animals) still viewed as the primary means of production, and a subsidiary part (oxen, steers, old animals) which is marketed as product. (Rigby 1985:162)

We might expect, then, reading the work of Rigby and of the other authors described immediately above, to be able to graph the advance of pastoralist societies toward full-scale commoditization as an orderly continuum, with different pastoralist communities, differentially exposed to capitalist formations and outside influences—as well as differentially vulnerable to the siren song of those influences owing to differing environmental and cultural factors—gradually wading further and further off the comfortable sandy beach of their traditional economies into the ever-deepening waters toward full market engagement.

What is happening in Nyaheiya, however, is a good deal more chaotic—one might even say messy. Everyone in Nyaheiya needs to have at least a tiny bit of money: for children's school fees; for clothing, matches, and other store-bought essentials; for bribes to officials; for the annual district tax on their cattle; for emergency health-care costs and other family-hardship needs. It is unclear whether they are more deeply engaged with the market economy than Rigby's Maasai. But while some of Nyaheiya's cattle holders may be buying cattle and selling cattle primarily as part of a herd management strategy calculated to maintain some semblance of a "traditional" status quo, others are more profoundly engaged with the market through their involvement in cattle raiding or through deriving economic benefits from others who are involved.

Still other members of the Nyaheiya community, who have no cattle, are shrewdly scoping out the corrals of those who do have cattle and targeting them for cattle raids, often in complicity with outsiders, with the goal of selling the cattle they steal to acquire the money with which to acquire beer and clothing, wives and cattle, this last representing an important component of *their,* somewhat *less* "traditional," herd-management strategy.

Different cattle-keeping peoples are indeed differentially articulated with the commoditization process, but different individuals and groups of individuals within the same community are also differentially articulated with that process, as this book will show.

CHAPTER 2

The Ethnographic Setting

Tanzania

With a land area of approximately 937,000 square kilometers and a population of about thirty million people, the United Republic of Tanzania—formed by the union, in 1964, of the newly independent state of Tanganyika and the islands of Zanzibar and Pemba—is the largest country in East Africa and the second-largest producer of cattle in all of Africa, after Ethiopia (see map 2.1). A German possession from 1891 to 1918, during which time it was known as German East Africa, Tanganyika was administered as a mandated territory by Great Britain—first under the League of Nations, and then, from 1945 onward, the United Nations Trusteeship Council, which replaced it—from 1918 until the achievement of independence by Tanganyika in 1961. Two years later, the Indian Ocean island of Zanzibar also achieved independence from Britain, and Tanganyika merged with Zanzibar and Pemba to form the United Republic of Tanzania in 1964.

Tanzania is divided into twenty-five *mikoa* (Swa.), or regions. One of these, Mara Region (see map 2.2), situated in northeast Tanzania, east of Lake Victoria, with its headquarters at Musoma township, covers a land area of 21,780 square kilometers and is in turn subdivided into five distinct *wilaya* (Swa.), or districts: Musoma Urban, Musoma Rural, Bunda, Serengeti, and Tarime.

Mara Region takes its name from the Mara River, whose impact on the ecology—including the human ecology—of the region is profound. Originating in the Nakuru highlands of Kenya, the river traverses Tarime District—forming the dividing line between Tarime District and the adjacent Musoma Rural and Serengeti districts—and empties its waters into Lake Victoria, northeast of Musoma, in a wide estuary at Kirumi, where a bridge links Serengeti District with Tarime District, the most agriculturally fertile portion of the Mara Region and the district where the research for this volume was conducted (see map 2.3).

Tarime District

Bounded by the Mara River and part of Serengeti District on the south; by Lake Victoria, with its numerous bays and estuaries, on the west; and by

MAP 2.1.   Africa (with mainland Tanzania emphasized)

the Kenya/Tanzania boundary, extending in a straight line from the northeastern midpoint of Lake Victoria to the Indian Ocean, on the north and east, Tarime District has an area of 3,885 square kilometers and an estimated 1994 population of 398,827 according to the district commissioner's office, located at the district's administrative headquarters, in Tarime town.

Geographically, the district divides readily into three distinct zones: the Tarime highlands, or uplands; the plateau, or midlands; and the Mara River valley, or lowlands.

Uplands.   Located in the northeast corner of the district, abutting the Kenya boundary, and rising from a height of about 1,500 meters to over 1,800 meters above sea level, the uplands experience annual rainfall in the 1,200 to 1,800 mm range, with occasional yearly highs of up to 2,000

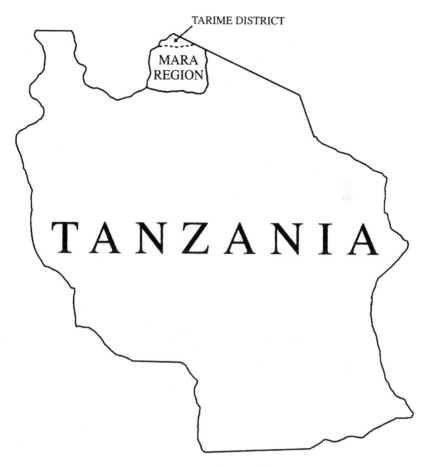

TARIME DISTRICT

MARA REGION

TANZANIA

MAP 2.2.   Outline map of mainland Tanzania (showing Mara Region and Tarime District)

mm, distributed more or less evenly throughout the year but with peaks in April and December. Soils are loamy sand, with good drainage (Hathout 1983), making the uplands the most fertile of the district's three zones. Food crops include maize, sorghum, cassava, bananas, finger millet, Irish potatoes, sweet potatoes, and onions. Coffee and maize are the primary cash crops.

Although the highland area was described by Tanner as having already become "overcrowded" by the mid-1950s (1966:36), cattle were still being "reared in large numbers" there when Rwezaura did his research there from 1979 to 1980 (1985:8). Today, however, the Tarime highlands

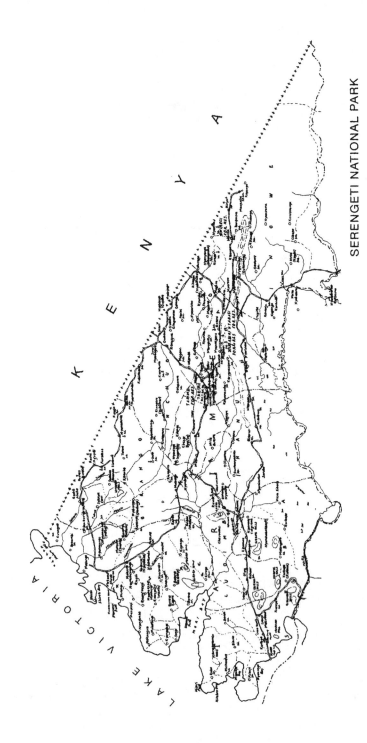

MAP 2.3. Tarime District

are largely denuded of cattle as a consequence of an extraordinary surge in human population growth in the district—up from 253,010 in 1978 (according to the *1988 Population Census: Mara Regional Profile*) to 398,827 in 1994, a rise of 57.6 percent—and, to a lesser extent, the explosion in cattle raiding that occurred during that same period.

While many highland families own only one or two head of cattle today—often exotic dairy breeds, or "grade" cows, that can be maintained in small cowsheds and thus require no land for grazing—many other highlanders have merely relocated their herds to the lowland areas, where pastureland is still plentiful, often placing them in the care of relatives, or acquiring a wife in the lowlands and setting up a separate homestead there to enable her to look after them, or putting them out in the lowland area under the Kuria system of stock associateship (*ogosagaria*).

Midlands. Comprising the central portion of the district, the midlands are situated at an altitude of from about 1,200 to 1,500 meters above sea level and experience rainfall in the range of 1,000 to 1,450 mm per annum. Food crops include millet, sorghum, cassava, sweet potatoes, and small amounts of maize. Cash crops include small amounts of coffee, and sometimes sunflower and groundnuts.

Lowlands. Extending along the banks of the Mara River at a height of from about 1,100 to 1,200 meters above sea level, the lowlands are characterized by an erratic rainfall pattern in the range of about 700 to 1,000 mm annually, with occasional yearly highs of up to 1,100 mm, according to the district government agriculture office in Tarime, which was the source for all of these rainfall estimates. The lowlands are warmer than the highlands, receive less rainfall, and have a higher rate of evaporation. Soils are generally clayey, with poor drainage, which means that the soils are drier, and less fertile, than upland soils.

Lowland villages are by no means equally blessed, or cursed, in this regard, however. Some, watered only by fragile streams that all but vanish in the dry period (roughly June through September) that occurs between the season of long rains (roughly March through May) and the period of lesser rainfall, or short rains (roughly October through February), suffer from serious periodic water shortages and infertile soil. Others, nestled close to wider, deeper stretches of the Mara River, enjoy the benefits of plentiful, year-round water and far more fertile soil created by the layers of silt deposited by the river when it overflows its banks during the long rains.

Lowland food crops include sorghum, bulrush millet, cassava, and sweet potatoes. Cash crops include cotton and, occasionally, sunflower and groundnuts. Cattle thrive in this area owing to the highly favorable climatic conditions, plentiful pastureland, and abundant, nutritious grasses.

For much of the colonial period, Tarime District, then known as

North Mara, was part of Musoma District, which was itself encompassed
by a larger administrative entity known as Lake Province. In 1947, however, North Mara was declared a separate district, and, in 1973, the name
North Mara was changed to Tarime District (Tobisson 1986:30 n. 12).

The district's population consists overwhelmingly of members of two
tribes, the Kuria and the Luo. Each tribe dominates four of the eight
tarafa (Swa.), or divisions, into which Tarime District is divided, and each
dispatches a single representative to Tanzania's parliament. Each of the
four Kuria divisions bears the name, in the Kuria language, of the totem
animal belonging to the specific Kuria clan or clans whose members
inhabit it: Inchage (zebra) Division is home to the Nyabasi and Timbaru
clans; Inchugu (elephant) Division is inhabited by members of the Kira
clan; Inano (baboon) Division is dominated by the Sweta clan; and Ingwe
(leopard) is the domain of the Irege and Nyamongo clans (see map 2.4,
which illustrates the distribution of Kuria clans in the eastern half of the
district; the Kira, Nyabasi, and Irege clans are all part of larger populations of these same clans that are bisected by the Tanzania/Kenya border).

The research on which this book is based was carried out in Ingwe
Division, the large "fishtail" comprising the southeastern portion of
Tarime District, in one of the five villages of the Nyamongo clan. With an
area of 927 square kilometers and an estimated 1994 population of 82,381,
Ingwe is the largest of Tarime District's eight divisions, encompassing
within its area nineteen villages, fourteen of them Irege and five of them
Nyamongo. Ingwe comprises portions of both the highlands and lowlands, its terrain plunging precipitously southward down a steep escarpment, from the Irege highland village of Keisangora, in Ingwe's own
northwest, into the Mara River valley lowlands some 615 meters below.

Ingwe Division is further subdivided into six *kata* (Swa.), or wards,
one of which, Kemambo—Kuria for "mountain" or "hill"—consists
entirely of the Nyamongo clan's five villages. One of these five, here pseudonymously designated as Nyaheiya—"a beautiful place," in Kuria—constituted the primary field site for this research.

The Kuria

The Kuria people—who are also referred to in the literature and in
archival documents by other names, or by variants of the same name,
including the Bakuria, Wakuria, Abakuria, Tende, Batende, Watende,
Kurya, and Kulia—are a Bantu-language-speaking agropastoral people
inhabiting an area of rolling, hilly grassland east of Lake Victoria, mainly
between the Mara and Migori rivers, straddling the border between Tanzania and Kenya (Binagi 1976:13), with the majority (about 213,000 in

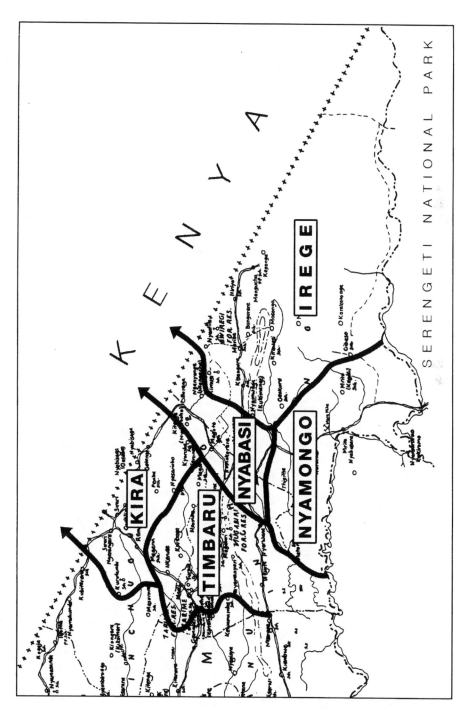

MAP 2.4.   Kuria clan distribution in eastern Tarime District

1987) residing on the Tanzania side and the minority (about 135,000 in 1994) living in Kenya.

Because present-day Kuria society has "evolved from many different sources" (Abuso 1974:13) brought together over centuries of intermingling and migration, any attempt to draw a rigid distinction between Kuria and non-Kuria is problematic, and "'being a Kuria' in fact designates little beyond the vague recognition of a common cultural identity" (Tobisson 1986:95).

In fact, the application of the name *Kuria*—a verb in the Kuria language (*-kuria*) meaning to "tread or paw the ground," as bulls do before fighting—to what were then, and still remain, a cluster of a dozen or more autonomous clans seems to be of fairly recent origin (Seba 1985:2), having apparently come into use during the early colonial period in the course of the consolidation of "indirect rule," possibly as a political ploy on the part of colonially appointed chiefs (Abuso 1980:7; Tobisson 1986:94–95). Membership in an *ikiaro* (pl., *ibiaro*), or clan—which was in precolonial times, and still remains, a sociopolitical as well as a territorial unit—has always been of greater significance to a Kuria than his tribal affiliation. Asked to identify the group to which he belongs, a Kuria will almost invariably reply with the name of his clan. Kuria use the name of an *ikiaro*—Nyamongo, for example—to refer not only to the people (pl., *abaNyamongo;* sing., *umuNyamongo*) whose clan bears that name, but also to the geographical area which that clan occupies (*buNyamongo*).

As was the case with all Kuria clans in precolonial times, the Nyamongo continue to have their own secret council of elders and their own ritual center, at Nyangoto, where they carry out certain major rituals and perform certain ceremonies. Chief among these are circumcisions (*ichisaaro;* sing., *esaaro*) entailing complete removal of the foreskin for males, and, until recent years, clitoridectomy and removal of the labia minora for females, which has now been replaced, among the Nyamongo, by partial excision of the clitoris only. Typically performed at two-year intervals—by a lone male circumciser, in the case of boys, or a lone female circumciser, in the case of girls—on scores or even hundreds of youngsters at a time, in a series of heavily attended ceremonies, these circumcisions are physically painful and are borne with stoicism, for Kuria of both sexes are expected to be brave, and to flinch or cry out at circumcision is to be branded a coward for life. In precolonial times, it was the circumcised young men, the warrior-youths, who bore the responsibility of fighting to defend the clan and of raiding other clans for booty in the form of cattle.

Origins

Notwithstanding the autonomy of their various clans and the recent origin of their tribal name, virtually all Kuria recognize themselves as having descended from a single common ancestor, Mkuria (or Mukuria), who led the migration of his people from the land of Misri—identified by Were with the Lake Rudolf area (1969:190)—where he lived with his two wives, Chuuma and Saai.

The Mkuria myth has many localized variants (Ruel 1959:28; Tobisson 1986:95; Prazak 1992:38–40, 42). In the version related in Nyaheiya, a village of the Nyamongo clan, which has the leopard as its totem, Mkuria sired six sons by these two wives—Wangwe, Wanchage, Wanguge, Wambeba, Wangeri, and Wanchugu—who became the eponymous totemic ancestors of the various Kuria clans and clan groupings. In the names of Mkuria's six sons, all of which remain in common usage as names among the Kuria people today, the names of the totem animals of the clans that *their* sons (Mkuria's grandsons) later founded are clearly evident: *ingwe* is the Kuria word for "leopard"; *inchage* means "zebra"; *inguge* means "baboon"; *imbeba* means "rat"; *ingeri* means "warthog"; *inchugu* means "elephant."

All six of Mkuria's sons went on to have sons of their own. Wangwe, the eponymous ancestor of the leopard (*ingwe*) totemic grouping, had three of them: Mnyamongo, the eponymous ancestor of the Nyamongo clan, with whose people and territory this book is primarily concerned and whose clan population is found only in Tanzania; Mwirege, the eponymous ancestor of the far-more-populous Irege clan, who reside both in Tanzania and in Kenya and who like to boast that they are descended from the more powerful male leopard and the Nyamongo from the weaker female leopard; and Mrenchoka, the eponymous ancestor of the Renchoka clan, who live solely in Kenya.

In precolonial times, "brother" clans like these, sharing a common totemic affiliation, were precluded from raiding one another, were obliged to assist one another in warfare if requested, and had an obligation to compensate one another in cases of homicide (Ruel 1959:27). It is a source of anguish and dismay for elders in Nyaheiya today that these rules of totemic alliance are no longer respected by young people.

The Homestead

In descending order of inclusiveness, the major units of Kuria precolonial sociopolitical organization—units that, for the most part, remain viable in Kuria communities today—were the *ikiaro* (pl., *ibiaro*), or clan; the *egesaku* (pl., *ibisaku*), or descent section; the *irigiha* (pl., *amagiha*), or clan segment; and the *eeka* (pl., *icika* or *ichika*), or lineage.[1]

These *icika,* each consisting of all the male descendants of a known

---

1. Kuria social organization has been extensively described by Ruel (1959, 1962).

ancestor, usually a grandfather or great-grandfather, traceable through definite, named links, are in turn divided into numerous *imigi* (sing., *umugi*), that is, homesteads or father-centered families. In precolonial times, Kuria society was acephalous, with all legitimate authority vested in the individual homestead heads, called *abagaaka* (sing., *omogaaka*) or *abiene imigi* (sing., *umuene umugi*). Within the homestead, the mother-centered unit consisting of a wife and her children is called an *inyumba* (pl., *ichinyumba*), or house.

A typical homestead consists of the homestead head, his wife or wives and all their unmarried children, and all their married sons, their wives, and their children. The widowed mother of the homestead head, and sometimes other guests and relatives, may also make their home within the homestead. Once a homestead head's son has had his eldest child—of whichever sex—circumcised, this son, his wife or wives, and their children typically move out of the homestead in order to establish a new one of their own.

The Precolonial and Colonial Periods

Prior to the advent of colonialism, the Kuria lived in concentrated fortified settlements (*amagori;* sing., *irigori*) built on easily defensible sites—usually on the summits or slopes of hills—that offered easy proximity to pastureland, fuel, and water (Baker 1935:19; Ruel 1959:30). Consisting of anywhere from the inhabitants of a few homesteads to a total population of several hundred people (Ruel 1959:30)—usually, but not invariably, belonging to a single descent section (*egesaku*)—these settlements were typically

> fortified by walls of stones . . . or by a very dense hedge of euphorbia. Outside the fortification were not the fields but a very broad belt of land for pasture. The fields were outside this belt. The part of the land under cultivation was called *ekeremero.* The idea was to have the cattle, all the time, near the houses, since grass is lower than mtama [Swa., millet] and, therefore, a surprise from approaching enemy was rendered more difficult. The fields were cultivated individually by the family members of each house and between the fields were planted rows of mtama as boundaries. The land under cultivation was in one block so that the people working in the fields could help each other in case of danger. (Cory 1947:70–71)

Only with the advent of colonial administration, bringing with it an enforced prohibition of intertribal and intratribal warfare and a consequently less urgent need to employ defensive measures, did the Kuria begin to abandon their stone-walled hilltop settlements and to fan out across the previously uninhabited countryside, with each homestead head establishing his homestead more or less where he chose to, so long as it was within the boundaries of his own clan's territory, and with his family farming the land immediately surrounding it (Ruel 1959:9–10, 56).

Although this settlement dispersal seems to have begun at about the time of the demarcation of the Tanganyika/Kenya border (Ruel 1959:150) in 1902, it apparently occurred somewhat later than this in the Tarime lowlands, which, because of their relative remoteness from the outposts of German authority, remained largely unaffected by the German occupation.

Indeed, it was not until the end of World War I, with the advent of British rule in Tanganyika—and, more particularly, with the establishment of an administrative office at Tarime town in 1928—that the lives of the lowland Kuria really began to be directly affected by colonial rule.

Documents left behind by those engaged in the British colonial enterprise disclose a striking, somehow curious ambivalence toward North Mara (now Tarime District) and its people: it was seen, on the one hand, as "a fertile area with vast possibilities" (TNA 13747 [Secretariat] 2/26/32:4)[2] and, on the other, as

> unruly and turbulent, a cross . . . between a lunatic asylum and a bear garden. (Sillery n.d.:61, quoted in Tobisson 1986:17)

> The intervening months [between January and December 1943] were amongst the Kuria taken up with the usual cattle thefts, litigation, acts of violence and complaints which go up to make the daily round in North Mara. (TNA 20/g/11 [Accession 83] 12/21/43:1)

The Kuria are depicted as

> an unruly and backward people for whom normal administrative methods as applied elsewhere . . . have seemed to be inadequate (TNA 13747 [Secretariat] 11/2/31:1)

and as

> a tribe which enjoys ample share with the Irishman in his traditional dislike of the law. (TNA 20/g/11 [Accession 83] 12/21/43:4)

---

2. Throughout this volume, the dates provided for documents from the Tanzania National Archives (TNA) are presented in accordance with the American system of dating, i.e., month/day/year. All date from the British colonial period.

But there is no denying the frank admiration that finds its way into many colonial reports—admiration for the Kuria as farmers:

> Amongst the Kuria are many able agriculturalists, interested in new ideas and a fine contrast to the lethargic Luo and Suba. (TNA 20/g/11 [Accession 83] 1/2/46:1)

> The African cultivator in North Mara in no sense resembles a sheep to be led or driven but rather an intelligent human being to be persuaded. (TNA 20/g/11 [Accession 83] 12/28/46:6)

And, during World War II, as soldiers in the East African forces:

> The recruiting effort varies considerably, from the superb offerings of the Kurya and other fighting tribes to the meagre and grudging dribble begotten by the Jita. (TNA 20/g/11 [Accession 83] 1/14/43:2)

> These young bloods create a very favourable impression on boat passengers (mostly soldiers themselves), when they embark for service each week, but that is nothing compared to the "panache" of the seasoned warrior home on leave. He is a truly magnificent fellow, and he knows it and the District, it is feared, will also know it when the cease-fire blows. (TNA 20/g/11 [Accession 83] 1/14/43:1)

The policies imposed by the colonialists, and the Kuria response to them, are treated in detail in chapter 4. Suffice it to say here that colonially imposed taxation and market-economy penetration created a host of new opportunities for the Kuria people, who worked in area gold mines, including the Mara Mine, in the heart of Nyamongo country; crossed the border into Kenya to labor on its sisal, coffee, and tea plantations; and served in the colonial police and armed forces in numbers far out of proportion to their representation in the populations of Tanganyika and Kenya. Their military service during World War II took them to such far-off places as Ethiopia, Egypt, Libya, Burma, India, and Ceylon.

By the end of 1942, the number of soldiers serving specifically from Musoma District, of which North Mara Division was then a part, had officially surpassed 5,500 (TNA 20/g/11 [Accession 83] 1/14/43:1), and by the close of 1946, the size of the contingent from North Mara Division alone was put at 5,200 men (TNA 20/g/11 [Accession 83] 12/28/46:1).

By the end of 1943, over 2,000 regular family remittances were being paid out to dependents of soldiers serving from Musoma District (TNA 20/g/11 [Accession 83] 12/21/43:3), and by the end of 1944, North Mara

Division families alone were dispatching at least 1,000 letters a month to their men overseas and about 3,000 family remittances were being paid out to them (TNA 20/g/11 [Accession 83] n.d.:2). By the close of 1945, with the war ended, "practically every household" in North Mara was said to include among its members someone who had served in the Allied forces (TNA 20/g/11 [Accession 83] 1/2/46:1).

"With the Kuria," commented the district officer, North Mara, in his 1944 annual report,

> provided their interest could be aroused, their political system overhauled, and their lawlessness curbed, nothing is impossible of achievement. (TNA 20/g/11 [Accession 83] n.d.:2)

The "lawlessness" in this just-quoted extract refers to Kuria cattle raiding, which was the overriding administrative concern of North Mara officials. As *The Handbook of Tanganyika* put it:

> The Kuria are intelligent but very highly strung and temperamental. They crave excitement, finding life tedious without it, and if they cannot allay their restlessness by making war on their neighbours or stealing cattle they must find some other outlet for their energies; these of recent years have often taken the form of litigation in the local courts, but the national sport of cattle stealing still thrives. (Moffett 1958:188)

The Nyamongo and Irege Clans

The Tarime District lowlands—now home to all of the Nyamongo clan and part of the Irege clan—were settled later than the highlands, first by the Nyamongo, who, if Baker is correct, constituted a single "sub-tribe" (what we are calling a "clan") together with the Irege, prior to budding off from the Irege in the latter part of the nineteenth century to form a much smaller clan of their own (Baker 1935:5, 10). Irege settlers followed the Nyamongo into the lowlands decades afterward, migrating down the escarpment in search of new farmland and grazing land for their livestock as their population in the highlands grew. Crumbled ruins of gray-stone settlements inhabited by Kuria in former times still pockmark the lowlands, whose residents, in common with those in the Irege-occupied area of the highlands, lived under constant threat of Maasai attack—both from the Kenya Maasai and from those inhabiting the Loliondo area of present-day Arsuha Region, Tanzania. The Maasai, it is said, would sweep through their lowland area in large numbers, knocking down the stone walls of the Kuria settlements (which were never held together by any mortar), slaughtering the occupants, and absconding with their cattle.

Due to the remoteness of these Tarime lowlands from spheres of German colonial administration, it is entirely possible that the inhabitants of the Tarime lowlands never even saw a German, but, in the years following the advent of British administration, and the Pax Britannica that accompanied it, the lowland Kuria began moving out of their isolated fortresslike settlements and into villages. Notwithstanding the British presence, however, frequent Maasai depredations continued to plague the Irege and Nyamongo area until the early 1950s, by which time the Irege population, both highland and lowland, had attained sufficient size and strength to enable the Irege to turn back a major Maasai assault, thereby shielding both themselves and the Nyamongo from further attacks and bringing the era of free Maasai access to the region to a close.

The overwhelming majority of what has been written about the Kuria people concerns the highland Kuria, but A. Sillery, a British district officer who was transferred from Musoma to North Mara in the early 1930s, left behind an unpublished memoir containing his reminiscences of various Kuria clans. Sillery had warm feelings for the Irege and the Nyabasi:

> The Iregi . . . were in many ways the most admirable people in Kuria. In a community of handsome people they were perhaps the most handsome; they lived on the high plateau, and were somewhat reserved, interfering little with the rest of Kuria, except for an occasional boundary tiff round the headwaters of the Mori river with their neighbours of Nyabasi, and generally keeping themselves aloof from the feverish life of the rest of Kuria. . . . The plateau in Bwiregi reached a height of 6000 feet above sea level, the air was always keen and invigorating, and a tour as far as the extreme easterly border was a delight, for the country compared favourably with Kenya at its best, and the views over the escarpment were superb.
>
> My favourite chiefship for some reason was Nyabasi. . . .
>
> I had more personal friends in Nyabasi than elsewhere. There were few huts along that road where I could not drop in and pass the time of the day and get a friendly greeting. My favourite view was on the edge of the escarpment just opposite the house of headman Rupilia. There was an overhanging rock, from which I could see the whole of Mara valley as from an aeroplane, Nyamongo below me; beyond, the hills of Nguimi and in the distance, behind them, the Serengeti plains. I always went there whenever I passed, and . . . look[ed] out over the peaceful blue spaces. (Sillery n.d.:94–96)

But his enthusiasm for the Nyamongo was more restrained:

The view also included Nyamongo, a detestable place, the "thieves' kitchen" of Kuria. It was below the escarpment in the valley of the Mara, and was ruled by a lame old man called Marwa Masero, completely under the influence of his ruffianly sons. They were capable of any infamy, but it took us some years to get rid of the family and substitute a prominent headman called Muhochi. . . .

Nyamongo was very well placed as a mart for stolen property since it dominated one of the few fords over the Mara passable in most weathers. The Nguimi on the southern bank were always co-operative and trade was brisk and profitable.

A tour of Nyamongo was something of a penance. First you had to scramble down the escarpment, 2000 feet of it, then across a rather dreary plain to the mosquito-infested camping ground. . . . It is typical of the perversity of the metal that when gold was found in North Mara the only substantial "strike" should be in Nyamongo. (Sillery n.d.:96–97)

Nyaheiya Village

Nyaheiya was founded as a village in 1974 under Tanzania's program of forced villagization, known as *ujamaa* (Swa., familyhood), with a founding population of about 1,500. Located about 90 kilometers from Tarime town, it has an area of approximately 11,000 hectares (or about 110 square kilometers) and an estimated 1996 population of 2,232 people residing in 350 separate homesteads. In 1995, there were about 5,800 cattle in Nyaheiya and an uncounted number of sheep and goats.

Nyaheiya is governed by a 26-member Village Council, including a village chairman and a village secretary, all of whom stand for election every five years. In addition, each of Nyaheiya's *vitongoji* (Swa., sing., *kitongoji*), or "neighborhoods," is represented by an *mkuu wa kitongoji* (Swa., pl., *wakuu wa vitongoji*), or "neighborhood head," who is elected by all the adult members of the *kitongoji,* and a *balozi* (Swa., pl., *mabalozi*), or "ten-cell leader"—called that because, at one time, his job was to serve as representative of only ten homesteads—who is a political representative of CCM, the ruling political party, and who is elected by all the adult residents of the *kitongoji* who are registered party members (CCM stands for *Chama cha Mapinduzi,* Swahili for "Revolutionary Party").

Although land for farming and grazing has been in short supply for decades in the heavily populated Tarime highlands, it is still plentiful in Nyaheiya, although cattle holders do often graze their cattle in open land beyond the village boundaries. Farm plots can be obtained from the village government as needed and can be passed on to heirs as an inheritance, but they may not be sold; if a landholder moves, his land reverts to the village, whose officials will allot it to other applicants as needed.

Nyaheiya is also blessed by the presence of several natural wells, which provide sediment-free water for cooking and drinking, and by its proximity to the Mara River, which guarantees a plentiful, year-round supply of water, colored brown by river sediment, for bathing and numerous household uses and for the watering of livestock. A field note recorded in August, during the dry season preceding the short rains, reveals something of the life of the river and of its place in the lives of the people of Nyaheiya:

> The Mara River, which flows into Lake Victoria, is the boundary between Tarime & Serengeti districts, & the Ngoreme, who live in Serengeti District, wade across to search for gold on the Nyamongo side. At the wide, shallow beach where the women go to swim and bathe their children, you can cross the river while standing on the bottom—although the water is too deep for that in some places & you have to watch where you step. The water flows by, muddy & brown. The river is at a very low level during this season, but in the season of the long rains [around March through May] it will overflow its banks and enrich the land around it with a layer of silt.
>
> The river is scenic & beautiful. At one point, a local teenager who lives near the river took me in tow and showed me the sights.
>
> We saw 2 crowned cranes on the far bank, come down to the river to drink, and 2 male baboons—plus a female w/ an infant—that also came to drink, the males making a few lackadaisical, & unsuccessful, attempts to sneak up on a group of resting ducks, which easily slipped into the water & eluded them, swimming effortlessly out of reach.
>
> We saw 3 baby crocodiles—one each on three separate occasions—basking on rocks or pieces of wood or banks of mud in the river.
>
> At the "beach" place, we saw 50–60 girls & women, many w/ children, bathing, swimming, playing in the water—& also washing children, clothes, & cooking pots and other household items they'd carried to the river w/ them. We also saw about a dozen other women bathing at a smaller spot.
>
> At 11:30 A.M. we saw herders driving their cattle down to the river to drink—at a spot not at all far from the bathers—about 30–35 head at a time.
>
> We saw 8 oxen pass by, hauling one of those giant granary baskets.

We passed a red-colored plant that reminded me of goldenrod. It's called *mchicha,* which my Swa. Dict. calls "spinach," but I'm betting it's what we call "kale." [It is not. *Mchicha* is a spinach-like vegetable.]

At a homestead close by the river, a young man was pounding up a cultivated green plant in a section of hollow log cut in half lengthwise. He said they throw the pounded-up plant-stuff in the river, and it poisons the fish, which rise to the surface in large numbers (perhaps it drives oxygen from the water, like the poisons Amazon Indians use), and the men wade into the river & dispatch the fish w/ *pangas* [Swa., machetes]. I know that large catfish [Swa., *kambare*] are fished out of the river here, because a man tried to sell me one soon after I first arrived.

It is this proximity to the Mara River, in addition to Nyaheiya's plentiful and nutritious grasses, that make it such a bountiful location for the keeping and raising of livestock. Although lack of adequate, or seasonably reliable, rainfall can be, and often is, seriously disruptive of local agricultural regimes, the availability of year-round river water largely insulates Nyaheiya cattle holders from serious losses even in periods of severe drought.

The blessings of their natural environment notwithstanding, the people of Nyaheiya are not self-sufficient in the production of their own food and are dependent upon the purchase of food—maize, millet, sorghum, bananas—from the area around Mugumu, administrative headquarters of the adjacent Serengeti District, as well as from the agriculturally plentiful Tarime highland area, in order to augment their supply.

Exactly why this is so is a complex question (discussed in chap. 8), but certainly an important element in the food-buying equation is the ability of all those living in the Nyamongo area, including the residents of Nyaheiya, to earn cash income by engaging in small-scale, low-technology gold mining in any one of the half-dozen ore-rich mining areas close by.

The British-operated Mara Mine, where Kuria miners began working for wages in the early 1930s, is defunct now, its crumbling stone buildings, which once housed miners, now housing the staff of Kemambo ward's lone police post, established in 1983, which sits atop a lofty hill offering a magnificent, commanding view of the surrounding countryside. Although an Australian company was engaged in exploratory drilling in the Nyamongo area as a prelude to launching a commercial gold mine there, all of the actual mining being done in this area (as of early 1996) was being carried out by local people employing only the rudimentary technologies available to them.

The two principal—but by no means the only—mining areas in the Nyamongo area are Nyabilama, near Nyangoto, which has been producing gold since colonial times but is no longer nearly as productive as it once was, and Nyabigena, known also as Nyaraguso, located between Nyangoto and Nyamwaga, which was founded in 1987 and enjoyed a boom period in the years from 1989 to 1992, only to see its yield begin to decline in 1993 owing to the problem of water seeping into the mine shafts and the lack of the equipment needed to pump it out.

Typically, an individual or a group of individuals invests the necessary money to dig the mine shaft—a rectangular hole in the ground anywhere from 75 to 250 feet deep, braced with a network of saplings that also serve as a makeshift ladder for descending and ascending—and then, having staked an official claim with the government, hires workers to dig out the gold in return for a share of whatever gold they find, usually 50 percent of it, in lieu of wages.

If A owns the shaft, for example, and hires B, C, and D to work for him, B, C, and D will typically work a six-day week in the mine, keeping whatever they bring out on Monday, Tuesday, and Wednesday as their compensation, while the gold they find on Thursday, Friday, and Saturday belongs to A, the owner.

In the case of multiple owners—say, for example, there are three of them—each owner might receive whatever gold the mine produces on one of the owners' allotted three days. Or the owners might agree among themselves to divide each of the owners' days into three segments, with each owner receiving whatever gold is brought out of the mine during his particular segment.

The miners work in shifts, usually one or two at a time, descending into the blackness with flashlights strapped to the side of their head with a rubber strap scavenged from an old inner tube and hammering away at the gold-bearing rock with chisels and short-handled nine-pound sledgehammers. On all sides, there is a good deal of unscrupulousness. If the workers are digging away on the days that have been allotted to them, and the owner sees that the vein of exposed gold in the shaft is visibly widening, he is likely to order the workers to cease digging for themselves and to spend the remainder of the day digging for him instead. The workers will surely grumble, but there are no written contracts that can be enforced and the workers have no recourse other than to quit and be easily replaced.

The workers, for their part, routinely steal from the owner—by hiding and sneaking out gold-bearing rock that they dig out on *his* days, or by burying it down in the mine and then sneaking back to the shaft at night to retrieve it when the owner is not there.

Only men work in the mine shafts, but women also earn income in the mining areas: sorting through the piles of slag for rocks bearing even faint visible signs of gold, selling food to the miners, working as clerks in the small shops, and providing sexual services.

Notwithstanding the slump that began at Nyabigena in 1993, there were still as many as 1,000 people prospecting for gold at Nyabilama and Nyabigena as late as March and April 1994. By June 1995, however, that number had been reduced to a bare shadow of what it had once been, the great majority of gold seekers having been driven out by the problems of deep standing water and unbreathable air in the mine shafts.

This fate is typical of low-technology gold mining in third world countries. Lacking access to expensive technology, and therefore unable to exploit any but high-grade ore containing gold visible to the naked eye, the miners experience a brief, heady boom, such as the one at Nyabigena, only to find themselves thwarted by poor ventilation, water-clogged mine shafts, and rock that is too hard for them to hammer-and-chisel through. Plagued by these sorts of obstacles, the mines all but close down, but even the small amounts of cash income they do continue to produce, along with the occasional lucky strike, mean a lot to the people of Nyaheiya and of the other villages in the Nyamongo area.

With income from the mines at a low ebb, cattle raiding has become the preeminent means of generating cash income in Nyaheiya, with many men who had once been miners moving opportunistically into cattle raiding. Cattle raiding is a more reliable income-producer than lowland agriculture, and far more remunerative. In common with mining, cattle raiding is both physically demanding and dangerous, but cattle raiding is *more* dangerous, not only to the cattle raiders themselves, but also to their victims, bystanders, and policemen. The use of guns, now widespread, has resulted in the loss of many lives.

> It is customary for Kuria to steal cattle, customary for Kuria to be killed stealing cattle, customary for Kuria to be killed guarding their cattle. It is a customary part of life in this region.

These are not the words of a colonial functionary, culled from some musty archive. They are the considered opinion of a contemporary Tanzanian official residing in Tarime town. To read them, one might imagine that little about cattle raiding has changed in the past hundred years or so, but, in fact, the very nature of cattle raiding has been radically transformed in that time. To understand this transformation, its causes and its far-reaching consequences, we shall first have to explore the past.

CHAPTER 3

"Better to Be Killed in the Cows . . .": Cattle Raiding in Its Precolonial Context

The Kuria have a saying: *"Ubuya witwe guching'ombe gokera gwitwa gokerogi ke omokari."* English-speaking Kuria tend to translate this saying as "It's better to be killed stealing cows than committing adultery," but this glibly sardonic translation in fact does considerable violence both to the Kuria language and to the values and meanings immanent in the original, Kuria-language version:

Ubuya means "better."

Witwe, a passive form of the verb *ugwita,* "to kill," means "to be killed."

Guching'ombe means "in the cows" or "with the cows." Although there are many words in Kuria for the various types and categories of cattle, the word most generally used for "cow" (*eng'ombe;* pl., *iching'ombe*) also means "[one head of] cattle," without regard to the animal's sex.

Gokera means "more than" or "rather than."

Gwitwa, also a passive form derived, like *witwe* (above), from the verb *ugwita,* "to kill," means "being killed."

Gokerogi is derived from the word *ikiruugi,* which means "to be caught red-handed," as in flagrante delicto. The prefix *"go-,"* which means "in" (as well as "at," "on," or "to"), denotes that the actor is in the very midst of carrying out the action.

Ke means "of" or "belongs to."

Omokari means "married woman" or "wife."

"Better to be killed in the cows," say the Kuria, "than being killed while in the act [of having sex] with another man's wife.[1]

---

1. Suzette Heald, based upon her research among the Kenya Kuria, notes (pers. com.) that *gokerogi* may alternatively be derived from the verb *-roga* (bewitch), thus imbuing this saying with the additional implication that it is better to die "in the cows" than to be bewitched by a (married) woman.

To be killed "in the cows," in Kuria parlance, is to be killed in the act of fighting for cattle. The very phrase is evocative of courage displayed amid the swirling dust of combat, whether in the cause of defending the cattle of one's own clan against enemy raiders or of striving valiantly to enlarge the clan's cattle holdings by executing daring raids against those who have been culturally defined as "others," that is, members of other tribes, such as the Maasai, or of totemically unaffiliated Kuria clans. Both the raiding of others' cattle and the defending of one's own stock are valorous deeds in this context. To die "in the cows" is to die a warrior's death.

Cattle raiding may take a variety of forms, as this chapter will show. But whether the raiders "capture" (-*roona,* a verb used especially to designate the capture of cattle) the animals in an open daylight raid while the animals are in pasture, or "capture [them] by stealth" (-*seeta*) in the nighttime while the animals are shut up inside their homestead's central cattle enclosure (*oboori*), the use of the verb "steal" (-*iba*), tarnishing the act by which the cattle are taken with a negative moral valuation, is, in the traditional context to which the saying applies, wholly inappropriate.

The appropriate Kuria verb in this context is, rather, -*soora,* which means "bring," in the sense of fetch, go and get, collect. Kjerland quotes a Kuria informant as saying that "when raiders go a long distance they *bring* good quality cattle" (1995:292, my emphasis). Kuria raiders travel far, then, "to bring" home cattle that they have "captured" either from other tribes or from other Kuria clans. Theirs is a meritorious, glorious undertaking.

"Stealing," or "thieving," as our own common understanding of these words makes clear, is a different matter entirely, and the Kuria have a number of words for such illicit activity, all of them appropriately pejorative. An *umwibi* is a thief, but the infinitive *ukwiba,* "to steal," may be applied to the stealing of *anything.* A speaker who, having used this verb, wishes to indicate the object of the stealing must specify it: *ukwiba iching'ombe,* for example, is "to steal cattle."

When the verb -*chunchuuri* (steal [cattle] by stealth) is used, however, the word "cattle" (*iching'ombe*) is understood, and the implication that one who behaves in this way—designated by the noun *obochunchuuri,* or a sneak thief of cattle—is engaged in dishonorable behavior is unambigu-

---

This idea that a death incurred through cattle raiding is ennobling while one incurred through adultery is demeaning appears also in these lines of a Kenya Kuria praise poem collected by Heald (1997):

When you are killed out raiding
Then you are a hero of cattle
When you are killed through love*
Then you are a rat which has dropped in water.
(*The use of the Kuria verb -*tuara* here implies an affair with a married woman.)

ous, for it is derived from the verb -*chunchuura* (move in a crouch, with one's back bent, in the manner of an old man), whose causative form is -*chunchuuria* (be furtive, move in a crouch, with the motive of concealing something).

What makes *ubuchunchuuri* "stealing," and therefore morally reprehensible, is certainly not the fact that cattle are appropriated or that they are taken by stealth as opposed to overtly—indeed, both -*seeta* and -*chunchuuri* entail the taking of cattle by stealth—but rather who it is that the cattle are appropriated *from*. What makes the *obochunchuuri* (pl., *abachunchuuri*) a thief—*not* a raider—and his act of taking cattle a crime is that he appropriates cattle from members of his own clan or from Kuria clans with whom his own clan is totemically affiliated. He is compelled to stealth because, particularly in the precolonial context, he will be branded a coward and pariah, and liable to penalties, should his identity and activities ever become known. We are doing no more than employing native categories, therefore, when we dub such men "thieves." Their activities stand at a wide remove from those of the raiders, or brave youths, whose exploits were honored, celebrated, heroized.

Cattle "theft," as Kuria themselves define it, must have been rare in precolonial times: "Natives state that stock thieving was practically unknown in [the] old days," wrote Baker in 1935 (45), and elderly informants in Nyaheiya today, recalling their own lives, maintained that even as late as the 1930s, the number of *abachunchuuri* in all of Nyamongo could be counted on the fingers of a single hand. At least a decade and a half before then, however, the line separating raiders from thieves had begun to blur and fade, ultimately to vanish entirely, under the pressures and policies of colonial administration and the steady, inexorable penetration of the money economy. Today, the raider-thief distinction is extinct or all but extinct, the casualty of a dramatic transformation that has played itself out over the course of this century.[2]

"A major element of the pre-colonial political scene," notes Ruel, was "fighting between countries, raiding for cattle, and withstanding Maasai attacks" (1991:343). In those days, the Kuria were "surrounded by enemies" (Baker 1935:29):

> Each province [clan] had its own traditional enemies (*ababisa,* literally "those who hide"), usually neighbouring provinces [clans] with whom no totemic alliance existed but always including the Maasai. (Ruel 1959:51)

---

2. Accordingly, in the chapters that follow, I will employ the term *cattle raiding* to designate any violent or illicit appropriation of cattle, and the term *cattle raider* to refer to any person who engages in this type of activity.

Defensive considerations played an important role in the selection of homestead sites (Baker 1935:19). "In addition to building their villages near the granite outcrops which served as a shelter for the women and cattle," notes Baker,

> if sufficient warning was given to enable them to escape from their huts, the Ba-Kuria also fortified a number of hills with a stone wall circling the entire foot of the hill and one or two more similar walls near the summit. The women and children used to retire to the innermost circle as soon as it became known that an attack was imminent and when the enemy appeared the warriors defended the outer line of defences, retiring on the inner fortifications if necessity arose. (1935:53)

The "fear of marauding Masai" was constant (Baker 1935:2). "A raid by Masai or Jaluo used to devastate all the villages on the route taken by the raiders" (44).

"Raids by the Masai and Jaluo usually took place at night or early morning," continues Baker, and,

> if the scouts of the Ba-Kuria failed to bring in warning, the unfortunate villager[s] were burnt in their huts or speared as they attempted to leave the flaming buildings, their womenfolk sharing the fate of the men or being carried off by the raiders together with the cattle. (1935:53)

Ruel's observation, in the 1950s, that "a notable feature of Kuria society is the lack of 'tribal' unity," is no less true today, and it was a dominant fact of life in precolonial times (1959:51):

> [N]ot only were provinces [clans] hostile amongst themselves but there are also instances . . . of provinces [clans] combining with outsiders, the Masai, to fight against fellow Kuria of another province [clan]. (51)

This interclan hostility, and the struggle to lay hold of strategic resources that lay at the heart of it, was played out in microcosm at the natural salt licks (*eng'eeng'i* or *engenye*), like the one at Monanka (or Mnanka), a swampy area located northwest of the present-day Nyamongo village of Matongo, at the southern end of the area now inhabited by the Timbaru clan. Here, men of different clans would bring their cattle herds and jostle violently for priority of access to the choicest spots. One Nyaheiya elder claimed that herders from totemically affiliated clans used to clash with herders representing clans with which they were not affiliated, with the victors seizing for themselves the cattle of those they had vanquished. These battles for primacy at Monanka, the Nyaheiya elder insisted, are where Kuria interclan warfare began.

Whether or not this is literally true, there is no question that Monanka and the other salt licks like it—such as the one at Nyarwana (or Nyaruana), just north of Monanka, "where cattle low nicely" (Kjerland 1995:52)—were places where the threat of violence was never far distant:

> Cattle were taken to the saline earths (*engenye*) twice monthly. Saline earths were non-tribal areas and it was against the "rule" to close the roads to *engenye*. . . .
>
> Nyaruana was a saline earth place between Nyabasiland and Nyamongoland, near Mara River. . . . An umuIrege drove his cattle straight through the stock of an umuNyabasi. This was against the rules of the saline earths and he was killed on the spot. (Kjerland 1995:291)

"Fighting," writes Ruel, "was not only a necessity; it was also a virtue":

> Courage in fighting is one of the most admired qualities of the Kuria, a test of manhood, and the deeds most recounted of the past are those of combat. Apart from its glory, fighting also brought booty in the shape of cattle—beyond their economic worth objects of prime value in Kuria culture. . . . That fighting was not a mere sordid necessity is apparent from the embellishments which were given to it—the special dress, the ornamentation of body and weapons. (1959:51)

For Kuria, the "virtue" of fighting, reinforced by martial ideology and attitude, was one born of necessity and circumstance—of being surrounded by enemies, of being embroiled in unrelenting competition for strategic resources: the grass, the water.

The Kuria distinguish between large-scale fighting, called *iriihi* (or *irihi*), meaning "war" or "conflict," and the various types of raiding collectively designated by the word *iniko,* which means both "raiding party" and "enmity" (cf. Ruel 1959:52; Kjerland 1995:291 n. 31). Most interclan fighting fell under the heading of *iniko,* but *iniko* could escalate to *iriihi* when, in the aftermath of a cattle raid, those who had been raided endeavored to overtake the raiders and recover their cattle, and the raiders' fellow clansmen turned out in force to defend their raiders (Ruel 1959:52; Kjerland 1995:291 n. 31). While *iniko* might involve a raiding party of more than a hundred young men, a smaller-scale raid, *egekomo* (a small gathering of people), typically involved a group of between five and fifteen participants, but never seven, as the Kuria regard this number as being extremely unlucky.

Ruel notes,

> A raiding party could be made up from the known bravest men selected from the total province [clan] or from the warriors (of any circumcision set) over a limited area. Raids varied in scale, but were normally directed . . . by . . . a "spokesman," "dream-prophet," or "war-leader," and were not organised simply by the warriors themselves. (1959:53)

Spokesmen

"Spokesmen" (*abagambi;* sing., *omogambi*) is the word used to describe men of high social standing whose influence in clan affairs flowed from their personal charisma, insight, and power to persuade others, for example, at formal gatherings, rather than from any sort of formal authority—which, in fact, they did not have. Derived from the verb *-gamba,* which means "say" or "speak," *abagambi* is also closely related to the verb *-gambana,* meaning to "testify" on one's own behalf, as in a formally adjudicated dispute or court case. Like the "big men" of Melanesia, "they were leaders only because they were followed" (Ruel 1959:43; see also Ruel 1991:343).[3]

Interclan fighting was one of the areas in which spokesmen exercised influence. "It is described in Renchoka," writes Ruel,

> how at a general meeting the spokesman would outline the plan of attack, concluding with the challenge: "Who will give me warriors?" At this point the warrior-youths made a mock attack on him, and he might even be knocked down by one of them. The attack was taken as a show of fearlessness on the part of the warriors and a promise of future strength and courage in fighting. (1959:44)

Dream-Prophets

"Dream-prophets" (*abarooti;* sing., *omorooti*) were men who prophesied future events through what was believed to be their ability to foretell the future by means of their dreams—although Ruel notes that "it is clear too that 'dreaming' was a verbal idiom for insights and intuitions obtained by

---

3. Dyson-Hudson describes a similar role for "spokesmen" among the Karamojong (1966:222–24).

other means" (1991:346). The noun *ekerooto* means "dream" in Kuria, and the verb *-roota* means "dream" or "foretell by dreaming." Dream-prophets, whom Ruel (1991) also refers to as "seers,"

> are said to have predicted such matters as: future attacks from outsiders; potential catastrophes in the form of disease, famine or loss of crops, which needed to be diverted [*sic,* averted] by rit-ual means; [and] successful future raids by the warriors of the province [clan]. (Ruel 1959:44)

Scouts (*erooti*) were sent out in advance of the raid, with instructions to search out the grazing places of desirable cattle herds, spy on the herds-men watching over them to evaluate their vigilance and preparedness, and gather up samples of the cattle's dung, earth from their hoofprints, and grass that had fallen off their mouths as they grazed for the dream-prophet to employ as omens for evaluating the propitiousness of the planned raid. (The Kuria verb *-hura,* meaning "watch over," applies most particularly either to keeping watch over one's own cattle to guard against their being taken or to spying on others' cattle in preparation for taking them.) Armed with the intelligence brought back by the scouts,

> The seer used his powers to give precise, detailed instructions about the circumstances the youths would meet and their conse-quent strategy for the raid: for example, they would first encounter a cow of such-and-such a colour, which they should ignore, before finding a further herd of cattle grazing in such-and-such circumstances, which were the ones to be seized, and so on. The seer himself never took part in a raid, and the warrior youths were expected to bring back all the cattle taken, for the spoils to be divided by the warrior leader [war-leader]. In some cases the seer foretold cattle of special markings that were to be brought back for his own use. (Ruel 1991:344; see also Ruel 1959:44–45 and Kjerland 1995:293)

He also provided the raiders with special leaves that they were sup-posed to burn, a kind of "sacrifice," known as *ekoroso,* to help ensure the success of the raid—a form of protection additional to that which was pro-vided by the secret council of elder males known as *inchaama* (see below).

War-Leaders

Dream-prophets advised on raids, but it was "war-leaders" who organized them (Ruel 1959:45; 1991:344). Although the role of the war-leader (*omo-ceena, omocaina,* or *umunciina;* pl., *abaceena, abanceena, abaciina,* or *aba-*

caina) had already ceased to exist by the time Ruel studied the Kuria in the 1950s, he found it still being commemorated in the lines of a popular beer-party song, "*Nyagorio eng'ombe, sobokera omocaina, nawe nakuruusia egorio,*" which he translates as "You who long for cattle, make up to the *omocaina,* it is he who will remove your longing" (1991:344, 352 n. 1).

The verb *sobokera,* which Ruel had previously translated, some three decades earlier, as "cherish" (1959:53), rather than as "make up to" (1991:344), actually means "sleep facing [someone]" and is usually used of a husband and wife, or of a mother and her child, suggesting a marital/sexual connection or, at the very least, a warmly intimate one, borne out by the related noun *umusubukiri,* which means "sleeping partner." From his own reading, which the one stated here by no means refutes, but rather supports and helps to substantiate, Ruel concludes the existence of a meaningful link between the role of the war-leader and marriage, which the war-leader's efforts facilitate by setting the stage for the warriors' acquisition of bridewealth cattle. In Ruel's words:

> The surface meaning [of the beer-party song] is that warrior leaders can help you to get cattle, but the overtones come from the use of words more appropriate to a sexual relationship and from the importance of cattle as bridewealth. Thus a secondary implicit meaning emerges: you who long for marriage, join a raiding party; that will assuage your longing. (1991:352 n. 1)

Baker, in addition to noting that "girls refuse to marry a man who has no stolen animals in the cattle which he brings to her father" (1935:45), also records a custom whereby a newly circumcised youth was presented with "a bow strung with a new cord" and warned

> not to break the bowstring for, should he do so, he will find difficulty in marrying, since it would be thought that his wife would die prematurely. (1935:104)

Like the popular beer-party song cited by Ruel, this belief also evokes the link between raiding and marriage—the former the means by which a young man acquires the bridewealth cattle he needs to marry, the latter the means by which he acquires the daughters who will one day bring bridewealth cattle into their father's homestead when they marry. The belief resonates in the conviction prevalent today among Kuria cattle raiders that if a man's bowstring snaps while he is en route with his comrades to the area from which cattle are to be taken, he is sent home immediately—otherwise, it is said, he would die in the raid—while the other cattle raiders press on without him.

The status of war-leader, writes Ruel,

is closely associated with that of the prophet, particularly regarding the latter's function in foretelling and directing raids. Today the term is often used as a synonym for prophet, with whom the war-leader's role is in any case merged, and in some provinces [clans] the term and its associations do not appear at all. (1959:45)

Conclave

A fourth politically important status was that of membership in what Ruel (1959) terms the "conclave" (*inchaama*), a secret council of elder males charged with the ritual protection and well-being of the clan and its territory. Although Ruel expressed doubt as to whether the *inchaama* had survived the changes in administrative structure wrought by colonialism (1991:343), Tobisson found the institution still very much alive among the Timbaru clan in the late 1970s (1986:104), and it continues to enjoy a robust existence today among the Nyamongo, who refer to it as the *ikimiira,* a word derived from *mila,* the Swahili term for "custom" or "culture."

As an august council, the men of the *ikimiira* play no role in the market-oriented cattle raiding with which this book is mainly concerned, but in the present, as in the past, they continue to play a role in the area's sporadic interclan warfare, in which raiding the enemy's cattle plays no small part, preparing magic medicine to protect their own fighters, to destroy the enemy's, and, in the case of night raiding from enemy cattle corrals, to ensure that the enemy will sleep through the raids and that their dogs will not bark.

In Nyaheiya today, even during intervals where there is no clan warfare, a sympathetic elder who is wise in the ways of making such magic may elect to assist a son or other cattle raider by providing him with protective medicine (*iriogo*), in the form of a small stick worn in the hair near the front of the head, to keep him safe throughout the course of a raid.

"In the past," writes Ruel, "the herding of cattle was the task of older boys . . . and of warrior-youths, who if attacked could defend the cattle" (1959:22). "Large, collective herds were then taken to graze in the outlying pastures surrounding the main settlement areas of the province [clan territory]" (120). This was dangerous work. *Abamura nguching'ombe bagukwera,* runs a well-known saying: "Young men die in the cows."

During cattle raids, the uncircumcised boys (*abariisia;* sing., *umuriisia*) served a kind of apprenticeship to these warriors, accompanying them on raids but entrusted with the least hazardous tasks, such as rounding up the sheep and goats and helping to drive the captured livestock home (see also Kjerland 1995:289).

Every few years, whenever the elders came to feel that enough boys and girls had attained the appropriate age, circumcision ceremonies (*ichisaaro;* sing., *esaaro*) were held, normally after harvest time. Ruel notes that "boys were expected first to show their valour and their right to the status of warriors by raiding and killing [an] outsider" (1959:123), but Kjerland was told by one of her informants that

> "Not every boy killed a man prior to initiation. Or a lion. If one or two in the group did, this was a signal that their group was mature enough to be initiated." (1995:138)

Once having passed through *esaaro* and the lengthy initiation period that followed it, the Kuria boys emerged as *abamura* (sing., *umumura*), which means "young (circumcised) men," "youths," "warriors." Ruel calls the *abamura* "warrior-youths" (1959). The verb *-mura* has the meaning "to be healthy and physically unblemished," with a skin that shines as when the body has been rubbed with oil—a semantic indication of the extent to which the welfare of society was invested in these young men.

Their role, notes Ruel,

> was especially that of fighting to protect the province [clan] or of raiding other provinces [clans] for cattle and the qualities most praised in them were courage, loyalty to age-mates (particularly of the same circumcision set), deference to elders and smartness of appearance. (1959:120)

Whether in raiding or warfare, a warrior displayed his courage by capturing cattle and by killing or capturing enemy warriors (Ruel 1959:53). Captives would be held for ransom—a ransom to be paid in cattle. "In this way," notes Ruel, "the acquistition [*sic,* acquisition] of cattle was associated with manliness and courage, and at beer parties or on the dancing ground individuals would boast in formal declaration of the [*sic,* their] prowess" (1958:155).

For young men newly become warriors, then, raiding was a way to win prestige, to demonstrate that the men of their circumcision set had the will and the courage to defend the clan. Raiding also offered a means of obtaining bridewealth cattle:

> A custom followed in the past when a warrior-youth wishing to marry lacked cattle was for him to present a bow or spear to his father-in-law as token of the cattle which he later hoped to capture. With this pledge the marriage proceeded. When the youth had then been successful in a raid the pledge was redeemed

with cattle proudly brought to his father-in-law. (Ruel
1959:111–12; see also 1958:154)

Because interclan marriages did occur, however, creating affinal and
consanguineal links between clans, sometimes even between hostile clans,
it was regarded as "a grave offence" to attempt to capture bridewealth cattle in the process of being driven from one clan's territory to that of
another (Ruel 1959:55). Kjerland says that Nyabasi raiders sometimes utilized this prohibition as a ruse, pretending to be escorting bridewealth cattle through another clan's territory as a means of concealing the fact that
they were herding captured cattle (1995:293).

"The favourite time of the year for a raid," writes Baker,

> was after the harvest had been gathered in especially if the
> younger men had been circumcised. If this was the case they
> would almost certainly want to blood their spears on some
> enemy or other, and their boastings would be carried over the
> countryside. (1935:53)

Raiding was carried out both by day and by night. Ruel states
unequivocally that Kuria raids "were not carried out by night as were the
Maasai raids, but by day, usually as planned attacks on cattle then being
herded" (1959:52), while Kjerland describes the Maasai as "masters" of
daytime raiding and the Nyabasi Kuria clan in Kenya, among whom she
did her research, as "experts" at nighttime raiding (1995:292). For the
Maasai, Baker splits the difference, telling us that their raids "usually took
place at night or early morning" (1935:53). Berntsen, a historian who has
done fieldwork among the Maasai, writes that the larger Maasai raiding
parties "never attacked at night," but rather "travelled to their target area
only by day, and arranged to strike at dawn" (1979b:234). Smaller groups
of raiders, operating without "the full approval of secular society and the
chief prophet," did attack at night, he notes, but such raids, and the warriors who engaged in them, were regarded with disdain (1979b:235).
Although raids on enemy cattle herds in the context of warfare are
said to have been carried out only in daytime, much Kuria cattle raiding in
the precolonial period was probably carried out at night, and probably for
much the same reason that cattle raiders have operated mainly at night
from at least the late 1950s (Tanner 1966:33) onward: because it is safer.
Unquestionably, the glamour and prestige lay in daytime raiding, but the
easy—or at least easier—plunder in cattle can only have lain in raiding by
night. Newly initiated warriors, and boys eager for the adult status con-
ferred by circumcision, needed to demonstrate that they possessed the
courage and discipline to protect and defend the clan. To accomplish this

they needed to kill enemies, to capture enemies, to seize the enemy's weapons, to drive off his cattle (Ruel 1959:53). To validate their worth as warriors, they had to attack in the open, not by stealth.

The war horn (*irongwe*) was sounded and the raiding party set out, led by a "brave youth" (*umumura omokare*) who had already demonstrated his valor in combat (Ruel 1991:352). Scouts who had been sent out earlier and returned had already provided those directing the raid with the intelligence they had gathered on the area to be raided (Ruel 1959:52), along with the cattle dung, partially chewed grass, and whatever other portentous materials the dream-prophet might have required to enable him to augur the likely success of the raid. His detailed, highly specific instructions to the raiders, regarding the obstacles they would encounter and precisely which sorts of cattle they ought to capture, functioned, as Ruel notes, to inspire confidence in the raiders and to instill in them a sense of discipline and mission (Ruel 1991:344).

Cattle raiding, to borrow Mao Zedong's famous remark about revolution, was not a dinner party. Once inside enemy territory, a standard strategy of the raiders was to kill whichever members of the enemy clan or tribe had the misfortune to cross their path, strewing the trail with corpses as a means of terrorizing the enemy and discouraging their attempts either to intervene in the raid or to pursue the raiders as they fled with the cattle. One nonagenarian in Nyaheiya insisted that a Kuria raider, unlike a Maasai, would never kill a child, or a woman, even if she cried out an alarm (*ikuurate*), citing what he claimed was a Kuria belief that "if you kill a woman, your family will die out." Many Nyaheiya residents, in fact, expressed dismay and revulsion at the conduct of contemporary cattle raiders for what is widely seen as their indiscriminate killing of women, children, and old people. But Kjerland's Nyabasi informants told her the diametrical opposite: that it was the Maasai who, in the old days, would never kill women or children, and that if they do so now it is because they are emulating the Kuria (1995:276).

Arriving home from a successful raid, the raiders signaled their success by their cries, the same cries that can still be heard in Nyaheiya today whenever its men return after having successfully recovered cattle that invading cattle raiders have taken from them. "A special cry was made by someone who had killed another," notes Ruel, adding that "in the latter case a certain ritual had to be observed to prevent the ghost of the dead man from returning to harm his killer" (1959:53).

Throngs of joyously ululating women greeted the returning raiders, bearing baskets of *ubukima,* the stiff porridge made from flour and water that is the staple food of the Kuria, and *obosara,* a nonalcoholic millet drink. An informant told Kjerland that "When a rustler came home women greeted him by spraying milk in the air" (1995:294).

The cattle captured in the raid, writes Ruel,

were driven back to the homestead of the spokesman, prophet or
war-leader who directed it and were there divided, the war-leader
(or other director) first taking his share and the remainder being
divided amongst the warriors who took part. (1959:53)

While Ruel asserts that "Those who had shown greater courage than
others were given a larger share" (1959:53), Nyaheiya informants claimed
that the raiders all received an equal number of cattle, but that those who
had been most courageous were awarded the "fattest" animals. Any raider
who attempted to bypass this formal distribution of the captured cattle by
diverting cattle to his own homestead would be disciplined by the group
(Ruel 1991:344). Captives were held prisoner in the homesteads of the men
who had captured them until their kinsmen bought their release by paying
a ransom in cattle (Ruel 1959:53).

Nighttime raiding was a very different sort of business, involving, as it
invariably did, the taking of cattle from inside cattle enclosures, practically
under the noses of the owners, who were sound asleep—if the raiders were
lucky—inside huts constructed all around the circumference of the central
corral. On the one hand, the nighttime darkness served to hide the raiders,
but, on the other hand, preraid reconnaissance notwithstanding, it left
them skulking around in the blackness in unfamiliar and hostile territory.
Anyone who has ever lived in rural Africa can testify to how difficult it is
to thread one's way through and around even a fairly familiar area, late at
night, even with the moon shining, even carrying a flashlight, let alone in
practically pitch darkness, moving at a dead run, in an area of homesteads
one may never have even seen before, and then endeavoring to drive away
sometimes recalcitrant animals that may start lowing at any time, giving
the game away.
    Certainly by the 1930s, and quite possibly even well before then,
nighttime cattle raiding was carried out with the aid of accomplices in the
target clans or tribes who provided the would-be raiders with the advance
intelligence they needed regarding the choicest targets of opportunity, the
safest routes in and out, the sleeping and sentry habits of the homesteads'
inhabitants, and other vital information, and who endeavored, insofar as
possible, to stall or misdirect the pursuit of the raiders by their own people
once the raid was discovered. The quid pro quo was that the raiders would
serve as accomplices for a raid into *their* territory at some later date.
    Pace Ruel (1959:178), there is no self-evident reason why such coop-
eration would not have been feasible in precolonial times: totemic affilia-
tions aside, peace pacts between Kuria clans were made and unmade (54);
Kuria clans made common cause even with the Maasai against other
Kuria (51); and there were affinal links between even non–totemically
affiliated clans and family visits between them (Ruel 1959:55; Kjerland

1995:293, 293 n. 36). There were, in short, plenty of opportunities for an enterprising Kuria to acquire allies among people he might like to raid. And while there is no evidence that these sorts of partnership arrangements actually existed prior to the colonial era, it may be as naive to assume that cattle raiding was all blood-and-guts heroism before 1890 as it most certainly is naive to believe that cattle raiding was ever a happy-go-lucky, non–contact sport.

What does seem plain, in either event, is that nighttime raiders had as their principal objective to lay hold of the cattle and escape with them, without, if at all possible, risking a fight. Nothing as meaningfully distinguishes daytime raiding from nighttime raiding as the fact that, in daytime raiding, killing enemies was both a strategy and a goal of the raid, whereas, in nighttime raiding, killing in the territory of the enemy was taboo—which did *not* mean that the raiders went unarmed, since the victims of these raids would have been more than happy to kill *them.*

Nighttime raids, like daytime raids, were organized by spokesmen, dream-prophets, and war-leaders, and magic medicine was provided to safeguard the raiders. Assuming that accomplices were in fact not available, then careful reconnaissance would have been indispensable. Raiding was avoided on bright moonlit nights that might betray the movements of the raiders, and after a heavy rainfall, when soggy ground would slow down the escape (Kjerland 1995:292).

On the night of the raid, the wife of one of the raiders would serve a meal to the raiders before they departed: if a hole appeared in the *ubukima* while it was cooking, that portended disaster and the raid was abandoned. This is a form of divination still practiced by the wives of cattle raiders in Nyaheiya today.

Among the Nyabasi clansmen of Kenya, Kjerland notes that

> A small star, *inyunyuriri* [*sic:* should be *inyunyuunyi, inyinyuunyi,* or *inyunyinyunyi*] was closely observed. Its closeness to, or remoteness from, the moon foretold if the cattle's owner was guarding his stock. If the black feathers of the black and white birds, *irokoro* and *enserechoe,* were seen facing the men, they would return to their homes immediately. Black foretold death and sorrow. . . . Immediate cancellation also followed the sound of an howling hyena. (Kjerland 1995:292–93)

Typically, one of the raiders would climb over the log wall of the cattle corral (*oboori*) and, once inside, would remove the log pole (*umuhingo*) barring the cattle gate (*ikihita*) so as to release the cattle to his companions waiting outside. It was also possible to gain entry to the *oboori* by uprooting some of the dead trees (*amasancho*) that formed its wall, but, in either event, the cattle were nearly always removed through the cattle gate because they were considered unsuitable for use as bridewealth if their removal was effected otherwise (Baker 1935:21; Kjerland 1995:292). Entering the cattle corral was an extremely hazardous undertaking, for two reasons: (1) in what was probably the most common homestead design, although not one that is employed today in Nyaheiya, a long pole, called the *umusiiri* (or *umusieri*), ran horizontally through the cattle gate and extended literally into the hut of the homestead head's eldest son, situated directly to the right of the cattle gate, through a special round opening in the hut wall made for that purpose; a bell tied to the pole, or a rope tied from the end of the pole to the bed on which the young man slept, ensured that any surreptitious attempt to open the gate would awaken him; (2) once inside the *oboori,* a raider became a target for poisoned arrows fired at him through other cutout openings in the walls of the huts. Consequently, the raider who performed this task was considered a hero, and upon safe return home was awarded the fattest of the cattle taken.

For the raiders themselves, killing during the course of these raids—so long as the raiders were on enemy soil—was strictly prohibited, a prohibition that was underlain with penances and rituals that had to be observed if the taboo was violated. In Nyaheiya, it is often said that, in the old days, even the cry of a sleeping baby, or the cough of a man who might be on the verge of wakefulness, was sufficient to make the raiders break off the raid and leave the cattle behind. Anyone rash enough to pursue the raiders onto their own territory, however, was fair game, and the killing of such an intruder was a cause for formal boasting and rejoicing (see also Kjerland 1995:292, 294).

Ubuchunchuuri, the "stealing [of cattle] by stealth"—what we would call cattle theft—was an altogether different matter from "raiding," for it entailed the taking of cattle belonging to members of either one's own *eeka* (lineage), one's own *irigiha* (clan segment), or one's own *ikiaro* (clan).

> Prior to the European occupation of the country there was but little stock theft in Bukuria. The watertight compartments into which each tribe was divided rendered it dangerous for individuals to wander outside the boundaries of their clans and so difficult for them to dispose of stock stolen from their fellow-clansmen. (TNA 13747 [Secretariat] 10/29/31:1; see also Baker 1935:45)

Moreover:

> Once a large number of cattle had been stolen, and their owners were searching for them, it was dangerous for the thieves to

attempt to hide the stolen animals in the bush—unprotected from wild animals and tsetse fly, with little water for the stock and no food for the men. Furthermore, men found with cattle in the bush were openly showing guilt, so for successful theft of a large number the cattle had to be merged into the herds of a community sympathetic to the thieves and hostile to the owners. Conditions for a large-scale raid did not exist within a unified tribal community, because the stolen herd could not be absorbed into existing herds with any explanations which were likely to satisfy the neighbours. (Tanner 1966:33)

What is more, effective mechanisms were in place for the punishment of violators, in that

cattle stealing within the group was punished by fining the thief double the number of cattle stolen—amongst the Wabwassi and Bakenye living south of the Mara the award is said to have been ten times the number of the cattle stolen. If the thief or thieves were unable to pay the full amount of the fine the balance was collected from their relatives (i.e. the clan)—communal punishment is therefore an established Kuria custom. All the cattle awarded were handed to the man who had been deprived of his property and the extra beasts provided him with the wherewithal to reward informants liberally. . . . An inveterate stock thief was strangled by his clan as his actions caused an incessant drain on their resources. (TNA 13747 [Secretariat] 10/29/31:1; see also Baker 1935:45, 78)

Public opinion, then, was the greatest deterrent of all and it is regrettable that no such sanction operates nowadays. (Baker 1935:45)

Indeed, by the time Baker penned those lines, cattle raiding, in its very essence, had become completely transformed—by the penetration of the market economy, by the imposition of colonialist policies, and by the Kuria response to them.

CHAPTER 4

"A Retarding and Corrupting Influence": Cattle Raiding in Its Colonial Context

With the signing of the Anglo-German agreement of 1890, the area that would, following World War I, come to be known as Tanganyika—and, some years later, as mainland Tanzania—was inscribed on the maps of the Western world as German East Africa. A series of military expeditions was dispatched throughout the new colony to consolidate German rule, and local headquarters were established in pacified areas (Rwezaura 1985:34). A British report of 1909 states that "it is not possible to mention a clan within a day's march of the Anglo-German border which was not punished forcibly by the Government of German East Africa" (South Kavirondo District Annual Report of 1909, quoted in Ruel 1959:149 and Kjerland 1995:166). Iliffe writes that "with their brutal soldiers and police, German officials inspired great terror" (1979:119).

Arriving at Shirati, on the shores of Lake Victoria, west of Kuria country, in 1902, the Germans erected a fort there, initiated construction of a road network, and traversed Lake Victoria by canoe in order to extend their control to Musoma and adjacent areas (Rwezaura 1985:34). Located forty-two kilometers west of Tarime, Shirati was ideally situated to serve as a depot for the exportation of cash crops, and its proximity to the Kenya border made it an excellent base for confronting the British as well as for thwarting cattle raids by the Nilotic Luo people living on the British side (Anacleti 1979:1).

To facilitate the levying of taxes, the imposition of fines and punishments, and the recruitment of forced African labor, the Germans installed local collaborators as chiefs over the indigenous peoples, notwithstanding the fact that most of them—including the Kuria—had no tradition of chiefly rule (Rwezaura 1985:34; Kjerland 1995:81 n. 81). In the Kuria case, this entailed bypassing the council of elders (*inchaama*) and other traditional leaders in favor of an appointed chief for every clan (Baker 1935:11). Chiefs who failed to carry out their duties satisfactorily were executed (Cory 1947:73; Ruel 1959:148–49; Rwezaura 1985:35 n. 1).

Although cattle raiding was outlawed, the "raiding" of other clans and tribes for cattle continued, albeit apparently at a much reduced rate after 1900, as the Germans successfully imposed their authority. Cattle "theft," in the sense of taking cattle from one's own clan or serving as an accomplice to outsiders who did so, "was apparently still rare" (TNA 13747 [Secretariat] 10/29/31:1–2). Cattle raiders whom the Germans captured, writes Baker,

> were punished with corporal punishment of not less than twenty-five lashes and with a term of imprisonment, during which the culprit is said to have been obliged to pay for his food and provide his own clothes. (TNA 13747 [Secretariat] 10/29/31:2)

For the evolution of cattle raiding among the Kuria, the years from about 1900 to 1914 were crucial, for this was the period when the line between cattle theft and cattle raiding—as these terms had been traditionally understood by the Kuria—began to blur, when it became, if not socially acceptable, at least thinkable for some young men to begin taking cattle by stealth from members of their own clan.

Kjerland, citing Berntsen's (1979b:285) Maasai research, attributes this sea change to the drastic shortages in livestock wrought by the rinderpest (*endoroe*) epizootics of the 1890s: with cattle so scarce, she argues, "people would even steal from those who were closely related to them" (Kjerland 1995:277). But, by all available accounts, taking cattle from one's own clansmen remained rare even after the herds had rebounded to their pre-rinderpest levels—which seems to have occurred, at least in Kenya Kurialand, by as early as 1909 if not earlier (215), suggesting that there may have been other factors at work promoting change as well.

By doing away with the authority of the councils of elders and appointing their own hand-picked chiefs to be Kuria leaders, the Germans had imposed a form of administration that was wholly alien to the Kuria people. The Germans also imposed taxes and then seized livestock in the event those taxes were not paid (Rwezaura 1985:39). "'If we did not pay tax,'" one of Kjerland's informants told her,

> "a cow or some goats were taken by force. Sometimes they took the animals of your brother instead; or they simply sent people to Shirati to prison." (1995:167)

The colonizers also appropriated large numbers of Kuria livestock arbitrarily, without compensation (Tobisson 1986:15), and often these livestock would be deposited for safekeeping in the corral of a friendly chief, who might well be a member of the same clan (*ikiaro*) as the man whose cattle had been confiscated but of a different clan segment (*irigiha*). Many of these chiefs had already engendered considerable antagonism in their own communities by unscrupulously seizing upon their newfound authority as an opportunity for defrauding their people. It thus came to be seen as acceptable, or at least as more acceptable than it had been previously, for a man who felt that his cattle had been wrongfully taken from him to seek to recover his property by taking cattle from the chief or, by extension, from any other member of the chief's clan segment. The category of persons from whom it was socially acceptable to take cattle was thus expanded considerably (Anacleti 1979:6).

The inevitable slackening of German control over its East African colony during World War I allowed these trends a new freedom to assert themselves. "During the war," notes Baker,

> the general confusion in the area north of the Mara River afforded the stock thieves an ideal opportunity and cattle lifting increased considerably. (TNA 13747 [Secretariat] 10/29/31:2)

As the British victory drew near, and the Germans were forced to withdraw from the Mara region, the Kuria deposed all but one of their chiefs and reinstated the councils of elders abolished by the Germans. The new British administration, however, reinstated these chiefs, or, in instances where local opposition precluded that, installed a close relative of that chief in his stead (Baker 1935:11; Anacleti 1979:6; Rwezaura 1985:35).

What followed was a period of what Ruel has termed "unstructured" administration, during which, owing to the remoteness of Kuria country from the British administrative headquarters at Musoma, in Tanganyika, and at Kisii, in Kenya, local administration was left in the hands of the chiefs with only occasional, brief visits from British administrative personnel (Ruel 1959:152). Many of these chiefs were heavily involved in cattle raiding themselves, planning and organizing raids, shaking down cattle raiders for a share of the proceeds, sometimes even participating in raids themselves (TNA 13747 [Secretariat] 12/22/32 [a]:2).

During this period, from 1918 through the mid- to late 1920s, cattle raiding mushroomed to become "the major administrative problem" for the British colonial administration (Ruel 1959:152; see also TNA 23426 [Secretariat] 7/15/36 and Kjerland 1995:298–99). Contemplating this tumultuous period from the vantage point of the early 1930s, Baker observed:

> After the war intercommunication between the sub-tribes [clans] and with Kenya became much freer than was formerly the case and stock thieving became a habit especially amongst the Bakira, Batimbaru, Bakenye, and Banyamongo.
> When I came to the District in 1924 stock thieving was endemic. (TNA 13747 [Secretariat] 10/29/31:2)

It was "expressly to try to control and to prevent the habitual cattle thieving which was fast on the increase, firstly between the Maasai and the Kuria, and, secondly, between the Kuria and the Luo" (Anacleti 1979:2, my translation; see also Ruel 1959:152 and Kjerland 1995:71) that, in 1928, an administrative office was established at Tarime town, in the heart of Kuria country. Nonetheless, cattle raiding surged in the turbulent early years of the 1930s, fueled in part—but only in part—by the food scarcities inflicted by the disastrous drought of 1931.

> This assisted—though it was not a primary cause—in an enormous increase in cases of theft of goats and sheep from grazing—frequently for immediate slaughter and consumption there and then by the thieves. There are also a distressingly large proportion of juvenile thieves of small stock at grazing. (TNA 13747 [Secretariat] 12/22/32 [b]:2)

In North Mara, stated a 1936 colonial report:

> Stock theft is practically confined to the Bakuria, an excitable, violent but extremely virile and intelligent people. . . . It may be said that 75% of the working time of the Administrative Officer is taken up with cases connected with stock thefts. (TNA 23426 [Secretariat] 7/15/36)

Cattle raiding was by now a far cry from what it had been in the precolonial era. The British now confronted multiclan cattle-raiding groups—British colonial documents in the Tanzania National Archives refer to them variously as "gangs" (TNA 13747 [Secretariat] 11/2/31:2; TNA 13747 [Secretariat] 12/22/32 [a,b]) or "syndicates" (Letter [Kenya] No.ADM.15/1/1 of 2/9/31, quoted in TNA 13747 [Secretariat] 10/3/31:2)—that operated across a vast area, dividing up herds that had been taken from one place and then remixing them with animals from other herds to reduce the possibility of their being identified, pasturing them in secluded valleys while awaiting opportunities to market them, moving cattle effortlessly back and forth across a porous Tanganyika-Kenya border in response to regional price fluctuations and shifts in the subtle algebra of supply and demand (cf. Anderson 1986:399, 408):

> They . . . help each other out with any matter of false evidence that may be useful in Court, conceal each other's property when the time for levying of fines comes around, mutually deter witnesses, etc. etc. . . . Until such persons are either killed on a raid, or enter a respected elderhood, they are a constant menace. (TNA 13747 [Secretariat] 12/22/32 [b]:6)

This historical change, or transformation, in the nature, conduct, character, and, ultimately, even the cultural-ecological impacts (see chap. 8) of cattle raiding among the Kuria occurred as a consequence of the penetration and evolution of the colonial economy and constituted a response by the Kuria to the implementation of colonial policies designed to facilitate the imposition and growth of that economy in North Mara. As this transformation can only be understood in light of those colonial policies, they will be discussed in detail in the following pages.

Stated briefly, however, the principal goal of British colonial officials in North Mara was to transform the Kuria into peasant cultivators, that is, farmers who would grow whatever food they needed to live on while at the same time producing a surplus of cash crops to fuel the manufacturing and processing industries of Western Europe (Rwezaura 1985:47). In pursuit of this objective, the colonialists sought to promote agricultural production while undermining the pastoral component of the Kuria economy through taxation, destocking, and forced cattle sales; introduced drought-resistant crops to forestall peasant withdrawal from cash-crop production in the wake of periodic drought; made cash earnings mandatory for indigenous people through the imposition of fines and taxes; and calculatingly fostered their dependence on manufactured goods from such countries as Great Britain, India, Holland, Japan, Italy, Germany, and the United States (Rwezaura 1985:47, 50).

Intertribal and intratribal warfare, including cattle raiding, were criminalized, not as a means of protecting the lives and property of Africans—which would have been an impractical goal, in any event, owing to the paucity of available police manpower and the remoteness of the Kuria settlements—but rather as a means of forestalling the kind of turmoil that might jeopardize the dependability of cash-crop production. Tanner, himself a former colonial official who had served in the area, observed,

> The colonial Government from the start of its rule had been actively concerned with preventing inter-tribal raids and retaliations, regarding them as a major threat to overall peace and order, but it paid much less attention to the recovery of the stolen cattle and the arrest of the thieves—except in the case of mass raids. (1966:31)

On the local level, a number of factors and indigenous attitudes helped to sustain this policy. Although "stock thefts were common and nearly always resulted in a big loss to owners" who had the misfortune to become victims of cattle raids (TNA 13747 [Secretariat] 7/26/29), "the totals of cattle stolen never represented a severe economic loss to the community as a whole" (Tanner 1966:34). And while the threat of violence in the course of a cattle raid was always present, the actual incidence of violence was extremely low (35). Perhaps most importantly, however, "there was no generalised public opinion against cattle theft as such" (41), partly because

> too many local people were involved in such thefts for any public outcry to be possible. Few were robbed in comparison with

the total number of cattle holders, and more profited from the slaughtered beasts than were aggrieved. (Tanner 1966:35)

In one noteworthy incident, Chacha Ikengo, a Kuria chief

who was described by an Administrative Office many years ago as "afraid of the cattle stealing community in his chiefdom" was dismissed for countenancing active measures directed by his people against police investigation into cattle thefts in his area, which measures culminated in an attack by a mob upon the Bukira police post. (TNA 20/g/11 [Accession 83] 12/28/46:3)

All of this, not surprisingly, both reflected and helped to reinforce the prevailing attitude of colonial officials on the scene:

As a matter of fact stock lifting appears to be the national sport of the Bakuria and where there are no [European] settlers to complicate the matter I am afraid that I feel rather kindly towards the stock lifter if he is a stout fellow with a stick and not a mere sneak-thief, and I doubt if we need be unduly put out about it. The officers must see that serious violence is punished, and should derive healthy (and valuable) occupation from pitting their wits against the local stock thief. This will keep everyone amused except the stock owner, and he is no doubt an emeritus stock thief, and can in any case protect himself by associating with his fellow stock owners in insisting on the N. [Native] Authorities putting a stop to the thieving as they certainly could if they wanted to. (TNA 13747 [Secretariat] 4/8/30)

Furthermore, by outlawing intertribal warfare, the colonialists largely eliminated the threat of retaliation by a tribe that had been victimized by cattle raiding against the tribe from which the raiders had come—and thereby aided and abetted the transformation of cattle raiding from an undertaking in which the entire community had both a stake and an interest into an activity carried out by, and mainly for the benefit of, small groups of accomplices acting independently of the communities from which they came. By outlawing intratribal, including interclan, warfare, the colonialists effectively did away with the system of penalties and fines—imposed against "thieves" (in the indigenous Kuria sense) *and* their families—that had helped to curtail those forms of cattle raiding that had been regarded as illegitimate in precolonial times (see chap. 3). As Ruel succinctly summarizes it,

the sanctions of the traditional society which could be used against cattle-theft are now no longer allowed to operate; at the same time the sanctions of modern governmental organization have proved equally deficient. (1959:178)

Many colonial officials held to a narrowly cultural view of cattle raiding. Cattle raiding in North Mara is "practically synonymous with the Kuria tribe," note Sillery and Montague in a 1932 stock-theft memorandum; "the illegal acquisition of stock is in the blood of the people" (TNA 13747 [Secretariat] 12/22/32 [b]:5). Tanner, having seemingly ignored the abundant evidence of multiclan cattle-raiding groups and transborder marketing, and having decided that a "basic motive for [cattle] theft was the almost universal and voracious appetite for meat" (1966:37), goes on to conclude, incomprehensibly, that it is

> unlikely that cattle theft was the result of rural poverty, or that economic motives predominated. (41)
>
> It seems more likely that, with protein shortage, rural boredom and political inactivity the young men committed thefts out of bravado. (39–40)

Cash-crop agriculture, in any event, was seen as the key to transforming the Kuria's "economic outlook" and the "romantic admiration" of cattle raiding fostered by that outlook:

> [T]he long view should be taken that it was only by effecting some change in the economic outlook of the people that any radical improvement would come about. . . . The acceptance by the people of a mode of life in which agriculture played a greater part, might do away with the somewhat romantic admiration that the ordinary citizen still had for the successful raider. (TNA 23426 [Secretariat] 1936:3)

A faltering effort had been made by the Germans to introduce cotton into the area in 1912, and these efforts were renewed and intensified by the British (Rwezaura 1985:36). In 1922, a hut and poll tax (*irigooti* or *iriguuti*) was instituted that was applicable to every owner or occupant of a hut throughout Tanganyika. Polygynists were required

> to pay additional tax in respect of each additional wife. Every able-bodied male of sixteen and above, who was not the owner of a hut, was liable to pay an annual poll tax. In 1930 the Hut and Poll Tax rate for Mara region was ten shillings. This rate placed the Kuria as paying the third highest rate of tax among the 28 districts of Tanganyika. (Rwezaura 1985:42 n. 1)

Concerned that periodic food shortages would disrupt cash-crop production by forcing peasants to revert to production for subsistence exclusively, the British introduced new high-yield, antifamine crops such as maize and cassava and instituted a program of famine relief (Rwezaura 1985:37 n. 1). The main demand for maize meal came from the miners working the scores of gold mines in the region, many of which, including the Mara Mine, which began operations in 1929 and employed some 700 men, were situated in the Nyamongo area (TNA 23426 [Secretariat] 7/15/36; Rwezaura 1985:36).

Notwithstanding all these colonial efforts, however, the project of transforming North Mara into a region of cash-crop agriculture, although eventually successful, particularly in the highland area, was very slow in gaining widespread acceptance. One reason was that the Kuria had other means of earning cash income to pay their taxes and fines: they served in the colonial armed forces and joined the police, remained in the local area to work in its gold mines, or crossed the border to labor for wages on the coffee, tea, and sisal plantations of Kenya. If they were desperate enough, they could even sell one or two head of cattle, though this was never viewed as anything but an option of last resort (Ruel 1959:152–53; Rwezaura 1985:40).

Another reason for the Kuria reluctance to embrace cash crops was that the remoteness of their country from Shirati and the port of Musoma made the marketing of their crops in Tanganyika an extremely problematic enterprise. Geographically, the Kuria's natural market was Kenya, but the separate administration of the two territories, even after the British came to control them both, made the marketing of Tanganyika crops in Kenya untenable (Rwezaura 1985:40).

Indeed, North Mara—renamed Tarime District in 1973—is still wedded to Kenya geographically much as it was then, bounded by Kenya on the north and east and Lake Nyanza on the west, and separated on the south from other parts of Tanzania by the Mara River, which is crossable today (but was not then) by a bridge at Kirumi linking the neighboring Tarime and Serengeti Districts. "These island-like circumstances," notes Anacleti,

> have caused the entire history of North Mara to be greatly influenced by the neighboring country of Kenya. This situation is certainly strengthened by the fact that there is no part of North Mara which does not have kindred on the other side, in Kenya. For example, going from east to west, we find the Kenya Kuria and the Tanzania Kuria, and, similarly, the Kenya Luo and the Tanzania Luo. These people have carried on economic as well as kinship relations without heeding the boundaries set down by the colonialists. To many of them, therefore, an international border represents merely an inessential, non-obligatory separation of their people. (1979:2, my translation)

The third, and final, major impediment to Kuria involvement with cash crops lay in the fact that the Kuria were far more intent on rebuilding their cattle herds to the levels they had enjoyed prior to the epizootics of rinderpest and contagious bovine pleuropneumonia (CBPP) (*ekehaha*) that had devastated East Africa in the 1890s than they were on dedicating themselves to agriculture (Rwezaura 1985:38). In the wake of these disasters, which, in the Maasai case, are estimated to have killed between 70 and 95 percent of their cattle (Kjerland 1995:119), the Kuria bartered all of their surplus grain for livestock, or deployed it, in lieu of cattle, as bridewealth (Baker 1935:45; Ruel 1959:107). Veterinary control of bovine diseases, introduced early on by the colonialists, also significantly facilitated herd recovery (Rwezaura 1985:72), and, as the Kuria began to capitalize on opportunities to earn money through wage labor, they invested whatever extra money they earned in cattle (Ruel 1959:177), thereby enlarging their herds still further. Indeed,

> the need to acquire money and thus cattle for bridewealth seems to have been the main stimulant for the early labour migration and early Reports note how earnings were then brought home to buy stock. (Ruel 1959:176)

Colonial officials only rarely understood the complex interdependence of agriculture and livestock raising in the Kuria economy. Rather, they tended to view cattle keeping as uneconomic, as a profligate squandering of the time, labor, and resources that they felt could far more profitably be devoted to agriculture. It was in the hope of somehow making cattle keeping "economical" that the colonialists introduced the ox-plough and promoted the production of semifluid clarified butter, or ghee.

In actuality, of course, cattle were not, and never had been, mere uneconomic appendages to Kuria agricultural life. Cattle played a vital role in Kuria subsistence, in ritual, and in social relations—and, as money came to acquire increasing importance in the course of capitalist transformation, they proved to be

> a more reliable form of capital than agriculture—which was frequently affected by droughts. Cattle also lasted better than crops, and paid high interest through the birth of calves. (Tanner 1966:37)

By the time Ruel arrived on the scene, in the 1950s, the size of the Kuria cattle herd surpassed, by a wide margin, what it had been even in the pre-rinderpest, pre-CBPP years. The Kuria, he wrote,

> have now more cows, more grain and a greater number of crops than they ever had in the past. The increase on pre-rinderpest herds of cattle must have been at least five-fold and on the post-rinderpest herds of the late 19th century when the Germans first arrived, the increase is nearer twenty-fold. (Ruel 1959:170)

As Kuria herd size rose, Kuria bridewealth (*ikihingo*)—the number of cattle received by Kuria fathers for their daughters in marriage—rose with it. Max Weiss, a German photographer and administrator who visited the area in 1904, was told that Kuria bridewealth had amounted to between ten and twelve head of cattle in the pre-rinderpest years (Kjerland and Svensson 1988:5), an estimate supported by Ruel, who reports pre-rinderpest bridewealth as having stood at about ten head of cattle, with fifteen the maximum (1959:107).

In the wake of the bovine epidemics, however, Ruel writes that Kuria bridewealth plummeted to "only one or two cows or their equivalent in goats or finger-millet (one granary of the latter being reckoned as equivalent to a heifer)" (1959:107).

Baker, who asserts that five goats were the equivalent of one head of cattle (1935:39), seems to suggest that bridewealth immediately following the epidemics may have been even lower than that when he writes:

> In pre-European days the bride-price is said to have consisted of one foodbin full of grain or one goat and rose as the number of cattle in the district increased. (45)

With remarkable resiliency, however, the herds rebounded. Weiss reports that Kuria bridewealth was up to from three to four head by the time of his visit, in 1904 (Kjerland and Svensson 1988:5), and bridewealth continued to rise in the ensuing years—particularly during the period from about 1920 to 1935 (Ruel 1959:107)—climbing to eleven, then fifteen, then twenty head by 1935 (Baker 1935:45; TNA 13747 [Secretariat] 2/26/32); to twenty to thirty head, or "even more," by 1945 (Cory 1945:40); and then to thirty to thirty-five head, and "occasionally even more" than that, in the 1950s (Ruel 1959:107).

Kuria bridewealth rates, which are determined by negotiation, are influenced by a range of factors—certainly the number of males seeking brides and the availability of marriageable females is one of these—and the rates for individual marriages can vary quite widely from one another, even within the same village, even on the same day. Generally speaking, however, the market for brides is a market much like any other, and, all other things being equal, as the amount of "currency"—in this case, cattle—in circulation increases, its value decreases, and the amount of it needed to effect a "purchase" climbs accordingly (Goldschmidt 1974; see also Ruel 1959:171).

Rwezaura argues that bridewealth rose in part because elder males became aware that their traditional control of society—hinging on their control over cattle and women, and, through this control, control over the rising male generation—was slipping away from them owing to the opportunities of their juniors to acquire cattle and, through cattle, women, with income they earned in the new money economy. Consequently, the elders lost confidence in the efficacy of the economic and social relations created by marriage and focused instead on maximizing their gains from lump-

sum bridewealth payments up front, thereby transforming bridewealth
from a mechanism of social integration into "an item of individual consumption" (1985:81).

Tobisson, arguing against Rwezaura, maintains that "the elders'
indisputable position of authority" remained intact during this period
(1986:27) and that the bridewealth rate rose steadily "to comply with a
growing livestock population" (187). Further, Ruel maintains that
bridewealth rose, in part, because the Kuria's "basic subsistence economy
has expanded but not developed" into a fully monetized, capitalist economy (1959:172), and, given that "no new outlet has been given to cattle as
wealth" (171)—that is, through the privatization of land and "the raising
of stock for sale" (173)—and that their economy therefore "remains the
same," the main purpose of Kuria cattle remains their use in bridewealth
transactions "and thus as an index of social wealth" (171).

What remains undisputed by all parties, however, is that the Kuria cattle
population soared in the course of the colonial era and that Kuria bridewealth
soared right along with it. Before long, the British colonial administration had
become persuaded that a crucial, causal link existed between high bridewealth
and the upwardly spiraling incidence of cattle raiding:

> No description of cattle would be complete without reference
> to stock-thieving, at which the Ba-Kuria are very expert. . . .
> Natives state that stock thieving was practically unknown in
> [the] old days and attribute the increase to the inordinate amount
> of cattle required by the present elders as bride-price.
> There is no doubt that the inflated bride-price did increase the
> number of stock thefts and avaricious parents often tell their
> sons that if they want to marry they must go and steal beasts for
> the bride-price. (Baker 1935:45)

> The Kuria rate of bridewealth is one of the highest for the whole
> of East Africa. . . . A high bridewealth has been thought to
> encourage cattle theft (since young men whose families lack cat-
> tle can obtain them only in this way). (Ruel 1959:174)

> Against an unduly high bridewealth it has been said that it makes
> marriage difficult for young men and so encourages either cattle-
> theft, or alternatively abduction of brides. (Ruel 1959:179–80)

Beginning in the 1920s, therefore, the British administrations of both
Tanganyika and Kenya undertook strenuous efforts to restrict the size of
bridewealth through the force of law. "This is an excellent thing," observed a
1921 Kenya government report, "allowing the young men to obtain wives,
and removing a fruitful cause of cattle theft" (quoted in Ruel 1959:175).

In Tanganyika, in 1929, the North Mara Federation Council issued an order limiting bridewealth to three head of cattle, plus one additional head to be slaughtered for the wedding feast (TNA 13747 [Secretariat] 2/26/32:6–7; Baker 1935:45), with infractions punishable by three months in prison plus a fine for both bridewealth giver and bridewealth taker—as well as the confiscation of all the cattle delivered in excess of the maximum (Rwezaura 1985:75; Tobisson 1986:18, 26, 30 n. 14).

In addition, regulations requiring official permission for the transfer of livestock between wards, originally promulgated to inhibit cattle theft and the spread of bovine diseases, were also used to monitor the movement and number of bridewealth cattle. "After 1930," writes Rwezaura,

> the prescribed procedure for transferring marriage cattle was for the intended husband to drive his herd to the Chiefs' Court where he handed them over before witnesses; with each beast being registered individually by name and sex in a special . . . book. (1985:76)

Infractions of the rules were unrelenting, however, and the legal maximum was increased to ten head of cattle in 1932 (TNA 13747 [Secretariat] 2/26/32:7; Kjerland 1995:90).

As should be obvious, the elder males of Kuria society—who, as wife givers, were the principal beneficiaries of high bridewealth payments, and who, as wife takers, were in the best position to make those payments—had not the slightest interest in complying with the bridewealth regulations. The chiefs, for their part, found in the regulations profitable new opportunities in helping others circumvent the regulations or in agreeing, for a price, to look the other way (Tobisson 1986:26–27). Viewed in economic terms, the bridewealth regulations were artificial price controls imposed on a thriving marriage market. Wife givers resolutely held out for what the market would bear and conjured innumerable stratagems for evading the regulations and getting the most they could for their daughters.

The Kuria system of stock associateship, or "putting out cattle for others to mind" (*ogosagaria*), provided the cover for one such subterfuge. Under the *ogosagaria* system, a man routinely lent out some of his animals to other stock holders, both as a means of spreading the risk of stock losses owing to disease and cattle raiding and as a means of fostering ties with others. A cattle owner might place, for example, a total of twenty of his cattle in the enclosures of friends and relatives while at the same time taking into his own corral a larger, smaller, or identical number of cattle belonging to some wholly different, or only partly different, assortment of holders. The consequence of all this, for the authorities, was that

> No one, therefore, can really say how many beasts a man owns for those with whom cattle are left will not say who is the real

owner though ready enough, when fined by the Native Court, to
way [*sic,* say] that none of the beasts in their kraal [cattle enclo-
sure] is their own property and that they themselves have not the
where withall [*sic,* wherewithal] to pay the fine or award. (Baker
1935:44)

To evade the bridewealth restrictions, the wife taker would drive the legal
number of bridewealth cattle to the chief's court while depositing the
bridewealth cattle in excess of that number in the corral of an agreed-upon
third party, who would deliver them to the wife giver at a later date (Ruel
1959:108, 177).

Another ruse entailed including, among the legally sanctioned ten
head of cattle, cows that were about to calf, or augmenting the legal maximum with young calves that, the wife takers would disingenuously claim,
were too young to be separated from their mothers right now but would
certainly be returned when they were a little older (Rwezaura 1985:76).
And some fathers found husbands for their daughters in areas far from
home where regulations governing bridewealth were nonexistent, more
lenient, or less stringently enforced (Rwezaura 1985:77).

In the final analysis, the British colonial effort to limit bridewealth
failed spectacularly:

Rules restricting the amount of bridewealth payable have been
issued under the Native Authority Ordinance. These rules are
not followed and there are very few cases in which legal
bridewealth is [not exceeded]. (Cory 1945, quoted in Rwezaura
1985:78)

The attempts made at different times in both territories to
reduce cattle-theft by legislation restricting bridewealth have
surely failed: the bridewealth law has been ignored and the effect
on cattle-theft has been negligible. (Ruel 1959:180)

Beyond their concern for high bridewealth as a cause of cattle raiding,
the colonialists also saw it as leading inexorably to the buildup of large cattle herds, overstocking, and land degradation, a problem that absorbed
much of their attention from the 1920s onward (Ruel 1959:174; Rwezaura
1985:73). In addition to being uneconomical, it was felt, pastoralist pursuits accompanied by unchecked marriage payments would invariably
ravage the land and stifle their efforts at agricultural development. The
administration had levied fines and imposed taxes as a means of coercing
the Kuria and other pastoral peoples into selling off their cattle to acquire
the cash with which to pay them. A system of markets had been organized,
and many cattle keepers, throughout Tanganyika, had found themselves
with little alternative other than to auction off a portion of their livestock
to satisfy their tax obligation (Rwezaura 1985:42).

These markets also became an important mechanism by which Tanganyika's indigenous peoples, including the Kuria, came gradually to be enfolded into the embrace of the world capitalist system. Griffiths, describing a Tanganyika cattle market attended by Maasai in the 1930s, writes that,

> as beasts are sold, a long queue of pig-tailed warriors has formed, waiting to pay tax and clerks are kept busy early and late making out tax tickets. Then, with what remains of the price of his beast, the owner finds his way to the lines of Indian stalls, where in tents piles of blankets are for sale, and rings of beads are temptingly displayed on large bamboo frames. On the ground are mugs and pots of iron and brass, and steel swords and spearheads for the men. (Griffiths 1938:100; see also Winter 1962:465)

Rwezaura correctly argues that, over time, the Kuria's steadfast determination not to part with their cattle was steadily eroded by their increasing reliance on European manufactured goods (Rwezaura 1985:41; see also Murmann 1974:105), and, indeed, sales of cattle by Africans in Tanganyika did rise dramatically during the 1920s, attaining their highest level in 1928 (Kjerland 1995:284). But the strategy the Kuria mainly employed was one of using the money they earned from marketing cash crops, police work, gold mining, and other pursuits to pay their taxes and then ploughing whatever surplus remained back into livestock. Cash-crop production was thus harnessed to the engine of livestock expansion, and the colonialists never succeeded in meeting their destocking quotas.

With the onset of World War II, however, the struggling efforts to bring about destocking and restrict bridewealth conveniently coincided with the need to provide beef to the men at the front. Every Mara taxpayer was required to contribute either one head of cattle or its cash equivalent to the war effort, and an urgent effort was instituted to persuade the cattle-keeping peoples of Tanganyika to bring forth cattle for sale to buyers for the meat canneries, in Tanganyika and in Kenya, that had been designated the task of slaughtering and processing the meat for the troops (Rwezaura 1985:42). In the notes for his 1943 Annual Report, however, the assistant district officer, North Mara, noted that "[a]ppeals to produce slaughter cattle for sale to the Kenya Livestock Control met with poor response: owners were not anxious to sell and the high prices offered made little appeal to an area which is at present saturated with money" owing to "the golden stream of army remittances which pours in [to North Mara] each month from relatives in the Services" (TNA 20/g/11 [Accession 83] 12/21/43:4, 1/14/43:10).

Accordingly, when the meat-packers proved unable to procure their quotas, the British took what they saw as the essential next step and imposed a program of compulsory stock sales (Rwezaura 1985:42–43, 74; Tobisson 1986:26).

In 1944, a "storm of cattle requisition" broke upon the people of North Mara (TNA 20/g/11 [Accession 83] 12/21/43:5). District quotas were assigned based on cattle-population estimates, with Musoma District required to provide 4,000 head of cattle within four months' time (Rwezaura 1985:43).

> The livestock attached to each house [homestead] were counted and the householder [homestead head] was required to sell a given number. (Winter 1962:467)

When cattle owners still refused to market their stock,

> chiefs' messengers were deployed throughout the district and given powers to seize cattle from specified homesteads. (Rwezaura 1985:43, citing TNA 47/36/1940)

The markets at which cattle were compulsorily auctioned were

> supervised by a European government official, a Livestock Marketing Officer, who is employed by the territorial Veterinary Department. . . . Assisting him is a small African staff. . . . The important members of this group are the market master, who is in direct charge of the marketing procedures, the auctioneer and his assistant, and the clerks who record the sales. (Winter 1962:465)

In an effort to ensure a government monopoly on the cattle trade, it was made "an offence for any cattle to be bartered or sold . . . other than at a declared market" (TNA 23426 [Secretariat] 4/18/36:2).

This policy was vigorously resisted by stock owners throughout Tanganyika, by none more than the Kuria, who utilized their stock associateship system and relocated portions of their herds under cover of darkness to conceal the size of their holdings. Sometimes they even entirely abandoned their homesteads in the highlands in favor of new, more remote settlements in the Mara River valley bottoms, farther from the reach of government intervention (Tobisson 1986:27–28).

Even many of those who were willing to sell—it is impossible to estimate *how* many—circumvented the official prohibition against selling their stock other than at the officially sanctioned auctions in Tanganyika and instead smuggled them across the border to sell to private buyers in Kenya, where cattle prices have invariably been higher than those in Tanganyika from the early 1930s onward (Kjerland 1995:284; see also Rwezaura 1985:42). Indeed, as early as 1937, according to Kjerland, "it was estimated that 50% of the stock which was slaughtered in Kenya came from Tanganyika" (1995:284).

The border dividing Kenya from German East Africa—later to become Tanganyika—had represented a major administrative distraction for the German and British colonial regimes from the time of its demarcation in 1902. Although some have stated that the Kuria population was artificially divided by this border, Kjerland argues that the Kuria essentially divided themselves by fleeing the German side for the British side in large numbers, particularly during the period from 1905 through 1912, to escape the Germans' demand for forced labor and other brutalities of German rule (1995:69, 92 n. 128, 142–48). German efforts to stem this emigration by setting up armed border-police posts and imposing pass restrictions proved ineffective (Letter [Kenya] No.ADM.15/1/1 of 2/9/31, quoted in TNA 13747 [Secretariat] 10/3/31:2; Ruel 1959:151).

Certainly, the Kuria had been migrating back and forth across the interterritorial line even before there *was* a line for the same reasons they continue to do so today: to visit relatives, take their cattle to salt licks, make marriages, collect debts, and secure new land for raising crops and pasturing their cattle (TNA 13747 [Secretariat] 9/24/31:7; TNA 13747 [Secretariat] 10/3/31:1). The colonial imposition of the boundary and of regulations designed to regulate movement back and forth across it, however, combined with the Kuria's early response to those measures, did have the ultimate effect of dividing their population in half, cleaving several Kuria clans (*not* including the Nyamongo clan, which remained entirely on what was ultimately to become the Tanzania side) in two and making the carrying-out of everyday-life-as-usual problematic for the Kuria (Prazak 1992:61–70).

It was never possible to patrol the border with sufficient effectiveness to cut off the traffic across it, however, and cattle raiders soon became adroit at exploiting the fact that the two territories were governed by separate administrations, first by the British and the Germans, and then, following World War I, by two separate, autonomous British administrations:

> There is very little doubt that the natives of this [Kenya] location indulge to a great extent in the pastime of stealing stock from their neighbours. . . . [They] steal from one another and run stock into Tanganyika Territory to hide it. The Tanganyika natives repeat the performance on their side and hide it in Kenya. (Hodge 1927, quoted in Kjerland 1995:71)

> [The] Kuria have taken advantage of the line drawn through their territory and across their provinces [clan territories] to be— or to convey their property to—whichever side of it is most to their profit; the boundary and the proximity of the differently administered Masai territory in Kenya have both helped to provide an escape route for stolen cattle. (Ruel 1959:151)

Cattle raiders were only rarely apprehended. Indeed, the vast majority of cattle-raiding incidents went completely unreported because victims, for a variety of reasons—the inadequacy of the police response, the alien nature of the colonial court system, social considerations in their home villages—deemed it not in their interest to file a complaint:

> No record is available of the number of cases of stock theft in which the offenders were not detected but such cases are very numerous and there are always a certain number of persons wandering about the country searching the Kraals [cattle enclosures] for their stolen beasts. (TNA 13747 [Secretariat] 10/29/31:3–4)

Tanner's study of cattle theft in Musoma District during the year 1958–59 yielded a grand total of 447 thefts, only 50—or 11.2 percent—of which had been previously known to the police (1966:31).

Evidence was hard to come by, in part because the venerable system of "putting out cattle for others to mind," which the Kuria employed skillfully to help them evade colonial attempts to restrict bridewealth and to impose compulsory cattle sales, also greatly facilitated the hiding of stolen livestock:

> As soon as the herd of the accused is detained, a string of his fellow thieves, mingled with aged female relations, is liable to appear, *all* of whom have placed their little all with [the] accused for safe custody. If the Administrative Officer is of an unsuspicious nature, he will find that of a promising herd of stock he shortly has only a barren cow without a tail and a one-eyed bullock left with which he will have the task of compensati[ng] an indignant tribesman for the loss of 10 head or so of breeding stock. (TNA 13747 [Secretariat] 12/22/32 [b]:7, emphasis in original)

Many of the chiefs appointed by the colonialists were themselves involved in cattle raiding, either directly or indirectly, and had no interest, therefore, in helping to suppress it:

> [A] thief would come and tell a Chief that he had stolen cattle from somebody in another area and the Chief would promise to help him provided he brought his (the Chief's) share which, however, must not come out of the stolen beasts but from the thief's own property. The thief would tell the Chief exactly where the stolen cattle were deposited and in return for his share the Chief would do all he could to prevent the stolen beasts being discovered. (TNA 13747 [Secretariat] 12/22/32 [a]:4)

The corruptness of the chiefs compelled the colonial authorities to attempt to combat cattle raiding with the aid of "special agents," their identities kept secret from the Native Authorities, who, "at a risk, bring us news of thefts, composition of gangs and whereabouts of stolen property" (TNA 13747 [Secretariat] 12/22/32 [b]:8).

They are a strictly confidential and quite fluid body. Their work—the tracing and reporting of stolen stock, and reports on activities of the various thieves gangs—is dangerous. (TNA 13747 [Secretariat] 12/22/32 [b]:4)

Even when cattle raiders were apprehended, however, efforts to prosecute them were severely hampered by the inconsistency of laws and punishments between the two territories.

The result of this anomalous position is to confer absolute immunity in respect of Kenya cattle on many well known receivers on the Territorial Border, and well-nigh complete immunity on any thief who can steal in Kenya and get the spoil safely over in to Tanganyika. (TNA 23426 [Secretariat] 4/18/36:6)

[The Kuria] are quick to play off one administration against another and have already learned that it is no offence in Tanganyika to be found in possession of cattle stolen in Kenya. (South Kavirondo District Annual Report 1936, quoted in Kjerland 1995:97)

The thief who keeps his stolen beasts in [Tanganyika] Kuria [land] will probably be caught now in a few days—but if he runs them all at once over into Kenya, and gets safe over, he may regard himself as out of danger.

There are regular "thieves exchanges" along the border: at these meetings Tanganyika thieves barter their takings with those of gangs working in Kenya, for their mutual security, and to the great confusion of the law! (TNA 13747 [Secretariat] 12/22/32 [b]:8)

In reporting the results of his Musoma study, Tanner estimated that "the number of men who were actively engaged in cattle theft during the twelve-month period may have been over 1,000," with several thousand more involved as accessories. Only eighty-nine men were ever convicted, however, a number Tanner called

a very meagre reply to [the year's total of] 447 cattle thefts, and there seems to have been at least a ten-to-one chance of not being caught and of retaining three-quarters of the stolen cattle. (1966:34)

Even for those who were convicted, moreover, imprisonment appears not to have served as a deterrent, either before the fact or after it:

The peculiar temperament of the Bakuria is that they almost disregard a short term of imprisonment. In many cases they

know that on their exit from gaol they return to the proceeds of
the theft for which they have suffered. (TNA 13747 [Secretariat]
5/22/30:2)

And when the thief has finished his term of imprisonment and is
released he always comes and explains to his companions that
imprisonment is nothing—he considers it play. (TNA 13747
[Secretariat] 10/18/31:2)

[T]he present form of imprisonment has a tendency to increase
rather than diminish stock thieving. . . . [A]fter serving their sen-
tence in Central Gaols they return to their homes more accomplished in the art of thieving than ever before. (TNA 13747 [Sec-
retariat] 2/26/32:10)

Beginning in the mid-1920s, and continuing for several decades,
officials began to bandy about the idea of redrawing the territorial boundary for the purpose of uniting all of the Kuria under a single administration, on the Tanganyika side, both as a means of reducing the burgeoning
incidence of cattle raiding and to facilitate the coordination of policies
concerning agricultural development, the movement of livestock, and land
degradation (Prazak 1992:66–67):

In the neighbourhood of Lake Victoria, the boundary between
Tanganyika and Kenya is an arbitrary compass boundary pass-
ing through the middle of a certain group of tribes which, for
convenience, we may call Bakuria. This has the effect that there
is a constant movement of stock across the boundary to grazing
or salt licks and for bride price and so on. In addition, there is an
increasing serious amount of stock thefts leading in some cases
to violence, and responsible for a number of homicides in the
past. (TNA 13747 [Secretariat] 12/19/31)

The position is unsatisfactory, it cannot be said that there is anything approaching adequate Administration. A solution would
appear to [be to] alter the boundary and allow all the Bakoria
[Kuria] to revert to Tanganyika. (South Kavirondo District
Annual Report 1925, quoted in Kjerland 1995:71)

Another theft of cattle reported from Ukiria. . . . A heavy punishment . . . might have some result—although the only two
alternatives of any use would appear to me (1) to put this whole
district under T.T. [Tanganyika Territory] (2) have a resident
District Officer here for 6 months to a year. The first is the obvious solution and it is difficult to understand why . . . the Kenyan

Government should stick to this area—especially when all tribal control is completely checkmated by having tribes divided ½ in Kenya, ½ in T.T. (Safari Diary, August 1931, quoted in Kjerland 1995:73)

[T]he whole question is one which resolves itself into stock theft and raiding and the movement of stock. . . .

A re-adjustment of the Boundary . . . is the only satisfactory solution. (TNA 13747 [Secretariat] 10/3/31:1)

Tanganyika Bukuria are attempting to come into Kenya in numbers for watering and grazing in one of their periodic movements and the erosion situation was somewhat acute. It is difficult to plan action, even with the fullest co-operation of the Tanganyika officials, which will be of lasting benefit unless the Colonial boundary is altered so that as to put all the Bukuria under one administration and control. (Monthly Intelligence Report—South Kavirondo, January 1946, quoted in Prazak 1992:67)

Notwithstanding the many knowledgeable voices raised in favor of a boundary alteration, however, and despite the fact that redrawing the Tanganyika border to include the Kenya Kuria would have cost the Kenya colony very little in the way of lost tax revenues (Kjerland 1995:73, 92), no boundary readjustment plan was ever implemented. Although various obstacles to a boundary alteration did exist, including the different political statuses of the two territories (Kenya was a colony while Tanganyika was a mandated territory and, later, a trustee area [Kjerland 1995:93, 94]) and the fear that tinkering with the border would lead to an unending cycle of adjustments and readjustments (Kjerland 1995:95), the principal stumbling block appears to have been the belief that gold might be present in the area that, in the event of an alteration, would have had to be ceded to Tanganyika.

It is generally admitted, both on the Kenya side and by our officers, that the only satisfactory solution is a boundary division, but it is said that there is little prospect of this being considered, and I think that is probably the case because it will involve a cession of territory from Kenya to Tanganyika in an area believed, by some people, to contain valuable gold deposits. (TNA 13747 [Secretariat] 12/19/31)

By the mid-1940s, the boundary-adjustment issue was dead:

I have to inform you that, after discussion of the matter during my recent visit to Dar es Salaam, it has been agreed that the difficulties involved . . . are so great that it is not worth while pursuing the problem further. (Mwanza District Book, November 1946, quoted in Kjerland 1995:94)

In the absence of a boundary adjustment, attempts at cooperation by authorities on both sides of the border became, by default, the only method available for attempting to control the illicit transborder cattle trade. In 1937, Tanganyikan law was amended to make it possible to prosecute, in Tanganyika, anyone found in possession of cattle that had been stolen in Kenya (Prazak 1992:81), and

> arrangements were made to allow chiefs and elders to attend *baraza* [public meetings] on both sides of the border, in order to bring with them any complainants and descriptions of stolen stock tracked into the opposite territory. (Prazak 1992:81)

The lengthy interterritorial border remained easily penetrable, however, notwithstanding the implementation of new police patrols (Prazak 1992:81), and transborder cattle raiding has continued unabated to the present day.

Indeed, by the mid-1930s, the new, "modern" form of cattle raiding had already established itself, a form very different from the community-sanctioned cattle raiding of precolonial times:

> From a study of Abakoria [Kuria] Stock Theft cases during [the] past year it seems likely that these crimes are perpetrated by Syndicates operating on both sides of the Border.
>
> The practice appears to be to have centres both in Kenya and Tanganyika to which stolen cattle are brought. When a small herd, the results of various thefts, has been obtained it is again split up into four or five lots, each lot consisting of cattle stolen from several places so as to make identification more difficult. Each lot is then run off again and handed over to one of the many receivers who work in with Syndicate both in Kenya and Tanganyika. (Letter [Kenya] No.ADM.15/1/1 of 2/9/31, quoted in TNA No. 13747 [Secretariat] 10/3/31:2)

Although the taking of cattle from other tribes and other, totemically unaffiliated clans was still looked upon favorably by the Kuria people while the taking of cattle from members of one's own clan was still sternly frowned upon, such intraclan cattle raiding was now a far more frequent occurrence, if not yet commonplace. It was easier and safer to take cattle from one's own clan than from another clan, or another tribe, inasmuch as taking cattle from one's fellow clansmen dispensed with the need to travel long distances and enabled one to avoid the dangers of operating in enemy territory.

Furthermore, the use of accomplices in the target villages of other clans and tribes, once unheard of, was now the norm. These accomplices also made cattle raiding easier and safer by dispensing with the need for dangerous scouting expeditions and providing a more effective means of targeting potential victims and learning their sleeping habits and security regimes. Nyaheiya elders who themselves had participated in cattle raids against the Maasai in the early 1930s insisted that two things were indispensable to such a venture's success: magic medicine to ensure that the members of the targeted homestead slept through the raid and that their dogs did not bark, and a Maasai accomplice to provide the Kuria raiders with advance intelligence and help facilitate their escape. Eventually, these Kuria would reciprocate by making it possible for their Maasai accomplice and *his* cohorts to take cattle from the settlements of *their* clansmen. In this way, a kind of underworld developed linking together cattle raiders even from clans and tribes that were hostile toward one another. Describing the raiders' method of operation, Baker writes:

> The herd of a defenceless old man, or of one who does not keep adequate watch, is marked down, usually by a neighbour who brings men of another sub-tribe [clan] to his village at night and acts as their guide. By next morning the stolen beasts are either hidden with friends or are being carried off by night marches to be exchanged for other beasts. (1935:46)

The role of the accomplice remained constant through the 1970s and remains the same today. His responsibilities

> are threefold: first, to make sure that the one guarding the cattle to be stolen is absent or asleep and to know where he sleeps; secondly, to open the gate of the cattle corral while his accomplices guard the hut doorways so that the herd's owners do not come out. And, once he has opened the cattle gate, he selects the best cattle and drives them out of the cattle corral. After that, he makes sure that he has escorted the thieves out of the village and then returns to his house and pretends to sleep while waiting to hear shouts for help. When he hears them, he comes out of his hut to join his fellow villagers in following the tracks [of the cattle]. His main job at that time is to delay the pursuit and to lead them astray in following the cattle. In that way, he gives his accomplices the opportunity to escape. (Anacleti 1979:10, my translation; see also Ruel 1959:177–78)

Cattle raiding had also become more brazen by the 1930s. Baker noted,

> On my return to Musoma in August 1931 I found stock thieving still very prevalent—in fact it appeared to have increased in

Lower Bukuria, at least, and in this area thefts were not only of nightly but of daily occurrence. . . .

Generally speaking the greater portion of the community is lawabiding and stock thieving is indulged in by a number of gangs who are in constant communication with each other. (TNA 13747 [Secretariat] 10/29/31:2–3)

Cases of [daylight] robbery are of frequent occurrence. One man will seize a youth who is herding in an isolated spot and hold him whilst his companions make off with the booty. He will then make off and will subsequently deny all knowledge of the robbery whilst the families of the thieves will establish perfect alibis for all concerned. (Baker 1935:46)

If a cattle raider was captured by local people, he usually

compromises with those who capture him by payment of stock. . . .

. . . [M]any complainants as well as most witnesses are so intimidated by thieves and their associates that it is most difficult to obtain convictions. (TNA 13747 [Secretariat] 2/26/32:9–12)

The difficulty of getting evidence against thieves and receivers is no small matter as these gangs are powerful and operate over large areas and fear of retaliation against those who dare to give them away is no mere word but is usually followed by swift action. This has been one of the greatest difficulties we have had to contend with. Valuable information has been given to us from time to time but our informants have definitely refused to give evidence in Court for fear of vengeance. (TNA 13747 [Secretariat] 12/22/32 [a]:8)

And when all else failed:

It not infrequently happens that a man will walk up to the District Office and say that he has stolen cattle and has come to surrender himself. On such occations [sic, occasions] one is apt to think that the "noble savage" is something more than a theory but his action merely means that the hue and cry after the stolen cattle is becoming too hot for the thieves and that the poorest of them has consented to screen his fellows by taking the entire balme [sic, blame] on condition that they give him so many head of the cattle each. (Baker 1935:46)

Pace Anacleti, who claims that cattle raiding "increased twofold" following the outbreak of World War II (Anacleti 1979:9, my translation), the war years seem to have been a relatively quiet time for crime generally

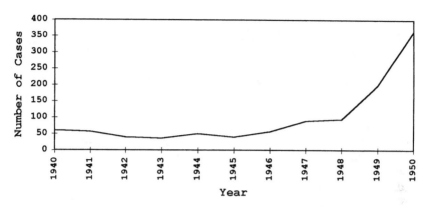

FIG. 4.1.   Criminal cases brought to North Mara District Court,
1940–50

in North Mara, including cattle raiding, judging by the yearly totals for all
criminal cases brought to District Court during that period (see fig. 4.1),
with the real rise coming after 1945, when so many young Kuria service-
men returned home, and skyrocketing in the years from 1948 through
1950 (TNA 1/65 [Accession 83] 1/9/51).

"The amount of stock stolen," noted the assistant superintendent of
police for North Mara in a 1950 memorandum, "increases daily" (TNA
6/46 [Accession 83] 2/18/50:2).

Many of those returning vets, eager to marry, settle down, and begin
building families and herds of their own, and with their pockets bulging
with army pay, drove cattle prices ever higher with their willingness to pay
as much as double the price the colonial government was offering for
heifers and calves (Rwezaura 1985:45). By early 1948, cattle prices were
roughly double what they had been before the war (TNA 36704 [Secre-
tariat] 1/16/48:3).

The demand for beef in the region also remained high, notwithstanding the fact that the war was now over, owing to the large number of gold
miners and the growing number of people living in towns (TNA 39092
[Secretariat] 7/14/49; Rwezaura 1985:43). Nonetheless, the compulsory
livestock sales that had been used to ensure a steady supply of beef during
wartime could no longer be justified now that the fighting had ended, and
the policy was officially abandoned in early 1946—but with the implicit
threat that compulsion could always be reintroduced if sufficient livestock
were not brought forth voluntarily (TNA 36704 [Secretariat] 2/10/48:11;
Rwezaura 1985:43). A Livestock Marketing Board was appointed to promote livestock sales, and a cattle sales tax that was to prove highly

unpalatable—levied against both buyers and sellers—was imposed to enhance revenue (Rwezaura 1985:43–44).

Among the ideas floated to improve livestock sales were (1) a poll-tax increase; (2) the imposition of compulsory herd-reduction quotas as a measure ostensibly to promote agricultural development; and (3) a stepped-up propaganda campaign to promote the sale of so-called "unproductive stock" (TNA 36704 [Secretariat] 1/16/48; Rwezaura 1985:44). Flooding the market with tempting European manufactured goods was also proposed (Rwezaura 1985:44) as a means of stimulating consumerism and the need for cash:

> Research is necessary to determine the range of goods required for particular tribes, and methods of popularising certain new items should be sought. There is room for the wide-awake sales-man. (TNA 36704 [Secretariat] 1/16/48:2)

Despite the colonialists' best efforts, however, cattle sales plummeted, and, by the end of 1946—"for lack of sellers"—the North Mara livestock markets had completely shut down (TNA 20/g/11 [Accession 83] 12/28/46:6).

By early 1948, cattle sales in Tanganyika, which had risen from about 100,000 head per annum before the war (TNA 39092 [Secretariat] 7/14/49:1) to about 300,000 head per annum during the war years, had fallen to 160,000 head (TNA 36704 [Secretariat] 2/10/48:10), a decline of 47 percent.

A crisis atmosphere surrounding the uncertainty of future beef supplies permeates the archival record for this period. In a confidential letter to the chief secretary to the government, in Dar es Salaam, the acting director of veterinary services wrote that:

> Quite frankly I feel somewhat apprehensive about future [beef] supplies, particularly in regard to Tanganyika Packers Limited at Dar es Salaam. . . .
>
> We have repeatedly claimed that there are sufficient cattle available in the Territory to supply the factory provided they can be got out, but I am quite certain that this entails compulsory annual destocking and to what extent is Government going to exercise compulsion? (TNA 36704 [Secretariat] 9/18/47)

According to the minutes of a provincial commissioners' conference convened at Tabora, Tanganyika, in January 1948, the provincial commissioner for Tanganyika's Eastern Province stated that he was

> dubious of the ability of the Territory to meet the rising demand for cattle and expressed anxiety as to the Tanganyika Packers project, in view of the fact that it would seem to depend to such an extent on culling and compulsion. He cited the failure of the

Liebigs Athi river factory in Kenya and recalled the political unrest which had resulted . . . when the Kenya Government endeavoured (unsuccessfully) to introduce culling. . . .

Pressed by the *Provincial Commissioner, Eastern Province,* the *Director of Veterinary Services agreed* that in his view the success of Tanganyika Packers would depend on culling and a degree of compulsion, and that unless that policy was accepted the project would be jeopardized. Nevertheless he felt that the long term benefit to the Territory of a concern such as Tanganyika Packers was so great, that every effort ought to be made to supply them with the cattle they would require. (TNA 36704 [Secretariat] 2/10/48:10–11, emphasis in original)

Another official commented that he was

much disturbed at . . . the words of the DVS [Director of Veterinary Services] that the success of T. Packers would "depend on culling and a degree of compulsion." From the very inception of the scheme I have stressed. . . that there cannot be [compulsion] or any degree of it. Culling of course is a very different thing. We must go very very carefully about this. (TNA 36704 [Secretariat] 2/16/48)

For the British authorities, the concern about the viability of meat supplies reverberated well beyond the borders of Tanganyika, as the following extracts from colonial documents make manifest:

Meat Supply to Troops in East Africa
1. Difficulties have recently arisen with regard to the supply of fresh meat for the troops stationed in East Africa. . . .
2. . . . [A]n acute meat shortage due to the unwillingness of the Africans to sell their cattle, made extensive cuts inevitable in the army ration scale. . . .
4. In view of this, and of the fact that the present position does not arise through any shortage of cattle . . . and bearing in mind that the shipment of frozen or tinned meat from Middle East Stocks will prove exceedingly expensive, it is felt that further action should be taken to see whether the Army's requirements can be met as normally from the abundant local resources of fresh meat.

Extract from Colonial Primary Products Committee
Interim Report
Animal Products.
(a) *Beef.*
The world meat outlook is serious. Post-war shortages of cattle and of feeding stuffs are likely to prolong the situation until

well into the 1950's. For the United Kingdom, depending very largely on imports, currency is an added impediment and all told it will be difficulty [*sic*] to obtain adequate supplies of meat for home consumption unless and until new sources of supply can be found. It is therefore urgent that additional supplies of meat should be made available, particularly from soft currency areas.

At first sight it would appear that dramatic opportunities exist in the Colonial Empire for establishing a meat export trade on a scale comparable to that of the Southern Dominions or of the Argentine. In the African Colonies, for example, it is estimated that the aggregate cattle population is 25 million head as compared with Australia's 13 million and the Argentine's 34 million. The Committee believe that, taking a really long view, there are great opportunities for deployment of the meat industry in Africa, both for internal use and for export. There are, however, certain basic difficulties which will first have to be overcome. . . .

. . . With the exception of Nyasaland and Northern Rhodesia (which will in any case be unable to export beef for many years to come owing to the scarcity of cattle to meet local demand) rinderpest exists in endemic form in all the African Colonies. Rinderpest is thus at present an insuperable obstacle to the development of an export trade in carcase beef from tropical Africa to this country. . . .

. . . [T]here could be no exports of carcase meat to the United Kingdom until either rinderpest had been eliminated or further research had proved that residual infection cannot exist in immunised animals. . . . [T]he campaign against rinderpest in the British territories in Africa should be intensified. . . .

. . . [T]here will have to be a great change in African animal husbandry; not only an economic but also a social change. Open-range grazing will have to give place to more intensive stock management and feeding and the owner will have to learn to regard his cattle as an article of commerce. At present, in many areas quantity is prized before quality, for the number of cattle a man owns establishes his status in the community. . . . A general improvement in the quality of African-owned herds must remain difficult until a complete change in social outlook of their owners has been brought about. (TNA 36704 [Secretariat] 11/26/47)

Memorandum No. 26 for Executive Council
Meat Supplies

During the war the provision of meat supplies was effected by means of compulsory sales. Now that these measures have been discontinued it is apparent that regular meat supplies will not be available under the present system of voluntary sales, and neither the Director of Veterinary Services nor myself are able to accept responsibility for the future.

2. It cannot be too strongly stressed that the situation is quite different from what it was when the formation of Tanganyika Packers was decided on. It was to some extent foreseen that as a result of army feeding thousands of Africans would have developed a taste for meat; but no one foresaw for one moment the groundnut scheme, with its immense demand for meat, both for Europeans and for African labour, particularly in the Southern Province where there are no cattle; nor the prospect of large European military forces in Kenya, who will most probably expect to take toll of the meat supplies of all the East African Territories. Finally, there is every indication that we shall be expected to do something to help to make up the meat shortage in the United Kingdom.

3. For these reasons it is considered that by the beginning of 1950 the situation, under present arrangements will have got out of hand. It is probable that compulsory sales can be avoided provided, amongst other means, a system of culling "by order" can be introduced and the present cattle sales tax be replaced by a cattle rate which latter has proved agreeable to stock owners in different parts of the Territory.

4. These measures will require a great deal of propaganda amongst African stock owners and no time should be lost should their introduction be approved. (TNA 36704 [Secretariat] 3/17/48)

[C]attle purchases by Tanganyika Packers . . . have fallen very seriously short of the numbers they require since the beginning of this year, and it is not too much to say that a crisis may develop if the situation does not improve. . . . [T]here has been an overall falling off of cattle coming on to the primary market. (TNA 41672 [Secretariat] 4/3/51)

The post–World War II effort to coax and intimidate the Kuria into selling their livestock foundered on the shoals of its own ineptness. The grievously unpopular sales tax served, predictably, to undermine cattle sales (Rwezaura 1985:45), and the newly established Livestock Marketing Board was relentlessly inefficient:

Auction centres were few and tended to serve much larger areas, thus making it inconvenient for distant cattle sellers to drive their beasts to auction. Furthermore, auctions were held infrequently. As the time interval between one auction day and another was about three months, the small butcher could not buy sufficient numbers of slaughter animals to last him that long. (Rwezaura 1985:46)

Operating without credit and with only a little capital, these small butchers therefore had no alternative but

to buy a few cattle at a time. When these were slaughtered and sold before the next auction day, the butchers had to buy cattle outside government auctions. (Rwezaura 1985:46)

None of this was in any way ameliorated by the fact that private buyers consistently offered higher prices for cattle than the Livestock Marketing Board. Although the government prohibition set in place during the war years to prevent the sale of cattle outside the official auction system remained in force even after the war was over, such private sales were in fact carried out wholesale, in what Rwezaura (1985:45) terms "utter disregard of the rule."

"All the veterinary laws in the world," declared North Mara's district commissioner, "will not prevent natives from taking their cattle into Kenya where excellent prices are obtainable" (TNA 1/24/472/2, quoted in Rwezaura 1985:45).

As the cash economy continued to make inroads, and as Africans in Tanganyika increasingly needed to acquire at least some money to meet their needs, the formal-sector livestock trade expanded, and the illicit trade in livestock expanded right along with it. For the Kuria of North Mara, cattle raiding, particularly transborder cattle raiding, had by now become "a part of the system of trade in the colonial underside of capitalism" (Anacleti 1979:10, my translation), and as important a means of acquiring cattle (or money, for that matter) as selling cash crops or any wage-labor occupation:

The Chief of Nguruimi, whose North boundary for many miles East and West of Mara Mine is the Mara River tells me that cattle raids into his Chiefdom by Kuria from North Mara are increasing considerably in number and violence lately and that his people are growing so restive that they are threatening to raid North Mara and seize Kuria cattle. I therefore ask you . . . to do what you can to point out to your people the danger they are bringing on themselves—and their cattle. (TNA 6/46 [Accession 83] 2/5/53)

As you know I have been very heavily committed on the northern side of my border, and it has not been possible for me to come down to see you again with reference to the compensation to be paid by the Kuria for stock stolen in the riad [*sic,* raid] of 24th/25th February.

. . . In the circumstances cannot these people be told to shell out as they are obviously bad hats and have been involved in pillage from the Masai? You will appreciate that I am extremely keen not to be involved in a major border incident in a time when there is so much to do elsewhere in the district. (TNA 6/46 [Accession 83] 7/5/53)

Then finally, in the mid-1950s, the British authorities, bowing to the inevitable, legalized the transborder cattle trade, thereby opening the Tanganyika cattle markets to buyers from Kenya (Kjerland 1995:88). A thriving legal trade in a commodity tends to damp down its illicit counterpart, because, for most buyers, the benefits of obtaining a commodity legitimately outweigh the risks of obtaining it through illicit channels, even where the illicit price is lower. Perhaps that is what explains the drop in reported cattle-theft cases in North Mara from 428 cases in 1952 to 191 cases in 1957—and not, as Ruel surmises,

the appointment on the Tanganyika side in December 1955 of a Stock Theft Prevention Officer, whose activities seemed at last to provide the answer to cattle theft. (1959:153–54)

Whatever the explanation, certainly no one had yet found "the answer to cattle theft." In the decades to follow, and particularly in the bloody 1980s, market-oriented cattle raiding would ascend to grand new heights of mayhem and violence. In 1961, the year that Tanganyika achieved its independence from Great Britain, the last, soon to be departing British district commissioner of North Mara reflected:

For generations, organised stock theft has been a retarding and corrupting influence in the public life of this district. Under present circumstances it is a serious threat to security. . . . The new Stock Theft Ordinance has been generally welcomed by responsible leaders and is proving a useful weapon.

However, Government is still not so well organised as the thieves. (TNA Acc. No. 544:1–2, quoted in Kjerland 1995:109)

CHAPTER 5

"Enemy Number One to the Two Nations": Cattle Raiding and the Postcolonial State

Notwithstanding the pious joint declaration of representatives of newly independent Kenya and Tanzania, following a meeting in October 1964, that "stock theft along ethnic and international borders should be regarded as enemy number one to the two nations" (TNA [Accession 544] 10/9/64, quoted in Kjerland 1995:262), it should come as no surprise that the intractable difficulties that had stymied both the German and British colonial administrations continued to bedevil the African administrations that succeeded them: the international border separating the two countries remained porous—both during the periods when it was officially open and, in the years following the collapse of the East African Union in 1977, officially closed—and pressing priorities elsewhere, a paucity of resources, police corruption, the remoteness of Kuria country, and a lack of cooperation from local people all continued to undermine official efforts to surmount the problem.

In 1974, the Tanzanian government of President Julius K. Nyerere reinstituted a system, first imposed by the German colonial administration in 1911, under which villagers following the tracks of their stolen cattle were instructed to hammer a tethering peg (Swa., *kigingi;* pl., *vigingi*) into the ground at the place where the tracks stopped, and police were authorized to confiscate ten head of cattle from every homestead in the nearest village if its residents failed to return the cattle and to surrender the cattle raiders who had taken them—but, in practice, this scheme fell apart early on and was never seriously implemented (Anacleti 1979:13, 14).

The Nyerere government also imposed an exile program under which individuals who had been denounced as cattle raiders by their fellow villagers were banished to remote areas of nonpastoralist southern Tanzania—to Lindi, Mtwara, Mbeya, and perhaps other places—typically without the benefit of formal legal charges or trials. As late as 1990, Tarime's district commissioner circulated plans for arresting and exiling twenty-nine suspected cattle raiders, at least four of them residents of Nyaheiya. Many of those exiled drifted back to their home villages after only a year or two, their surreptitious return facilitated by an inattentive and inefficient administrative bureaucracy, but others—including several Nyaheiya men—returned to their own homes only after having endured decades of exile.

While this harshly punitive program can have had no more than a negligible effect in damping down cattle raiding overall, other policies of the new government might as well have been tailor-made to *foster* cattle raiding, in particular the tight restrictions on the formal export trade in cattle, which served only to nurture its illicit twin. Within Tanzania, permits and fees were required even to move cattle over very short distances, and efforts by victims of cattle raids to recover their animals when they turned up for sale at local livestock markets were mired in bureaucratic restrictions: a man whose cattle had been taken first required a letter from his village chairman authorizing him to search for his animals at a market located in the area of another tribe or clan; after arriving at the market and showing the police there his letter, the searcher would survey the market, and, if he spotted any of his missing cattle, would report back to the police, who would instruct him to return to the market and, posing as a potential buyer, try to ferret out the name of the person who had his cattle up for sale; only after the searcher had managed to secure this information and returned to the police with it would the police step in to make an arrest— and even then, in practice, usually only after he had paid them a bribe.

Attempting to recover cattle that had been stolen in Tanzania and run across into Kenya was even more frustrating, and a successful outcome less likely, requiring first a letter of authorization from the district commissioner, on the Tanzanian side, and afterward the cooperation of the Kenya authorities, which was not forthcoming. Keng'ang'are Maswi, a Nyaheiya man who lost 141 head of cattle to cattle raiders in a single raid in 1986, painstakingly tracked his animals to Masanga, a Tanzanian village of the Irege clan close by the Kenya border, only to be compelled to abandon his pursuit when the Kenya police declined to take up the search for his cattle and his request for authorization to cross into Kenya to try to find them himself was denied. Evidence from the Kenya side indicates that Kenyan victims of cattle raids hoping to recover cattle driven into Tanzania met with similar intransigence on the part of the authorities in Tanzania (Kjerland 1995:263 n. 40).

More important, the suction pull of market forces grew inexorably more powerful during this postindependence period, as the demand for beef in both Kenya and Tanzania rose precipitously and as cattle prices rose right along with it, driven ever higher by the insufficient supply of cattle making its way onto the commercial market. In the late 1950s, in North Mara (now Tarime District), the average head of cattle fetched Tsh[1] 167;

---

1. Tanzania and Kenya both employ "shillings" as their national currency, but these two currencies have disparate values and are *not* to be confused with one another. Throughout this book, Tanzania shilling(s) is abbreviated as Tsh, and Kenya shilling(s) is abbreviated as Ksh. One hundred Tanzania shillings is therefore written as Tsh 100. During the fieldwork period, Ksh 1 was equivalent to approximately Tsh 10.

by the late 1970s, this figure had risen to Tsh 901, a more than fivefold increase over the course of two decades (Rwezaura 1985:85), with cattle prices unfailingly higher in Kenya than in Tanzania, a state of affairs that has continued unchanged since the early 1930s (Kjerland 1995:284). The oft-quoted saying "An ox never dies in Mara" encapsulates this reality, a wry reminder that even after an ox has grown too old for ploughing, his owner can still sell him across the border in Kenya for a higher price than he had originally paid for him as a young working ox in Tanzania.

There is, if truth be told, scant incentive on the Kenya side to stanch the illicit flow of cattle, for it is Kenya that most benefits from the illicit trade: its middlemen who buy the cattle at Migori and other Kenya markets; its transport companies that transport them in huge cattle trucks from the border-area markets to the Kenyan capital, Nairobi; its tanneries and factories that turn the cowhides into shoes and other leather products, and its jobbers and retailers who market those products; its butchers who sell the meat; its meat-packing companies that ship the cattle—both as live animals and as canned beef—to Somalia and the Persian Gulf, and, accepting at face value what many interviewees claimed is true, to Israel and Scandinavian countries as well.

Some portion of the cattle taken by cattle raiders in Tanzania remains in Tanzania, sold to, and then butchered and resold by, local-area Tanzanian butchers. For the cattle taken by Nyaheiya's cattle raiders specifically, this locally sold portion exceeded 50 percent during the fieldwork period, although where one sells a stolen cow is strongly dependent upon the presence or absence of clan warfare, geography, and other factors and is therefore liable to change from place to place as well as over time. Nonetheless, it is Tanzanian cattle that help to fuel Kenya's industries and to swell its bottom line, but mainly Tanzania's people—both the victims of cattle raiding and its perpetrators—who sustain this Tanzania/Kenya trade with their property and sometimes their lives.

Kjerland suggests that cattle raiding grew more violent in the 1960s, noting that delegates to a 1966 follow-up to the 1964 Kenya-Tanzania cattle-raiding conference mentioned above were apprised of the use of a gun in one recent raid and the killing of a cattle owner in another (1995:264)—expressions of heightened concern that seem almost quaint in light of what was to ensue a decade and a half later. Asked, on the Nyaheiya homestead survey, for example, to evaluate "the seriousness of the cattle-theft problem as it has manifested itself in this area" from decade to decade beginning with the 1950s (see table 5.1), the overwhelming majority of those offering an opinion dismissed the cattle raiding of the 1960s and 1970s as "not a serious problem," while cattle raiding in the 1980s and 1990s was described by more than 93 percent of *all* respondents as "extremely serious—out of control."

It is true that, for the 1960s and the 1970s, 56.3 and 43.2 percent, respectively, of those surveyed said either that they did not know how serious cattle raiding was in those decades or elected not to answer at all—probably because many of the respondents were simply too young to be able to recall those decades—but it is nonetheless noteworthy that *not a single one* of those who *did* respond with an opinion chose to label the cattle-raiding problem of those decades as "extremely serious—out of control."

For the 1980s and 1990s, however, not only did more than 93 percent of those surveyed characterize cattle raiding as "extremely serious—out of control" during those decades, but only a scant 0.5 percent of them expressed the opinion that cattle raiding during those periods was "not a serious problem." This radical perceptual shift reflects the abrupt, equally radical escalation in the frequency and intensity of cattle-raiding violence that followed hard upon the close of the Tanzania-Uganda War of 1978–79, known in Tanzania as the *Vita vya Kagera* (Swahili for the War of Kagera, after the area of Tanzania that the forces of Idi Amin invaded), which drove the dictator Idi Amin from power in neighboring Uganda.

Nyaheiya village had been founded in 1974, with the fourteen villages of the Tanzanian portion of the more populous Irege clan to the east of it, mainly in the Tarime highlands, and its four sister Nyamongo villages lying mainly to its west. The Nyamongo and the Irege clans are totemically affiliated, sharing the leopard (*ingwe;* pl., *ichingwe*) as their common totem and regarding themselves as the descendants of Wangwe, one of the six mythical sons of Mkuria, the eponymous ancestor of all the Kuria people. In precolonial times, totemically affiliated clans were allied in warfare and were prohibited from engaging in cattle raids against one another—principles that, to the dismay of many Kuria elders, are honored mainly in the breach today.

Nonetheless, relations between these two clans are said to have been extremely harmonious during this early villagization period, with as much

TABLE 5.1. *Question:* **"Please Compare the Seriousness of the Cattle-Theft Problem as It Has Manifested Itself in This Area over the Following Decades"** (*n* = 190)

	Extremely Serious (out of control)	Very Serious	Not Serious	Don't Know	No Answer
1950s	0%	.1%	6.8%	2.1%	91.6%
1960s	0%	5.8%	37.9%	49.5%	6.8%
1970s	0%	18.4%	38.4%	40.0%	3.2%
1980s	93.7%	1.1%	.5%	3.2%	1.6%
1990s	93.2%	2.1%	.5%	2.6%	1.6%

as one-quarter of the population of the nearby Irege village of
Ekeng'ooro—a village far less well-endowed than Nyaheiya is with pas-
turage and water—establishing homes for themselves in Nyaheiya, pasturing their plentiful herds of cattle there, working alongside Nyaheiya's miners at mining areas within Nyaheiya's borders, and sending their children
to study together with Nyamongo children in Nyaheiya's primary schools.
Many Nyaheiya residents said that during this tranquil period they came
to regard Nyaheiya and Ekeng'ooro as practically one village.

This era of good-fellowship ended abruptly, however, in the wake of
the Tanzania-Uganda War. The Kuria dominate the Tanzanian army,
which has served as a vehicle for the fulfillment of Kuria ambitions since
early colonial times. Although Tanzania is constituted of approximately
120 named ethnic or tribal groups, the Kuria, who represent less than 1
percent of Tanzania's population, are estimated to have comprised about
50 percent of the Tanzanian armed forces at the time of the Tanzania-
Uganda War. Military service has provided many Kuria men with unpar-
alleled opportunities for prestige and advancement, without the requirements of a formal education, in an environment that is congenial to the
expression of the qualities of firmness, courage, and self-discipline with
which many Kuria men identify. "They do a good job [in the armed forces]
because they have no fear, you see," explained a Kuria former MIG fighter
pilot who flew missions in Uganda. "They are without fear."

President Nyerere, who hailed from Kuria country and whose wife,
Maria, is herself a Kuria, recruited many Kuria into his personal body-
guard and relied heavily on Kuria fighting men throughout his adminis-
tration. It is a standing joke in Tanzania that the well-known initials
JWTZ do not really stand for *Jeshi la Wananchi Tanzania* (Swahili for
Army of the People of Tanzania), but rather for *Jeshi la Wakuria Tangu
Zamani* (Swahili for the Army of the Kuria since Long Ago). Today there
are more Kuria Tanzanian army officers than there are officers of any
other tribe, and more retired army officers living in Mara Region, of which
Tarime District is a part, than in any other region of Tanzania.

Another potential source of military manpower during the 1970s was
the *Mugambo,* or People's Militia. Amid a torrent of government warnings
that the white-minority apartheid government of South Africa was determined to smash Tanzania's experiment with socialism, People's Militia
units were established in villages throughout Tanzania, and citizens—both
men and women—received training in the use of arms to defend their villages. "Even a person like me," recalled a now-middle-aged non-Kuria
government clerk at the district government headquarters in Tarime town,
"if I were given a rifle right now, I could dismantle it, put it back together."

In 1978, after the Ugandan forces of Idi Amin had invaded the
Kagera region of Tanzania, the Nyerere government launched a full-scale
counterattack to drive Idi Amin from power:

The buildup of the first two months had involved drastically increasing the number of soldiers in the army. During the first week of hostilities, units of the People's Militia began training. . . . Volunteers were accepted from the ranks of peasants and the unemployed. The police force contributed two thousand men to become soldiers. . . .

A week after the invasion regional commissioners from all of Tanzania's twenty regions met in Dodoma to discuss recruitment. Each region was given a quota of two thousand and the commissioners were told to accept only those who had completed militia training.

However, the regional commissioner from Mara Region, on the eastern side of Lake Victoria, where unemployment is high and soldiering has been a tradition since the . . . First World War, put out the word that anyone who wanted to could join the army. (Avirgan and Honey 1982:71–72)

The result, as Avirgan and Honey note, was a veritable "flood of men from Mara":

In all about forty thousand militia were brought into the army, which grew to seventy-five thousand. Eventually, forty-five thousand Tanzanians went into Uganda. (1982:72)

Avirgan and Honey cite unemployment as the principal motivation for enlistment, noting, "In Tanzania, as in most African countries, soldiering is a steady, well-paying job and many people were anxious to go to Uganda with the hope of remaining in the army after the war" (1982:72). But they fail to acknowledge yet another prime cause of that "flood of men from Mara," that is,

the fantastic arsenal built up by Idi Amin. Almost from the start Amin's troops began abandoning arms and ammunition in such quantities that the biggest problem for the Tanzanians became transport to move the stuff. Everything from AK-47 assault rifles to Soviet T-54 medium tanks, equipped with infrared night viewing devices, fell into Tanzanian hands. (Avirgan and Honey 1982:77)

The pastoralist Karamojong of Uganda also soon became aware of the potential of this vast abandoned arms supply:

There had been a period when the barracks at Moroto [in Uganda] had been completely abandoned, the Nubians and Kakwas having fled and the other soldiers having gone temporarily into the bush. The local Karamajong had gone into the barracks and discovered a bigger treasure trove of weaponry than they had ever dreamed possible: Russian AK-47 assault rifles, French G-3s, machine guns, 87-mm mortars and more ammunition than could be used in a decade of cattle raiding. (Avirgan and Honey 1982:171)

All manner of subterfuge was employed by Tanzania's men at arms to smuggle captured and stolen military weapons back into Tanzania, the most common being to pack them into coffins and transport them back across the border on the pretext of returning fallen comrades to their home villages for burial. Mock funerals, with closed caskets, were held, ostensibly to spare loved ones the sight of the grisly remains said to be inside them—and then, after a suitably safe interval had passed, the contents of the caskets were "exhumed" and put to work in the service of cattle raiding.

Officers and commanders at higher levels also smuggled weapons, large numbers of which were ultimately funneled into the illicit transborder cattle trade. As a veritable tsunami of violent crime broke over Dar es Salaam and other Tanzanian towns at the onset of the 1980s, fueled by the crippling inflation and consequent increased desperation for cash that followed hard upon the war's end, Tanzanian police reported that recently demobilized People's Militiamen accounted for more than 60 percent of all arrests made (Avirgan and Honey 1982:236).

"In Nyaheiya," noted one villager who was a veteran of the Uganda conflict,

the Kagera War made everything change completely. People came back with guns, [with] new dreams of being as rich as they had seen rich people in other parts of Tanzania and Uganda, [with] madness to show themselves as brave people who have driven out Amin, so feared nothing, [and with] their loss of morality—killing a human being was like killing a fly to them. . . . These people started stealing from Nyamongo, and Nyamongo stole from the Irege.

Another Nyaheiya veteran, who had served with the Tanzanian army in the Seychelles and trained soldiers in Mozambique before going to fight in Uganda, said that when local youths

went to fight outside of the country [they] had a lot of experiences. They were used to having money and as everybody knows most soldiers like women and alcohol. In Mahe Island [in the Seychelles] they could find women dressed in their underpants and ready to go for sex with anybody for a few shillings. People who have been in places like these get used or become addicted to women or alcohol. These two things, once you are used to them it's not easy to do without them. Also, in order to win women, especially beautiful ones, you have to have a good amount of money. So the soldier who came back had no other source of income except stealing cows.

In places like ours, one cannot depend on agriculture and even if you do it you will have to wait for so many months to get the products and you may end up getting either no products at all or products but no market. But cows have a permanent market and you don't have to wait for so long. You only have to be brave.

Some people who went to the army had said final farewells to their family. They were not expecting to come back home alive. He has already decided to die. Now he comes back safe! Still what made him to say final farewells is because he hoped to get something to make him advance in life. Have a good house, eat nicely. His expectations are not fulfilled [by his army service]. So he doesn't care if he risks again to try to get or to fulfill his desire of a good life and [to satisfy] his addictions.

So people who became brave are those who are ready to die. They are ready to die knowing that they have wives and children and in case they die still their lineage will continue and they will be remembered.

In Tarime District and contiguous Serengeti District, where acquiring a military weapon was akin to winning the lottery—"If you have a gun," commented one Nyaheiya cattle raider, "you are a rich man"—the influx of smuggled weapons benefited mainly the Irege clan at the expense of the Nyamongo clan, because, first, with only five villages in Ingwe Division, as contrasted with the Irege's fourteen, the Nyamongo were greatly outnumbered; second, with their convenient access to cash earnings from gold prospecting in the Mara River valley's mines, the Nyamongo have generally been far less inclined toward careers in either the army or the civil service than their Irege brethren.

For the people of Nyaheiya, this arms disparity had devastating consequences. Cattle raids against Nyaheiya escalated alarmingly in the aftermath of the war, with brazen daylight raids, involving large numbers of cattle, becoming increasingly common. Sometimes, it was claimed, cattle raiders even went so far as to deliver a message to a village in advance of a raid, announcing their intention to come for the village's cattle at a specified day and time and warning the villagers not to try to stop them.

Mwikwabe Mangure's father and paternal grandmother were shot dead by cattle raiders in a 1980 raid on Nyaheiya in which thirty-nine head of cattle were taken. "The police did nothing," he said. "The only thing they did was take their bodies to Tarime."

It was not long before Nyaheiya's Nyamongo population became convinced that their coresident Irege were colluding with their fellow Irege in Ekeng'ooro to steal their cattle—and in 1981 they forcibly expelled the Irege, igniting a bloody interclan conflict and ushering in an era, still ongoing, of deep-seated clan enmity punctuated by intermittent interclan war. These conflicts entail, along with combat, raids on the enemy's cattle, but even after formal hostilities have ended, the ongoing enmity that these conflicts generate fosters a supportive climate for the continued raiding of the former adversary's cattle on a "private," ad hoc basis.

Prior to the war with Uganda, residents of a village whose cattle had been taken by cattle raiders had been free to follow the tracks into another clan's area. As the number of thefts mounted, however, and as, for example, the people of Nyamongo found the tracks of their cattle routinely heading eastward into Irege territory, the Nyamongo began accusing *all* Irege of complicity in the thefts for having failed to intercept and recover their stolen cattle as they passed through their area—notwithstanding the fact that purloined cattle often pass by a village in the dead of night, when most villagers are fast asleep.

In retaliation for this perceived collusion, the Nyamongo began recouping their losses by seizing cattle from *any* cattle enclosure belonging to an Irege, and the Irege countered by denying the Nyamongo free passage through their territory and firing volleys of arrows at them when they attempted to pass. The reverse, of course, was also true. This escalating cycle of violence greatly facilitates cattle raiding, not only because it makes it infinitely more difficult for victims of cattle raids to recover their cattle, but because it generates a climate that makes it easy for an Irege butcher, for example, to buy a stolen Nyamongo cow and sell the meat in his village without fear of censure or disclosure by his fellow villagers.

In 1981, four Kuria interclan wars raged simultaneously, all of them ignited by the new, technologically upgraded form of cattle raiding unleashed by the Tanzania-Uganda War: the Nyamongo fought the Irege, the Irege fought the Nyabasi, the Kira fought the Timbaru, and the Nyabasi fought the Kira. On 12 July 1981, in the climactic battle of the Nyamongo-Irege war, twelve Nyamongo fighters were killed.

The response was a massive crackdown by the Field Force Unit, the military wing of the Tanzania police, the first of three such crackdowns in Tarime District—in 1981, 1984, and 1986, respectively—designed to bring a halt to clan warfare, clamp down on cattle raiding, and effect large-scale confiscations of weapons. Other, similar crackdowns—referred to in Tanzania as "police operations"—were carried out in adjoining Serengeti District, where the use of military weaponry was even more pervasive and cattle raiding consequently even more violent. The pattern that has prevailed since 1981 has been one of periodic police crackdowns, accompanied by the seizing of weaponry and numerous arrests, followed by a brief lull in cattle raiding, followed by a resumption of cattle raiding as usual once the Field Force Unit has withdrawn from the area.

Indeed, no sooner had the Field Force left the area following the 1981 crackdown than cattle raiding resumed again. In October 1982, cattle raiders armed with submachine guns and semiautomatic rifles took eighty-seven head of Nyaheiya cattle in broad daylight. In November 1982, similarly armed cattle raiders took an additional ninety head from Nyaheiya in another daylight raid, while in nearby Kewanja, a Nyamongo village to the west, cattle raiders armed with a light machine gun made off with ninety-eight more. In December 1982, cattle raiders armed with a subma-chine gun and a French-made G-3 World War II army rifle broke into a Nyaheiya cattle enclosure around 4:00 A.M. and drove off sixty-eight head of cattle. Other villages in this area also sustained heavy losses.

Between 1978 and 1984, the size of the Nyaheiya cattle herd, as mea-sured by the nationwide cattle censuses conducted in those two years, plummeted from 11,656 head to 4,537 head—a decline of 61 percent—while the herd of nearby Ekeng'ooro, Nyaheiya's Irege neighbor village to the east, swelled from 6,383 head to 7,664 head, a rise of 20 percent. While all of these census totals probably represent undercounts (see chap. 8), the magnitude of the losses they reflect is probably real. A second Field Force crackdown in Tarime District, in 1984, proved to be as generally ineffec-tive as the first had been.

The legal cattle trade with Kenya had been snuffed out by the collapse of the East African Community and the closing of Tanzania's border with Kenya in 1977. Now, amid all the fear and violence, local cattle markets in Tanzania began to close down, too. The bustling weekly market at Nyamwaga village, an Irege center in the Tarime highlands whose strate-gic location had enabled it to attract cattle buyers and sellers from Kenya, the Nyamongo area, and Tarime town, shut down completely as people began staying away in droves, fearing for their own safety and that of their livestock.

For tribal groups such as the Maasai, who, although known as for-midable fighters, have never shown an interest in national military service and who therefore lacked a ready source of modern weaponry, these early days following the close of the Tanzania-Uganda War were extremely try-ing times. In Serengeti District, Kuria tell of a band of heavily armed Kuria cattle raiders who raided a Maasai village in the Ngorongoro area, terrorizing the populace and feasting on a slaughtered cow in leisurely fashion before absconding with the village's entire cattle herd.

In Tarime District, half Kuria and half Luo, where the herds of the Luo people were devastated by Kuria cattle raiders, the proceeds garnered by middlemen in the illicit cattle trade fueled a decade-long residential building boom in Tarime town that began in the early 1980s and did not slow till the early 1990s. "*Mji umejengwa kwa ng'ombe Wajaluo*" (Swa.), they say in Tarime town: "The town has been built from Luo cows."

There were alternative ways for acquiring guns besides the army, however. It was—and remains—possible to buy them from willing policemen, to rent a policeman's rifle for a single raid, or even to hire a policeman to accompany the raiders and intimidate the victims by firing shots into the air. (A night's gun rental cost from Tsh 60,000 to Tsh 80,000—or, alternatively, two head of cattle—during the fieldwork period, double that if the cop came along on the raid.) There are also local craftsmen who can be engaged to create crude, but still lethal, homemade guns (Swa., *migobole;* sing., *mgobole*) of the sawed-off-shotgun variety. Today, a cattle raider who brings a gun on a raid commands a larger share of the cows.

In Mugumu town, headquarters of the adjacent Serengeti District, a prison warden was murdered for his gun in the 1980s, and policemen are said to have been fearful of patrolling with their weapons for fear of being ambushed and killed for them. A brisk and lucrative underground business developed—in Serengeti District mainly, but in Tarime District also—in the hiring out of guns to cattle raiders by businessmen, who often commissioned raids and provided cattle raiders with advance cash up front. Their shops, hotels, and businesses—built with cattle-raiding profits—line the streets of Mugumu and Tarime town.

In Nyaheiya and its sister villages, an atmosphere of crisis prevailed during this period. Many residents emigrated to distant areas, seeking safe havens for themselves and their livestock. A village Committee of Guardianship and Security (Swa., *Kamati ya Ulinzi na Usalama*) was formed, and strenuous efforts were undertaken to safeguard the community. For men, militia participation was mandatory, and fines were imposed for failing to attend training sessions, for failing to show up for village guard patrol, for damaging a weapon, or for firing a weapon without proper justification.

Lists were compiled of all the village's ex-servicemen, with special attention focused on those who had taken part in combat in Uganda. Additional lists were compiled of those known to possess guns, some of whom fled Nyaheiya upon learning they had been identified, and of area cattle raiders known to employ firearms.

Strangers and visitors were immediately suspect. One Nyaheiya man was dragged before the committee, beaten, and interrogated regarding the group of Kuria visitors to whom he had recently played host—men of varied clan affiliation, from both Tanzania and Kenya, two of whom had been observed carrying a submachine gun and a semiautomatic rifle. The committee noted that the strangers had spent three days in the Nyaheiya man's homestead and that he had shown them traditional hospitality by slaughtering a goat for them.

A Nyaheiya man came forward to alert the committee to a warning message he'd received from relatives in Kenya listing the names of a nine-member Kenyan Kuria cattle-raiding group together with the names of a half-dozen Nyaheiya cattle holders whom the group had purportedly targeted for a raid.

Another Nyaheiya man told the committee that all his calves were dying for lack of milk as a consequence of his cows having been taken by cattle raiders, while others complained that their cattle were disappearing into Irege villages, but that the people there were refusing to pay compensation.

The committee strongly criticized the commander of the local police post for allowing relatives from Kenya to reside with his family.

As of March 1985, the Nyaheiya militia commanded an arsenal of 28 semiautomatic rifles and 223 rounds of ammunition. Eighteen months later, the committee petitioned the government to provide the local police post with submachine guns and light machine guns for defense against cattle raiders. It is not known whether this request was granted.

In 1986, probably the most devastating year of cattle raiding in this area in the twentieth century, fighting between the Nyamongo and the Irege broke out yet again. Kuria elders from throughout Tarime District, who had convened in Tarime town to deliberate the crisis at the government's behest, sharply criticized those Kuria elders who were in complicity with cattle raiders and denounced unnamed police and local officials who were "taking advantage of [clan] disunity to increase their income." They urged all youths to participate in following the tracks of cattle stolen from their villages; admonished all citizens to cooperate with efforts by outsiders to recover their stolen animals and to pay compensation for unrecoverable cattle stolen by their fellow villagers; and warned sorcerers (*abarogi;* sing., *omorogi*) against continuing to provide cattle raiders with magic medicine to enhance their courage. In addition:

> They also agreed that the elders who leak committee secrets to the thieves should be punished. Punish the villages in which all the people fail to follow the stolen cattle. Village officials who collaborate with thieves should be punished. . . . All thieves who are notorious should be exiled. Night patrols should be increased.

But it was simply not enough. According to police records, Nyaheiya alone lost 929 head of cattle in 13 separate raids in that year, an average of 71 head of cattle taken in each raid, only four head—0.4 percent—of which were ever recovered. This contrasts starkly with the results of Tanner's study of cattle theft in Musoma (now Tarime) District for the one-year period from 1958 to 1959, slightly more than twenty years earlier, during which the number of cattle taken averaged 11 per theft, 21 percent of which were ultimately recovered (1966:41).

In 1986, in neighboring Serengeti District, to which many members of the Kira, Timbaru, and Nyabasi clans had migrated in the 1950s and 1960s, two clan wars raged, one between the Kira and the Nyabasi, the other between the Kira and the Timbaru; and nearly two hundred people—cattle raiders, victims of cattle raids, and policemen—are estimated to have been killed in cattle-raiding-related incidents (see chap. 8).

There were a handful of Kuria cattle raiders who attained extraordinary notoriety during these turbulent 1980s—Musubi and Wang'eng'i are two of them—but it is the exploits of a third man, Nyamokara Nyamaganya, that have already acquired the aura of legend. A member of the Irege clan who lived, with his three wives, in Nyaheiya for a number of years as well as in nearby Ekeng'ooro, he served a stint in the Tanzanian army before returning to Tarime District to launch his cattle-raiding career. His Nyaheiya neighbors, and others who knew him, described him as "a brave man," "good in running, good in shooting," and as gifted with an uncanny sixth sense that warned him of impending danger and enabled him repeatedly to elude the police. Nyaheiya's village chairman swears that he had dug a fifteen-foot-deep escape tunnel from inside his house out onto the main road that runs through Nyaheiya.

In the mid-1980s, as one of a half-dozen members of a cattle-raiding group headed by Chacha Kangariani, another ex-soldier, who had somehow contrived to acquire guns from the police during the Field Force crackdown of 1984, Nyamaganya is believed to have killed Kangariani and taken over as leader in the wake of a dispute over Kangariani's division of the spoils of a cattle raid against the Maasai.

Nyamaganya and his followers, it is said, seized cattle in broad daylight and drove them brazenly through the countryside, brashly indifferent to whether or not people saw them, and some claim that they crafted their own homemade guns. Nyamaganya apparently also functioned as an ally, or receiver, for other cattle-raiding groups, using Nyaheiya as a hiding place for cattle that had been taken from villages elsewhere. Although he pretended to take cattle only from other tribes and other, totemically unaffiliated clans, it is said that, in actuality, he harbored no compunctions about also taking cattle from both the Nyamongo and Irege.

During a period when Nyaheiya and other Nyamongo villages were being relentlessly hammered by Irege cattle raiders, Nyamaganya and his men are said to have hauled down the Tanzanian flag at Nyamwaga, the headquarters of Ingwe Division—the administrative unit of Tarime District that encompasses the territory of both the Irege and the Nyamongo clans—and hoisted their own, leopard-skin standard in its place, proclaiming Ingwe as their personal fiefdom. Though possibly apocryphal, this story has received very wide circulation, both within Tarime District and well beyond it.

The Field Force crackdown of 1986 was the most brutal, and the most effective, of all the crackdowns that have been carried out in this region to date. Police units in the previous crackdowns, it is often alleged, had invariably been corrupted by their contact with local police and other officials who were themselves implicated in the illicit cattle trade—and had hence failed to accomplish their objectives. But the 1986 operation is said to have been carried out by Tanzanian army units disguised in Field Force uniforms—because the Tanzanian army is not legally authorized to operate within Tanzania—whose ranks had been purged of Kuria and packed with Zanzibaris, who are widely known for their antipathy toward mainland Tanzanians. Logistically self-sufficient, and bivouacked in rugged, bushy areas isolated from contact with local villagers, police, and officials, they swooped down on villages in early-morning raids, summoned villagers to meetings, and, announcing they had come to confiscate guns, urged villagers to point the finger at those who had them.

While many villagers are said to have been emboldened by the Field Force's presence to make denunciations, there are also widespread reports of atrocities. Anyone who had served in the army, or who had a relative who had served, was presumed to be hiding weaponry. Many men were brutally beaten, their testicles bashed with wooden cudgels; girls and women were raped. In Nyaheiya, a suspect was forced to doff his trousers and sit on a sheet of galvanized-iron roofing material that had been heated to red hot until he cried out in agony and agreed to surrender his weapon.

In the highland village of Nyamwaga, a Catholic nun from the United States, operating a small parish health clinic, recalls rapes and beatings, and remembers treating a baby for an ugly whiplash-wound on its forehead inadvertently inflicted by a Field Force officer in the course of whipping its mother while she was carrying the child on her back. In a village in neighboring Serengeti District, a man being interrogated by an officer was summarily shot to death.

Hundreds of weapons were confiscated, more than three hundred of them in the Mugumu area alone, many of them from cattle raiders who successfully negotiated for pardons before agreeing to surrender them. One recipient of such a pardon, now in his thirties, recalled being driven in a Field Force vehicle to the place where he had hidden his rifle, firing it into the air to exhaust his ammunition, and then handing it over to his Field Force escort. "I was very good," he reminisced with a smile, cocking his forefinger like a kid playing cowboy. "If I shoot at you, I do not miss."

The 1986 Field Force crackdown also marked the end of the cattle-raiding career of the notorious Nyamaganya, who had repeatedly infuriated and humiliated the police, moving elusively back and forth between Nyaheiya, Ekeng'ooro, Mugumu, and Tarime town, somehow contriving to remain always one step ahead of them. Cornered finally near a schoolhouse in Nyaheiya, however, a schoolhouse that had been closed down for lack of pupils in the wake of the expulsion of the Irege by the Nyamongo five years earlier, Nyamaganya, then about age thirty-nine, was beaten to death by Field Force officers with hippopotamus-hide whips (Swa., *viboko;* sing., *kiboko*) in full view of numerous onlookers.

The incompleteness of surviving records for the years 1987 and 1988 makes it impossible to quantify the impact of the 1986 crackdown on cattle raiding in the Nyamongo area, but we can be certain that any lull was brief. In Nyaheiya, in 1988, cattle raiders murdered the brother of Mokami Wambura's husband in the course of a cattle raid, then shot her mother-in-law dead when she tried to implore the raiders to let the family keep a single cow. Today, one of Mokami Wambura's sons is himself an active raider.

In 1989, Nyaheiya was raided eight times by cattle raiders—at a rate of once every six and a half weeks, on average—a frequency that was to double and then triple by 1994, although never matching, either in number of raids or casualties, the peak years of the 1980s.

In 1990, twelve cattle raiders, three of them armed with guns, shot two men dead in Nyaheiya, wounded two others, and made off with a herd of 270 cattle and 62 goats. In Mugumu town, in Serengeti District, that same year, cattle raiders in quest of guns attacked the district headquarters police station, only to be driven off after a heavy battle. The newly constructed fortresslike police post there stands as a stolid monument to these events.

In 1992, in Tarime District, fighting between the Nyamongo and the Irege erupted yet again, continuing sporadically off and on through late 1994, when the Nyabasi took up arms against the Nyamongo also. All of this fighting provided baptism by fire for many of the Nyaheiya men active in cattle raiding today.

"The enmity between Irege and Nyamongo is like Germany and Britain during World War II—it's like Hitler!" exclaimed one Nyaheiya man. "There is an Iron Curtain between Nyamongo and Irege!"

In early 1995, during a period when Nyaheiya was being raided about once every six days, on average, the member of Parliament representing Tarime District's four Kuria divisions arrived in Nyaheiya for a meeting with village officials to discuss how best to cope with the escalating cattle-raiding problem. "We don't like to bring in the police because we know the consequences," he told a group of villagers who gathered about him, in a pointed, implicit reference to the heavy-handed police operations of the 1980s. "The innocent people will suffer a lot and I am convinced that the solution to this problem is in our hands."

CHAPTER 6

"The Police Didn't Help Me at All!": Vigilantism and Sungusungu

Cattle raiding, as practiced by people living in Nyaheiya today, may be loosely divided into three separate categories, but an individual cattle-raiding career may embrace, at one time or another, any combination of these types.

In the first type, referred to locally as "tying off one cow," one or two village residents will take advantage of the inattentiveness of a herder (who, in Nyaheiya, may be male or female) in order to surreptitiously throw a rope around a grazing animal and hide it in the bush, or even inside an empty hut somewhere, until nightfall provides an opportunity to spirit the animal safely away to a place where it can be sold for cash.

In cattle raiding of the second type, a group usually of between four and ten raiders (never seven, which the Kuria regard as an extraordinarily unlucky number), all of whom reside in Nyaheiya, take cattle from other villages and sometimes even from other Nyaheiya residents, almost always under cover of darkness.

In cattle raiding of the third type, cattle raiders residing in Nyaheiya are members of cattle-raiding groups, also numbering between four and ten, that are made up of raiders affiliated with two or more clans (and, less frequently, tribes) who cooperate with one another in the raiding of each other's villages.

In a fourth type of cattle raiding, common during the 1960s and 1970s but now all but nonexistent—at least in the Tarime lowlands, where the atmosphere of intense hostility between the Nyamongo and Irege clans since 1981 (see chap. 5) has made it so much easier and safer to prey on cattle close to home—cattle-raiding groups usually numbering between twenty and thirty men would venture far from home, spying out distant cattle herds, waiting an opportunity to seize them, and then flee, usually with sizable numbers of cattle. Such long-distance raiding is especially dependent on the power of firearms to terrify, both during the raid itself and in the lengthy escape back to friendly clan territory. In Tarime District today, however, sporadic clan warfare, and the lingering enmity it engenders, enables some cattle raiders to pose as champions of their home village, ostensibly striking out vengefully against a nearby enemy village in righteous retaliation for previous raids carried out against the village where they live—even though, in practice, the raiders personally pocket the proceeds from their raids.

Quite a few informants claimed that a predilection for cattle raiding runs in families, with many raiders following in the footsteps of their fathers, who had been cattle raiders before them, but data collected on scores of Nyaheiya cattle raiders demonstrate convincingly that it is the specifics of household demography that constitute the strongest predictor of who becomes a cattle raider and who does not (see chap. 7).

The vast majority of cattle raids occur at night. Once a theft has been discovered, or the immediate threat of violence to the victims of the raid is past, a haunting, mournful cry (*ikuurate*) goes up from the women of the raided homestead and is taken up by the women of neighboring homesteads, friends and kinfolk alike. The precise nature of the cry differs from clan to clan, but among the Nyamongo it consists of a keening *Wuuu-eee,* followed by the words *Tatuturya iching'ombe!* (literally, "Help the cows!"). It is a cry of alarm, a call to action, and a plea to all and sundry to help recover the stolen cattle.

As the women move through the village, their plaintive wail alerting their fellow villagers to the theft and proclaiming the name of the homestead head whose cattle have been taken, the men of the village are silently grabbing up their weapons—bows and arrows, machetes, and short swords (*imichonge;* sing., *umuchonge*), but seldom guns, because only a very tiny minority of villagers are sufficiently affluent to be able to own guns—and racing to cut off the paths leading out of the village. This rush to action is not well-organized, and, in their haste to respond to the emergency, those villagers who respond most quickly may well find themselves confronted by a force of raiders who have them outnumbered and outgunned.

If the men arrive at the escape routes too late to prevent the cattle from being driven out of the village, then they will commence to follow the tracks, aided by cheap flashlights and the light of the moon. When a bovine animal walks, it pushes earth backward, creating a tiny mound of earth at the rear of its hoofprint, indicating clearly the direction from which it came and in which it is headed. The pursuers search the ground assiduously for fresh tracks, those that lead away from the village in the direction of enemy villages and not merely toward their own open grazing lands.

It is mainly village affiliation, not kinship, that governs which men follow the tracks. In practice, it is usually a contingent of about forty men that includes the men of the victimized homestead, some friends and neighbors, and, mainly, the men who happened to be on nighttime village sentry duty at the time the raid occurred. The women of the raided homestead, meanwhile, will carry their cry to other, nearby villages, where men who are members of the victims' *egesaku* (descent section)—but *only* men who are members of their *egesaku*—will grab up their weapons and join in the search.

Following the tracks is a hazardous undertaking, particularly for the man whose cattle have been taken, for it is usually he who leads the pursuit. If the raiders have only a small head start, they may well leave behind a rear guard for the express purpose of ambushing pursuers. If the pursuers get their hands on the raiders, they will kill them. In early 1995, a Nyaheiya man leading a band of pursuers on the trail of his cattle was shot dead by cattle raiders, and, in the violence that followed, the pursuers killed two raiders on the spot with machetes and arrows and mortally wounded a third raider, who staggered back to his home village and died.

More typically, however, cattle raiders who sense their pursuers closing in on them will adopt the more prudent strategy of abandoning the cattle and fading away into the nighttime blackness. When villagers succeed in recovering their stolen cattle, it is usually under these circumstances. Not infrequently, raiders endeavoring to flee an area from which they have taken cattle are confronted with the problem of recalcitrant animals that begin lowing loudly and/or attempting stubbornly to return home again. Cattle raiders slash the legs of these animals with their short swords and machetes to prevent their returning to their home corrals and thereby betraying the escape route the raiders have taken. While these crippled cattle are invariably recovered by their owners, these owners are left with no viable alternative but to slaughter the maimed animals on the spot and carry the meat home.

The factors of hunger and fatigue also favor the raiders: the rule of thumb is that six hours of hot pursuit will exhaust the pursuers' endurance, which means, in practice, that once the raiders have attained a six-hour advantage, the stolen cattle are generally unrecoverable.

During periods of clan warfare, or wherever and whenever clan enmity is intense, cattle raiders have the advantage of being able to drive the cattle they have taken safely and openly through the territories of clans who are hostile to their victims, and even to sell them to local butchers in those areas if they wish. Where clan relations are amicable, however, cattle raiders must exercise extra caution to avoid being seen driving the cattle until they have either crossed the Kenya border (e.g., into the Masai Mara Game Reserve) or concealed the animals in some secluded haven within Tanzania (e.g., a wooded area of the Serengeti National Park, or a certain valley close by the Irege village of Karakatonga, or near the Irege border village of Mangucha) from which the animals can be safely and easily moved across into Kenya.

Under circumstances like these, the raiders take care to avoid the

main roads, skirting populated areas in favor of what in Swahili are
termed *njia ya panya,* literally, "rat roads": irregular, unofficial bush roads
not marked on any map, traversable by men and animals but too narrow
for vehicles, evocative of the evasive, seemingly erratic path of a swiftly
scurrying rat. Implicit in the Swahili phrase is these roads' illegal aspect,
their use in connection with smuggling goods across the international border, bypassing and evading official checkpoints, customs posts, and crossing points. A portion of this intricate, ever fluid, immensely flexible "rat
roads" network, prominent in the illicit cattle trade, is traced in map 6.1.

Cattle taken from any of the five villages of the Nyamongo clan are
frequently driven first to the Irege village of Ekeng'ooro, then to the Mara
River at Masanga, then on to Kegonga, one of the illicit gateways to
Kenya. Alternatively, cattle taken from the Nyamongo villages of
Matongo or Kewanja may be driven first to the Irege village of Genkuru,
then to Kitawasi, from there to Mangucha, and then on to Kenya. Cattle
taken from Magoto, one of the villages of the Nyabasi clan, are likely to be
driven first to the highland Irege center at Nyamwaga, thence to Keisangora, then on to Muriba and Itiryo, and across the border to Kenya. Cattle taken from the Nyabasi village of Nyakunguru are moved first to
Genkuru, then to Kangariani, from there to Itiryo, and on to Kenya. Cattle taken from the Irege village of Nyamwaga are likely to be driven first to
the Nyabasi village of Magoto, then to Borega, and then across the border
to Kenya.

Clan affiliation is extremely important in this schema. Both the Irege
and Nyabasi clans have populations straddling the border between Tanzania and Kenya (see chap. 2 and map 2.4). If cattle are to be moved to
Kenya, as opposed to being both taken and sold within Tanzania, the
raiders' goal is to move the cattle swiftly into a clan territory either of
cooperating kin or other allies capable of facilitating the easy transfer of
the animals to fellow clansmen on the Kenya side of the border. The international border is thus best conceived of as a strategic resource whose
exploitation is greatly facilitated by having a reliable network of kin and
trusted friends living on both sides of it.

At small weekly and semiweekly cattle markets in Kenya, held in villages close by the border, such as Kwitembe, Suba Kuria, and Ntimaru,
receivers of cattle smuggled over from the Tanzania side mingle and hag-
gle over prices with Kenyan buyers. "Can I take these cattle to my corral?"
a buyer asks, an oblique way of inquiring whether the cattle are so hot that
prudence requires that they be slaughtered and sold as beef immediately,
or whether they can safely be held awhile and transported further into
Kenya for resale.

The illicit trade in cattle is not a neat, orderly enterprise in which each
entrepreneurial group performs exactly one fixed role in a scrupulously

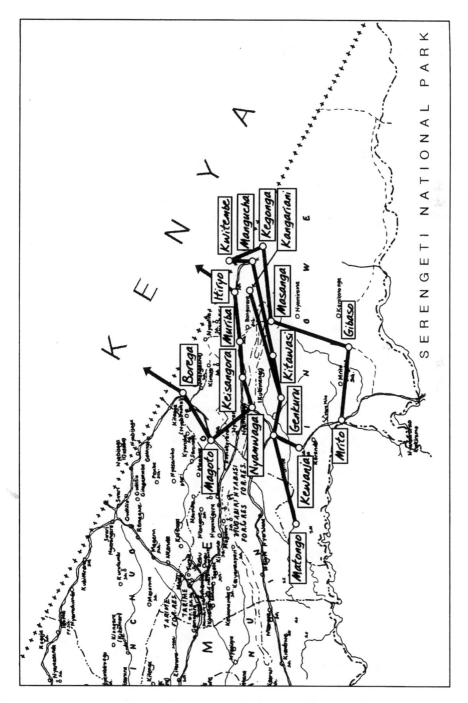

MAP 6.1. "Rat roads" network in eastern Tarime District

rationalized scheme of things. If a buyer has access to a truck this week, or can pool his resources with another man to hire one, he may buy a few head of cattle and truck them all the way to Nairobi in order to realize the largest possible profit. But, the following week, with less capital on hand, he may have to settle for doing what most buyers do with the cattle they buy at these small markets: hire a few herdsmen to drive them on foot to a larger market, further inside Kenya, such as the one held on Mondays at Migori town, about twenty-five minutes by car from the Tanzania/Kenya border, and resell them there for a more modest profit.

Some of the animals that change hands at Migori will be slaughtered, butchered, and sold locally by the kilo, but most will be herded aboard the line of waiting cattle trucks, each of which carries a maximum load of 28 head of cattle, and transported to Nairobi for a fee (in January 1996) of Ksh 28,000 per truckload.

Cattle prices rose dramatically during the fieldwork period, but the prices for the various types of cattle did not rise uniformly. In October 1994, for example, calves, the cheapest category of cattle, fetched Tsh 15,000 each in Nyaheiya, a price that villagers considered very high at that time, but by January 1996 the price of a calf had more than tripled, to Tsh 50,000. During that same period, however, the price of oxen merely doubled, from about Tsh 60,000 each to about Tsh 120,000.

Cattle prices also experience seasonal fluctuations that vary widely from category to category: the price of steers, the preferred animal for ploughing, for example, spikes upward during cultivation periods, when steers are in high demand but few are coming onto the market because their owners are using them for cultivation. The price of heifers rises whenever there is a strong demand for them to help rebuild herds.

As one leaves Nyaheiya, moving onward to Tarime town, crossing over into Kenya at the Tanzanian border town of Sirari, and then continuing on across Kenya to the large towns of Migori, Kisii, and finally Nairobi (see map 6.2), the price of beef and of all forms of livestock rises inexorably. In January 1996, a kilo of beef that sold for Tsh 900 in Nyaheiya fetched Ksh 300 (roughly Tsh 3,000) in a butcher shop in Nairobi, a markup of 333 percent.

A big ox that sold for Tsh 120,000 in Nyaheiya fetched about Ksh 20,000 (roughly Tsh 200,000) in Nairobi, a markup of only 67 percent. Once slaughtered and butchered, however, the 400 kilograms of meat supplied by that ox fetched about Ksh 120,000 (roughly Tsh 1,200,000) in Nairobi's butcher shops, an amount equal to $2,076.12 based on the prevailing January 1996 exchange rate of Ksh 57.8 = U.S.$1.00.

It is a lucrative business, particularly for the middlemen, and because the cattle supplied to the market by cattle raiders represent a substantial component of the overall trade in cattle—although no one knows precisely

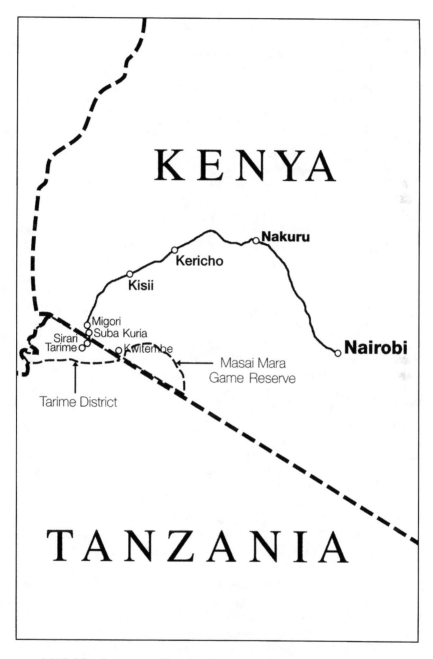

MAP 6.2.   Important villages and towns on the cattle marketing route
from Tarime District to Nairobi

how substantial—cattle raiders are generally able to demand, and receive, high prices for the cattle that they sell: as high as 83 percent of market value (i.e., Tsh 25,000 for an animal with a formal-sector market value of Tsh 30,000) at the place of sale.

The shortage of beef in Kenya is one important factor driving these high informal-sector prices, and the bureaucratic restrictions that Tanzania imposes on the formal-sector livestock trade is another. But a third factor was undoubtedly the lengthy contagious bovine pleuropneumonia (CBPP) (*ekehaha*) emergency quarantine imposed on Tanzania's own cattle markets during the fieldwork period, which not only prohibited cattle from Kenya from coming into Tanzania but also prohibited Tanzanian cattle from being driven for sale to nonlocal markets *within* Tanzania, thereby making many Tanzanian butchers—such as those at the Nyamongo-area mining town of Nyangoto—all but wholly dependent on illicitly obtained cattle merely to fulfill strictly local demand.

The high earnings and profits from the illicit cattle trade, however, come at a dreadful expense to those who own and raise the cattle, who have little defense against the raiding onslaught and who receive little help or protection from duly constituted state authority.

"We have no police in Tanzania," commented a Moscow-trained Kuria physician living in Musoma town. Citizens exact "mob justice" from cattle raiders and other criminals, he explained, because they know that if they turn them over to the police, the lawbreakers will simply bribe their way to freedom. A policeman earns his livelihood, in essence, through his ability to impose an illicit "tax" both on victims of crime and on those who have broken the law.

In the Nyamongo area, of which Nyaheiya is part, the local police demand a bribe before they will consent to investigate any complaint, and, having received it, they will then proceed to extort bribes from the alleged perpetrators and, having received those, will then go on to demand more money from the complainant, and so on, until one or both sides are either broke or tire of the game. Even an arrest, followed by detention in the local lockup, is only a gambit in the game of wringing further payments from complainants eager to keep the accused locked up and kinfolk of the alleged perpetrator anxious to see him freed. The real bread and butter of police work consists of arresting people involved in bar fights, or caught cultivating *bangi* (Swa., bhang), or distilling *gongo,* the local white lightning—minor infractions commonly referred to by local people as "mistakes"—and then extorting bribes from them to let them go.

Of the forty-two respondents to the homestead survey who answered affirmatively to the question "Has any person in this homestead ever been arrested?" fifteen of them, when asked, in a follow-up question, what the outcome of a cited case had been, volunteered that the arrestee in question had been released after paying a bribe to the police.

Police officers are easily found who will hire out their rifles to cattle raiders, or sell them their firearms outright, or accompany cattle raiders on nighttime raids for a fee (see chap. 5). Although there is as yet no established practice of paying regular protection payments to the police to buy immunity from arrest, as is common in developed countries, cattle-raiding groups and their buyers routinely deliver cash payments to the police to win the freedom of their comrades who have been arrested. For raiders who have been shot or otherwise wounded in the course of carrying out raids, local police will readily provide, for a fee, the official form (called a PF3) that any person seriously wounded or injured, whether in a crime or an accident, must present to a doctor or hospital before he can legally receive treatment. Policemen also extract a cut of all illicit livestock traffic that moves through their area and shake down known cattle raiders for bribes by threatening them with arrest.

Although the ledger books in which the police record citizens' reports of cattle thefts, along with the progress of the ensuing investigations, almost invariably contain entries stating that police have joined together with villagers in the aftermath of a cattle raid to follow the tracks of their stolen cattle, the truth is that the police seldom follow the cattle tracks by daylight, and never at night, when hot pursuit of the raiders and the cattle is highly dangerous—but also crucial if there is to be any chance of recovering the animals before they are "gone to Kenya." On those occasions when cattle are successfully recovered, it is either because local people followed and recovered them, sometimes through the use of force, or because the victim or a family member, wandering the countryside in search of the stolen animals, came upon them in some distant cattle corral and then summoned—and paid—the police to help him recover them.

"The police didn't help me at all," commented an elderly Nyaheiya man recalling the theft of his cattle in 1994.

> My wife was the one who followed the tracks to Bukira, at a village called Matanka, and she found the cows in a homestead and the wife of the homestead head was milking. She saw the cows and she pretended that she was sick so that she wanted the wife of the homestead head to give her medicine. Then [after ascertaining that the cattle were indeed her husband's] she came back and brought the police. The police went and captured the cows back.

On those infrequent occasions when the police *do* apprehend a cattle raider, noted one Nyaheiya cattle holder, "it's to ask for their share. Instead of stopping this business, they're pruning it."

It is hardly surprising, then, that when asked, on the homestead survey, to "rate police effectiveness in coping with the cattle-thieving problem in this area" (see table 6.1), an overwhelming majority of respondents—

93.2 percent of them—gave police the lowest rating made available to them on the survey: "ineffective."

Requests, in a follow-up question, to explain these low evaluations unleashed a torrent of criticisms:

> Like the day when my cows were stolen, a man went to call them [the police] but they said that their boss was not around. This was just a way to demand money and to avoid us. In the morning I went to see them again and they just came to see my place and wrote down their things and that was all.

> Many people are robbed here at Nyaheiya. And they make reports to the police but they [the police] don't help them. They are useless here at Nyaheiya.

> They [the police] fear them [the raiders] because the thieves have more powerful weapons than the policemen.

> They [police] are money minded and do not like to take risks. They are cowards.

> They [the police] are also thieves. They like bribes very much.

> They [the police] like bribes and then let the thieves go free and this frightens even the leaders. Therefore the police are contributing to the increase of cattle theft in this area.

> They cooperate with the thieves by drinking together and accepting bribes from them.

> A thief might be caught with evidence but within a short time he comes back.

> They are friendly with thieves. They are useless.

> They are useless.

> They lend the thieves their guns to steal. So they are also fighting us.

> The thieves are friends with the police. The police rent their guns to the thieves, so they also fight the people of Nyaheiya and they do not follow the tracks to help them when they are robbed.

TABLE 6.1. *Question:* **"How Would You Rate Police Effectiveness in Coping with the Cattle-Thieving Problem in This Area?" (*n* = 190)**

Extremely Effective	Reasonably Effective	Not Very Effective	Ineffective	Don't Know	No Answer
1.6%	2.6%	.5%	93.2%	1.1%	1.1%

They don't help the people follow the tracks, so they are useless.

The police are afraid to follow the tracks, so they are useless.

Because when they are informed of a theft they just pretend to go after the stolen cows but do not go very far. In this way, they discourage the people who are following the tracks.

When cows are stolen, you inform them [the police]. When they reach [a place] where there is a bar, they stop for a beer.

They don't like to follow the tracks. They like to catch people in small mistakes so that they can be paid bribes.

They are afraid to follow the tracks at night, and [after his cattle had been stolen] they waited till the morning. They are useless to me.

They have guns but they are also afraid of night, so they wait until in the morning to follow the tracks—after the cows have already reached Kenya.

They're afraid to follow the tracks at night.

They don't help following the tracks. They only like to go after someone who's made a small mistake so they can be paid a bribe.

They are also thieves because they don't help the people follow the tracks.

The police are themselves poorly paid men who are ill-equipped to cope seriously with the cattle-raiding problem. The raiders outgun and outnumber them. Lacking vehicles, the police are limited to negotiating the treacherous rain-gullied unpaved roads on bicycles. Many police posts lack shortwave radios or any other means of communicating either with their superiors in Tarime town or with other police posts. In an effort to discourage complicity between policemen and Kuria lawbreakers, the government has seen to it that no Kuria policemen are posted to Kuria country. The result, as residents of Nyaheiya often noted, is that most of the area's policemen, and their commanders, are indifferent, if not outright hostile, to local people. "They seem not to care about the situation of this place," noted one Nyaheiya man. "They say, 'Let Chacha kill Mwita [Chacha and Mwita are common Kuria names] and we don't care.'"

Many policemen in Tarime District frankly fear the Kuria, and exaggerated, or wholly apocryphal, anecdotes of Kuria ferocity are common currency in police circles. One is that Kuria have ceremonies at which they boast about the number of people they have killed and injured. Another is that a Kuria will never confess or betray information, "even if you cut him into little pieces." Yet another story, heard often from policemen throughout Kuria country, is that, even when they lack guns themselves, the Kuria have absolutely no fear of firearms. At night, able to identify the type and caliber of any weapon by its sound alone, goes the story, they will count the number of rounds fired by a policeman and then, when they know he is out of ammunition, they will close in on him and hack him to death with their short swords.

The upshot of all this is that the people of Nyaheiya and all the rest of Kurialand have scant alternatives open to them but to act as their own policemen, that is, to rely on mechanisms of self-help much as they did prior to the advent of colonialism.

Unlike the situation that prevailed in past decades, when "there was no generalised public opinion against cattle theft" in Kurialand (Tanner 1966:41), the people of Nyaheiya and other Kuria villages have come to oppose cattle raiding as the offtake from raiding has passed the point of sustainability and as the widespread use of firearms by cattle raiders has claimed the lives of many innocent people. Asked, on the homestead survey, to register the extent of their approval or disapproval of Nyaheiya residents carrying out cattle raids against the Maasai, the Luo, the Irege clan, or against their own Nyaheiya neighbors, overwhelming majorities of Nyaheiya respondents registered vehement disapproval of *all* such cattle-raiding activity (see table 6.2), an attitude that was also expressed at frequent village meetings in Nyaheiya and in innumerable private conversations throughout the fieldwork period. In the words of one local official, "Many people want peace." Three complicating factors, however, make it difficult for the people of Nyaheiya and other Kuria villages to put their opposition to cattle raiding into practice by taking effective steps to curb the cattle raiders in their midst. The first of these is that, in an area all but bereft of economic opportunities, cattle raiding—along with prospecting for gold—constitutes a crucial underpinning of the village economy. Many people benefit from it, directly or indirectly, and there is probably no one who is not either related to a cattle raider or a friend or neighbor of someone who is. It is not an easy thing in any close-knit community for a person to take an action that might help send the son of a relative, friend, or neighbor to prison.

A second reason, closely related to the first, is that cattle raiding is a major source—perhaps even *the* major source—of scarce and highly valued animal protein for the people of Nyaheiya. The knowledge that Nyaheiya's cattle corrals are home to thousands of cattle should not mislead one into believing that a meat meal in Nyaheiya is cheap. To ask a Nyaheiya man to slaughter a cow for its beef, which, in the absence of refrigeration, will go bad in three days, is functionally equivalent to asking an American farmer to sell his tractor to pay for a Thanksgiving dinner.

When a group of Nyaheiya cattle raiders return home from a raid, particularly against the hated Irege village of Ekeng'ooro, the three dozen or so village women living in homesteads along their path rush out to greet them, ululating joyfully, knowing that the raiders will often distribute all the sheep and goats they have taken to village women as gifts, retaining only the cattle to sell for cash. Where there is an insufficient number of animals for every woman to claim one, several women will usually share one, taking it to a nearby homestead to slaughter and dividing the meat. "We are happy!" exclaimed a Nyaheiya woman on one such occasion. "We are happy and joyful to have meat!"

Another woman, employing the Swahili word *mtumba*—a term widely used in East Africa to mean "second-hand clothing"—as a metaphor for illicitly obtained beef, bluntly stated her view that "people shouldn't be stopped from getting *mtumba*. We hate the Irege, and we like cows to be taken from them and we eat *mtumba*."

A third factor militating against effective opposition to cattle raiding is the fact of recurrent clan warfare, which not only serves to legitimate cattle raiding—as well as functioning as a kind of school, or training ground, for cattle raiders—for so long as the fighting rages, but also nurtures and reinforces a climate of interclan enmity that fosters at least a tolerance, if not full-scale support, for cattle raiding, particularly if it is carried out against certain groups.

"When we were going there [to Ekeng'ooro] and taking cows and bringing them here," recalled a young Nyaheiya man who had participated in a recent spate of clan warfare between the Nyamongo and Irege, "the women at Nyaheiya were very happy."

"War," commented a Nyaheiya member of a multiclan cattle-raiding group, "is good for thieving."

Clan warfare has two main causes. The first cause, animosity engendered by cattle raiding itself, has already been discussed in chapter 5. But clan warfare is also ignited by boundary adjustments initiated by the government, either for administrative reasons—for example, in response to population changes or demographic shifts—or, paradoxically, in an effort

TABLE 6.2. *Question:* **"If One of Your Fellow Villagers, or a Group of Your Fellow Villagers Working Together, Were to Steal Cattle from the Following Groups, How Would You Feel about It?"** (*n* = 190)

	Maasai	Luo	Irege	Nyaheiya
Strongly approve	.5%	.5%	0%	0%
Approve but with some reservations	.5%	0%	.5%	9.5%
Disapprove	3.2%	2.1%	1.1%	1.1%
Strongly disapprove	95.3%	96.8%	97.9%	89.0%
No answer	.5%	.5%	.5%	.5%

to resolve already ongoing disputes, which are at bottom disputes over pastoralism's primary strategic resources: grass and water. Invariably, any boundary adjustment angers someone, setting the stage for further conflict, often with one clan seeking to intimidate members of a rival clan from living or grazing their livestock near a disputed border so as to be able to acquire a de facto dominance over the disputed area.

Absent the presence of any legally sanctioned representative of state authority able and willing to safeguard their lives and property, the people of Nyaheiya and the other Kuria villages of Tanzania have little recourse but to do what they can to protect themselves. This is precisely the point of view that Gisieri Chambiri, the member of Parliament for the Kuria divisions of Tarime District, brought with him to Nyaheiya on 11 January 1995 when he proclaimed that "the solution to this problem is in our hands." After making a thinly veiled denunciation of the Field Force police operations of the 1980s (see chap. 5) for their persecution of innocent people and reminding his listeners that Tanzanian law empowers *all* citizens to arrest wrongdoers—"You are all policemen!" proclaimed the MP—Chambiri went on to advocate his own preferred means of combatting the cattle-raiding problem, including:

1. Public condemnation of the cattle raiders, "so that they become unfortunate in life."
2. Turning captured cattle raiders over to their victims to deal with as they see fit. "Then, when the thief is brought to you, you will decide yourselves what to do with him."
3. Utilization of a method currently being employed, according to the MP, elsewhere in Tarime District, in which cattle raiders residing in a village are taken into custody and their fathers compelled to administer severe public beatings to them on pain of being beaten themselves if they refuse.
4. Adoption of a method of punishment currently being applied, according to the MP, in Bukoba, Tanzania, seat of the country's Kagera Region, whereby the mucous secretions of slugs—or house snails—are smeared on the eyes of captured cattle raiders so as to render them permanently blind and make them living examples to others.

While none of these suggestions, excepting perhaps the first one, was ever specifically implemented in Nyaheiya, the broader idea of rough justice for cattle raiders was already well-established, both in principle and practice, long before the MP's visit. Indeed, killing cattle raiders, either in the course of their carrying out a raid or in the course of pursuing them to recover the cattle, is the preferred means of dealing with cattle raiders—provided that they are not fellow villagers.

Nyaheiya villagers killed three Irege cattle raiders in the course of the fieldwork period, and three Nyaheiya cattle raiders were killed while carrying out raids against the villages of other clans or tribes. A Canadian volunteer schoolteacher, working in Tarime town, unexpectedly became an eyewitness to an event of this kind while visiting Buhemba, a Kuria village of the Timbaru clan, in early 1995 (the "sticks" she refers to in her account are actually the *marungu* [Swa., cudgels or knobkerries; sing., *rungu*] that are carried by the men of some Kuria clans):

> A cow had been stolen from Buhemba village, and a day or so later a man came and he said, "I have a cow for sale. Does anybody want to buy my cow?" And a few men said, "Let us see this cow," and when they saw it they said, "This is *Juma's* cow!" and they started to beat the man.
>
> People came running from everywhere. I never saw a group of people gather so fast. There were a hundred—more than a hundred. They surrounded the man, so that I couldn't see him, but I could hear the sticks hitting his body. I will never forget the sound of the sticks hitting his body.
>
> I was standing with the women, and I asked them, "What are they doing? What is happening?" And they said, "He is a thief. They are going to beat him to death."
>
> I was new, so I still wasn't confident with my Swahili, and I would repeat everything anybody said to me. So I said, "You are saying he is a thief and they are going to beat him until he is dead." And they said, "Yes!"
>
> I'll never forget the sound of the sticks hitting his body. They said they beat him so hard his ears fell off. They—fell off. He must have been not right in his head, that man, to have tried to sell a cow in the same village he stole it from. I remember asking, "You say they are going to beat him until he is dead," and they said, "Yes!"
>
> Children came. Even children. Everyone was having a wonderful time. I didn't see him being beaten, but I saw his body. They put an arrow in his head and dumped him in front of the police station.

The visit of the MP to Nyaheiya in January 1995 took place in the wake of a decision by local officials, in concert with area elders, to respond to the area's cattle-theft problem by implementing, under government sponsorship, a form of village vigilantism known as *Sungusungu*[1] that had

---

1. *Sungusungu* is a Swahili word for a species of large black biting ant, and, throughout Tanzania Kurialand, this is the etymology that is offered. Among the Sukuma and Nyamwezi, however, people relate the name to the Sukuma word for poison (*busungu*), a reference to the poison-tipped arrows employed by *Sungusungu* members there (Bukurura 1996:265n. 3).

first arisen in the early 1980s (Abrahams 1987:181–83; Mesaki 1994:58; Bukurura 1996:260), among the Sukuma and Nyamwezi peoples of west-central Tanzania, as an indigenous response to cattle raiding and robbery and, in some communities although not in others, to the perceived problems of witch finding and witch eradication (Abrahams 1987:187; Mesaki 1994:58; Bukurura 1994:20, 1996:260). This embracing of the anticrime functions of *Sungusungu* by Tanzanian officialdom in Tarime District represented a marked turnaround from the 1980s, when police and judges arrested, tried, and sentenced some members of *Sungusungu* groups—although the popularity and spread of these groups, as well as personal sympathy with them, ultimately led Tanzania's president, Julius K. Nyerere, and his successor, Ali Hassan Mwinyi, to grant amnesties to some of those convicted (Abrahams 1987:189–90; Bukurura 1996:263–64, 265n. 10).

By late 1994, the institutional framework for this new, state-sponsored incarnation of *Sungusungu* in Tarime District was already in place. A district *Sungusungu* "commander" was elected to preside over all *Sungusungu* operations throughout Tarime District, and, under him, a division commander was appointed for each of Tarime District's eight divisions, including Ingwe Division, of which both Nyaheiya and the Irege village of Ekeng'ooro are a part. Each village, in turn, elected its own village commander, responsible for leadership of the *Sungusungu* contingent within his respective village, and a *Sungusungu* clerk and ten other men were selected to assist the village commander in carrying out his work.[2]

Village commanders were required to report to ward commanders, who reported to the division commanders, who in turn reported to their division officer, a district government official, who in turn reported directly to the district commissioner, the district's highest-ranking official. All villages pledged to cooperate in apprehending the cattle raiders in their midst and in returning cattle stolen from other villages.

In Nyaheiya, where all men between the ages of eighteen and fifty are required to perform *Sungusungu* service, thirty men—armed with bows and arrows and short swords—were assigned to patrol the village each night, with instructions to sneak up on invading cattle raiders, fire an arrow at them, and then sound the alarm.

In addition, *Sungusungu* members made the rounds of the various homesteads, soliciting accusations against anyone suspected of involvement in cattle raiding, and, throughout Tarime District, lists were compiled of cattle-raiding suspects, the places where they lived, and the specific

---

2. When, in late 1995, a villagewide meeting was held in Nyaheiya to elect a new village commander, the village chairman, who is an elected ruling party official, presided over the meeting, flanked by the outgoing *Sungusungu* commander and a pair of village officials, and by the police sergeant in command of the local police post.

crimes of which they had been accused. Inevitably, there were some deliberately false accusations made, by people who owed others money or who
harbored resentments over adultery or other grudges, and efforts were
made to substantiate accusations by seeking corroboration from other
accusers and by insisting that accusers persuasively link those whom they
named to particular raiding incidents.

Those who had been accused, and who were not already in prison,
were taken into custody by the village *Sungusungu* commander and his
men and hauled before a village *Sungusungu baraza* (Swa., council house,
from the verb *barizi,* to attend a council, but also used to denote any meeting held to discuss a public issue) attended by about fifteen people, including the village commander and his ten immediate subordinates, the village
chairman, selected village elders, and the accused. Accusers do not attend
these *baraza,* and their identities are not revealed to the accused, who are
confronted with the evidence against them, interrogated, and beaten with
a hippopotamus-hide whip (Swa., *kiboko;* pl., *viboko*) on the legs, back,
and buttocks in an effort to extract confessions. Whipping on the chest is
not engaged in, as it is said to be potentially lethal. Sometimes the whipping and interrogation of a single suspect or group of suspects continues
on and off for several days. While these methods are not sanctioned by
Tanzanian law, reports strongly suggest that suspects in official police custody do not fare much better.

In Nyaheiya, village men who had been caught red-handed with cattle belonging either to their fellow villagers or to residents of other Nyamongo-clan villages, or who had employed guns in the commission of
their crimes, were turned over to the police to be incarcerated at Tarime—
sometimes for years—while they await official investigation of their cases
and possible criminal trials. Of the resident accused cattle raiders remaining, those who confessed at their *baraza* were required to pay heavy fines
of from three to four head of cattle or from Tsh 20,000 to Tsh 50,000 in
cash, which were used to defray the expenses of the *Sungusungu* as well as
to support such village institutions as the primary school and the new
clinic, then under construction. Then these men were released, with an
admonition not to engage in cattle raiding again.

In those cases where those who had confessed were unable to pay
their fines, the *Sungusungu* was empowered to collect those fines from their
kin, seizing their property—livestock, furniture, cooking utensils—if need
be and selling it to raise the money needed to discharge the penalty. In the
first sixty days of the *Sungusungu* crackdown, the Nyaheiya *Sungusungu*
took into custody and interrogated some two dozen suspected Nyaheiya
cattle raiders.

It needs to be emphasized that, in Nyaheiya, these extremely harsh
procedures were utilized only against those Nyaheiya men who stood

accused either of committing or abetting cattle raiding within Nyaheiya itself, or against any of the other Nyamongo-clan villages, or against other specific groups with which the Nyamongo regarded themselves as being closely allied, such as the Ngoreme people of neighboring Serengeti District. No one in Nyaheiya was ever punished, for example, for taking cattle from the Irege. That is why, in early 1995, after a Nyaheiya man named Chacha Gotora had been mortally wounded in the course of a raid against the Ngoreme that had gone disastrously awry, Chacha's Nyaheiya comrades tried to hold to the story that they had *not* been guilty of raiding the Ngoreme, but rather that Chacha had been shotgunned to death in the course of their attempt to waylay and rob a band of Irege raiders who, the Nyaheiya men falsely claimed, had themselves taken cattle from the Ngoreme.

Although there *were* occasions when the Nyaheiya *Sungusungu* felt compelled to cooperate with the *Sungusungu* of other clans' villages, including the Irege, to the extent of recovering and returning cattle that had been taken from them by Nyaheiya cattle raiders, the Nyaheiya *Sungusungu* never went so far as to turn over one of its own "sons" to the *Sungusungu* of another village, or to the police, for cattle raids carried out against another tribe or clan, at least insofar as it was possible to determine.

Like many of Nyaheiya's young men, Chacha Gotora had become increasingly active in cattle raiding as the yield from prospecting for gold in the area declined. The local mines were not producing well during the fieldwork period, and many men accustomed to having cash in their pockets had switched over to engaging in cattle raiding full-time.

The stated, and perhaps honestly intended, justification for the implementation of *Sungusungu* in the villages is that local people are the ones best equipped to identify and bring to justice the cattle raiders in their midst—far better equipped, many argue, than the police, all of them corrupt, all of them outsiders, who are frequently contemptuous of local people and indifferent to their concerns. Apart from enhancing village security through beefed-up nighttime patrols, however, the main function of *Sungusungu,* whether deliberate or incidental, seems to have been to safeguard local people against police arrest and criminal prosecution while at the same time redirecting the illicit economic benefits of law enforcement from the pockets of police officers, wardens, and magistrates back into the local communities where the cattle raiders live. *Sungusungu* is thus a mechanism for keeping the graft at home.

If a Nyaheiya man's oxen are stolen, for example, he can report the theft to the village *Sungusungu* commander and his subordinates, who will agree to take up his case for a fee—but for a lower fee than is customarily demanded by the police. Then the *Sungusungu* will set to work, activating a local information network far superior to that of the police and chastened by the knowledge that their fellow villagers will vote them out of office if they habitually fail to perform their duties adequately—because, unlike the police, they are not invulnerable to community sentiment.

If the oxen are recovered, usually through the cooperation of the *Sungusungu* in other villages, the Nyaheiya *Sungusungu* will extract an additional fee from the oxen's owner, both as a reward for their success and because the *Sungusungu* men in the cooperating village(s) must be paid for their help. If the culprits are identified and turn out to be, or to include, Nyaheiya men, and if the oxen they stole are no longer recoverable, they or their families will be required to pay compensation to the oxen's owner in addition to the fines that will go to supporting the building of the new clinic and other village projects. In one 1995 case, in which fourteen calves were stolen by a multiclan gang and sold across the border in Kenya before they could be recovered, the families of two Nyaheiya men who confessed to involvement in the incident were required to pay a fine of Tsh 80,000—far less than the actual market value of the calves—Tsh 5,000 of which went to the *Sungusungu.*

Nonetheless, it is this possibility of being able to obtain at least some compensation from cattle raiders who come from one's own village that accounts for an apparent anomaly in table 6.2, the fact that nearly eighteen times as many survey respondents "approve, but with some reservations," of Nyaheiya residents stealing cattle from *other* Nyaheiya residents as approve of Nyaheiya residents stealing from the Maasai; similarly, nearly 98 percent of survey respondents "strongly disapprove" of Nyaheiya stealing cattle from the Irege, while 89 percent strongly disapprove of Nyaheiya residents stealing cattle from *other* Nyaheiya residents.

The reason for this seeming anomaly is *not* that Nyaheiya residents approve of stealing from one's neighbors as opposed to stealing from outsiders as a *moral* matter—on the contrary, their answers express a disapproval of *all* cattle theft—but rather that, as a *practical* matter, they know that if cattle are stolen from them by other Nyaheiya villagers, there is at least a decent chance that the *Sungusungu* will succeed in identifying the culprits and in compelling them to pay compensation, even if the animals themselves have already gone to Kenya. If one's cattle are stolen by outsiders, on the other hand, it is far less likely that the thieves will ever be identified or that compensation will ever be paid. Just as important, villagers know that their young men are in grave danger of being killed while attempting to steal cattle from other villages, whereas they are certain to be let off with a whipping and a stern admonition not to steal again if they are caught stealing cows at home—provided they have not employed guns against their fellow clansmen or been captured red-handed with Nyamongo cows.

Inevitably, however, the *Sungusungu* has proved to be vulnerable to the same abuses that have plagued all other efforts to resolve the cattle-raiding problem: some village *Sungusungu* commanders extort payoffs in cattle from cattle raiders, particularly those who have taken cattle from the villages of other clans or tribes; others extract advance payments from villagers needing assistance, but then fail to perform the required work; others actively assist cattle raiders in robbing their own people, capitalizing on their knowledge of people's sleeping habits and sentry routines acquired in the course of their nightly patrols. In Nyaheiya alone, three village *Sungusungu* commanders were ousted in the space of less than one year: two for corruption, the other for slashing an elderly woman with a short sword during an altercation over the up-front fee he demanded from her before undertaking to recover her stolen hoe. Even when operating with integrity and at its most efficient, the *Sungusungu* still have only bows and arrows and short swords to fight with, while many cattle raiders are armed with guns.

Beginning in early 1995, however, and continuing for some months thereafter, the *Sungusungu* crackdown did exert a dramatic effect on the incidence of cattle raiding in the Nyamongo area. In Kemambo *kata*, or ward, which comprises all five of the Nyamongo-clan villages, including Nyaheiya, forty-one cases of livestock theft were reported to the police in 1995, fifteen of them in January, before the crackdown really began to take hold, and then six more in February, as the crackdown began to take effect. In the ensuing ten months of 1995, however, only twenty more cases were reported altogether, an average of only two cases per month (see table 6.3)—although the number of reported cases did show a pronounced upturn in December, a sign that the intimidatory impact of the crackdown had begun to slacken.

Nyaheiya residents, who had reported a total of seventeen cattle-raiding incidents to the police in 1993 and twenty-five cattle-raiding incidents in 1994, reported only seven such incidents in 1995. Net cattle losses (number of cattle taken minus number recovered), as reported to the police by Nyaheiya residents during 1994 and 1995, declined by a dramatic 86 percent (see table 6.4). Although the numbers of cattle reported stolen may be exaggerated by villagers in hopes of receiving outsized compensation for their losses later on (see chap. 8), the number of thefts reported, and the percentage of rise or decline in numbers of cattle stolen from month to month and from year to year, are probably accurate.

The *Sungusungu* crackdown also produced a number of noteworthy side effects: the owners of small bars in Nyaheiya, whose stock in trade was bottled beer brought in from Kenya, suffered a devastating decline in their business because the cattle raiders, who had been their principal patrons, no longer had money to spend in the bars. And there was a

TABLE 6.3. **Cattle Thefts Reported to Police by the People of Kemambo Ward (including Nyaheiya), during the Year 1995**

Month	Number of Thefts Reported
January	15
February	6
March	1
April	1
May	2
June	1
July	0
August	3
September	2
October	3
November	2
December	5
Total	41

renewed surge of effort on the part of local people to attempt to eke out an income from gold prospecting, however meager, at the poorly producing area mines.

Most noticeable, however, was that beef for sale by the kilo, which had previously been available every single day in Nyaheiya, with only rare exceptions, was now available for purchase much less frequently, about six days a month, and far fewer people than before the crackdown had the wherewithal to buy it. This dearth of available beef supplies was marginally—but only marginally—compensated for by a shotgun-owning villager who occasionally killed a hippopotamus by the banks of the Mara River about a two hours' walk from Nyaheiya and sold the meat, which was much less expensive than beef, and by hunter-entrepreneurs from another Kuria village who sold dried meat (*kimoro*) from zebra, topi, and buffalo acquired in the Serengeti National Park, which was a good deal more costly than beef. The small group of Nyaheiya men who had been

TABLE 6.4. **Cattle Thefts Reported to Police by the People of Nyaheiya, 1993–95**

Year	Number of Thefts Reported	Number of Cattle Reported Stolen	Number of Cattle Recovered
1993	17	593	66
1994	25	412	36
1995	7	73	22

garnering a small cash income from selling the hides of stolen livestock found themselves, at least for the time being, out of business.

The *Sungusungu* crackdown had an undeniably chilling effect on cattle raiding in 1995, but it can have had no effect whatsoever on the root causes of cattle raiding, which are structural and economic. Indeed, by December of that same year, the total number of cattle-raiding incidents reported to the police by the people of Kemambo ward had all but returned to February's level (see table 6.3).

"Thieves of these days don't fear anybody," said one Nyaheiya man ruefully. "They come either to kill or to be killed."

CHAPTER 7

"They Can't Stop the Stealing":
An Analysis of the
Nyaheiya Cattle Raider Sample

Sixty-six Nyaheiya residents were identified in the course of fieldwork either as being actively involved in market-oriented cattle theft or as having been involved in market-oriented cattle theft at least at some time in the course of the five-year period from 1990 to 1995.

Cattle raiding is an illicit, ofttimes violent activity usually carried out by organized groups of four to ten men, typically (but not invariably) abetted by one or more accomplices in the target villages. If they are caught in the act, they are liable to be shot or beaten or hacked to death by their intended victims—as, indeed, three Nyaheiya cattle raiders were in the course of this fieldwork—and so there are compelling reasons for them to keep their identities secret, particularly from outsiders. There is thus no way of knowing whether the sixty-six men in this sample represent the absolute sum total of Nyaheiya residents who engaged in cattle raiding sometime within the course of that five-year period. Probably they do not. But the number is consistent with the educated guesses of a number of Nyaheiya informants, who variously estimated the probable number at somewhere between fifty and eighty.

Of these sixty-six, two were eliminated from further consideration in connection with this study because the collection of additional data regarding them proved impossible: one had fled to Kenya with his family to avoid prosecution for cattle theft; the other had been imprisoned for cattle theft, and his family had departed Nyaheiya for a distant area of Tanzania.

Of the sixty-four cattle raiders remaining, on whom data were collected, five were sent to prison for cattle theft either prior to or during fieldwork; three were killed while carrying out cattle raids in the course of the fieldwork period; one had been killed while defending his father's cattle from raiders during the early 1990s; and one had fled the village but left his family behind in Nyaheiya, where they were interviewed. The balance of the sixty-four-man sample, fifty-four cattle raiders in all, were all residing in Nyaheiya at the time of the study (see table 7.1).

Some of those in the sixty-four-man sample had been engaged in cattle raiding for as long as eight years and claimed to have participated in as many as 150 cattle raids, while others had been involved for much shorter periods and had taken part in only two or three raids. Some reveled in the cattle-raiding life, and some said they hated it. The money was good, they agreed, but many had seen friends die pointlessly and were sick of it, while others were bitter that, despite all their work, they had nothing to show for it. Some claimed they had quit for good, while others said they were merely lying low for a time—"resting," as one interviewee engagingly put it—in the wake of the *Sungusungu* (state-sponsored village vigilante) crackdown that began in late 1994, sharply reducing cattle raiding throughout the area, at least for a time.

All sixty-four of the cattle raiders in the study were males, the raiding of other villages for cattle being, like warfare, an activity engaged in exclusively by young men, at least insofar as it has been possible to determine. Of the 380 incidents of livestock theft occurring in Kemambo *kata* (Swa., ward), of which Nyaheiya is a part, between 1982 and the end of 1995, concerning which it has been possible to unearth documentation, only one of them, the 1984 theft of a single cow and its calf belonging to a Nyaheiya man from the area where the livestock were grazing, was alleged to have been perpetrated by a woman, who was also a resident of Nyaheiya.

Of the sixty cattle raiders in the sixty-four-man sample whose birth years were obtainable, thirty-four were in their twenties and twenty-six were in their thirties. Only one man in the group of sixty was over thirty-five; he was thirty-eight. In the course of fieldwork, men were identified in every decade of life in Nyaheiya who had participated in cattle raiding at one time or another, but none was found who had actually been active after reaching the age of forty. The thirty-four cattle raiders in their twenties represent 17 percent of the male population of Nyaheiya in that age group. The twenty-six in their thirties represent 31 percent of the male population in that age group. Taken as a group, the sixty cattle raiders whose birth years were obtainable represent 21 percent of the male population of Nyaheiya aged twenty to thirty-nine. This accords well with the thumbnail estimate offered by a number of villagers that Nyaheiya's active

TABLE 7.1.   The Nyaheiya Cattle Raider Sample
(*n* = 64)

In Prison	Killed in Cattle Raids	Residing in Nyaheiya	Residing Elsewhere
5	4[a]	54	1

[a]Of these four, three were killed in cattle raids against other villages, and one was killed in a cattle raid against Nyaheiya.

cattle-raider population consisted of about 25 percent of the village's young men.

A few of the cattle raiders in the sample had begun their careers in cattle raiding before reaching twenty, but always as members of a working group of older raiders, and invariably they had been assigned the least dangerous and least demanding task in a cattle raid, that of rounding up and herding away the victim's sheep and goats, while the group's more experienced members were the ones who broke into the victim's cattle enclosure (*oboori*), let out the cattle, and assumed responsibility for the group's offense and defense.

At the time these data regarding cattle raiders were collected, there were 350 separate homesteads in Nyaheiya, yet all sixty-four of the cattle raiders in the study had grown up in only forty-six homesteads. In other words, 100 percent of the cattle raiders in the study grew up in what amounts to just 13 percent of Nyaheiya's current homestead total. Thirty of the cattle raiders, or just under half (47 percent) of the total number, grew up in only twelve of Nyaheiya's homesteads, which is the same as saying that 47 percent of the cattle raiders identified during fieldwork came from only 3 percent of Nyaheiya's current homestead total of 350. Just two of Nyaheiya's homesteads accounted for a total of eight cattle raiders (two sets of four uterine brothers each); two other Nyaheiya homesteads accounted for a total of six cattle raiders (one having three uterine brothers and the other having two uterine brothers and one nonuterine brother from two separate households within the homestead); and eight of Nyaheiya's homesteads accounted for a total of sixteen cattle raiders (eight sets of two uterine brothers per homestead). The remaining thirty-four cattle raiders in the sample grew up in thirty-four separate Nyaheiya homesteads.

This heavy concentration of the sixty-four cattle raiders identified in the course of fieldwork in such a tiny percentage of Nyaheiya's homesteads almost certainly reflects, as we shall see, a real tendency for cattle raiders to cluster together in households where male siblings heavily outnumber female siblings, partly for the reason that brothers in these sister-poor households share a crucial social and economic dilemma: the lack of a sufficient number of uterine sisters to provide the brothers with enough bridewealth cattle to enable them all to marry; but it may also reflect the "snowballing" (Bernard 1988:98) strategy that made the collection of these data possible. The group of sixty-four cattle raiders reported on here is therefore not a random sample, but it is a large enough sample that telling inferences regarding Nyaheiya's cattle raiders may reasonably be drawn from it.

In their interviews, cattle raiders reported various reasons for turning to cattle raiding as an income-producing activity. They did it, they said, *kufanya starehe* (Swa., to make oneself comfortable, be at ease; in English we might say, to take life easy or to lead the good life) and because they found it to be a much faster means of earning money than gold mining, which was, for all intents and purposes, the only comparably remunerative alternative open to them.

They spent their money, they said, on clothing and other necessaries for themselves and their families, on beer and on women, and on the acquisition of cattle—mainly bridewealth cattle for themselves and/or their siblings, but occasionally also cattle with which to build their own herds. "The life of a cattle thief," proclaimed one raider, with what seemed like a mixture of bravado and regret, "is to sell cows, go to bars, and drink beer—*sana!*" (*sana* is an intensive in Swahili, used to heighten any kind of action or quality). Indeed, the sight of the cattle raiders drinking beer in the village bars when few others in Nyaheiya could afford to buy bottled beer—one bottle representing roughly 1 percent of Tanzania's estimated GNP per capita of U.S.$90.00 for the year 1993 (World Bank 1995:657)— was one of the most reliable indicators (especially since the local mines were not producing well, as was the case throughout the fieldwork period) of when cattle raiding was up or down and who the active players in it were. Notwithstanding the interviewees' stated list of motives, however, it is the inability of a set of male uterine siblings to rely on family assistance in the acquisition of bridewealth cattle, and their consequent need to acquire those cattle through their own efforts, that would seem to be the strongest motivating factor, or at least the best predictor, of who in Nya-heiya becomes a cattle raider.

For both males and females, marriage is central to a Kuria's life. For females, marriage is the means by which a woman gains access to cultivable land and, if she is lucky, cattle, the very stuff of subsistence. Marriage constitutes the arena in which she secures her validation as a woman and ensures the security of her old age as the mother of a large family of both sons and daughters. It is the mechanism by which she brings bridewealth cattle into her natal household, thereby making it possible for her uterine brothers to acquire wives of their own. "Our wealth," explained one Nyaheiya man, "is our women."

For males, the need to marry is also compelling. Although many people in Nyaheiya are keenly aware that their world is changing and that the acquisition of many wives and many children has come to entail increasing costs and responsibilities and not necessarily more wealth, a man must still marry if he is to acquire offspring and bind them to his lineage in order to secure his old age and if he is to lay claim to the labor of wives and offspring that will make it possible for him to cultivate crops and raise cattle; to mine for gold in the local mines and/or own and operate a small bar or shop; and to have his firewood and water fetched, his food cooked, his clothes washed, and a dizzying array of other homestead chores performed for him while still allowing him ample free time to attend village meetings, engage in networking activities and carry out business of various kinds, travel, play, and socialize. Fathers may bemoan the school fees and other costs attendant upon having large families, but prestige in Nyaheiya still accrues to the man who has married many wives and fathered many sons and daughters. It is no surprise that in the random survey sample of 190 homesteads, only one instance was found of a homestead head who had never married. Only eighteen of the sixty-four men in the cattle-raider sample either grew up or currently resided in homesteads that chanced to be included in the random survey sample, but all sixty-four, or members of their immediate families, were asked to provide the name of each cattle raider's father, the names of that cattle raider's father's wives, and, for each of his father's wives, the names of all her children, their sexes, and the years in which they were born, including the names, sexes, and birth years of all siblings who had died in infancy or were, for any reason, no longer alive. All siblings, both uterine and nonuterine, who had died before marrying were excluded from the following analysis on the self-evident ground that a male sibling who dies without marrying is no longer in need of a wife, while a female sibling who dies without marrying is no longer available as a potential provider of bridewealth cattle for her brothers.

The sixty-four cattle raiders in the study grew up in households having 191 male uterine siblings and 106 female uterine siblings, all of whom were either alive at the time of the study or had died subsequent to having acquired a spouse. This means that males accounted for 64 percent of the uterine-sibling population of the cattle raiders' natal households as opposed to merely 48 percent of the Nyaheiya population as a whole, based on responses to the homestead survey (see table 7.2).

For two of the cattle raiders, data were obtainable regarding their uterine siblings but not their nonuterine siblings. The sixty-two cattle raiders for whom both uterine- and nonuterine-sibling data *were* available grew up in households having a total of 185 uterine brothers and 100 uter-

TABLE 7.2.   The Nyaheiya Cattle Raider Sample: Uterine-Sibling Breakdown of Cattle Raiders' Natal Households by Gender ($n = 297$)

Males	Females
191[a]	106
(64%)	(36%)

Note: The population of Nyaheiya is 48 percent male, 52 percent female.

[a]The 64 cattle raiders in the Nyaheiya sample *are* included in this figure.

ine sisters, a uterine-sibling population, in other words, that was 65 percent male. By contrast, however, these same sixty-two cattle raiders had a total of 119 nonuterine brothers and 118 nonuterine sisters, a nonuterine-sibling population that was only 50 percent male. The sixty-two cattle raiders were thus part of a uterine- and nonuterine-sibling population that included a combined total of 304 brothers, both uterine and nonuterine, and 218 sisters, both uterine and nonuterine, with males representing 58 percent of that population (see table 7.3).

Setting aside deceased siblings who had died without marrying, forty-nine out of the sixty-four Nyaheiya cattle raiders for all of whom uterine-sibling data are available (nearly 77 percent of them) grew up in households having fewer female uterine siblings than male uterine siblings, creating the prospect that a substantial number of those male siblings would reach marriageable age without benefit of a sister to bring in the bridewealth cattle that would enable them to acquire wives of their own.

The sixty-two cattle raiders (out of the full sample of sixty-four) for whom both uterine- *and* nonuterine-sibling data are available came from homesteads having a total of 122 separate households, forty-five (or 37 percent) of which were the natal households of the cattle raiders themselves. Of these forty-five natal cattle-raider households, thirty-three (or 73 percent) had more brothers than sisters, four of them (or 9 percent) had more sisters than brothers, and eight (or 18 percent) of them had brothers and sisters in equal number.

Of the remaining seventy-seven households in these same homesteads, twenty-five (or 32 percent of them) had more brothers than sisters, twenty-nine (or 38 percent) had more sisters than brothers, fourteen (or 18 percent) had brothers and sisters in equal number, and nine (or 12 percent) had no children at all. In other words, whereas 73 percent of the natal households of the sixty-two cattle raiders had more brothers than sisters,

TABLE 7.3.   The Nyaheiya Cattle Raider Sample:
Uterine and Nonuterine Sibling Breakdown of Cattle
Raiders' Natal Homesteads by Gender
(*n* = 522 siblings)

	Males	Females
Uterine siblings	185 (65%)[a]	100 (35%)
Cattle raiders'		
nonuterine siblings	119 (50%)	118 (50%)

Note: Males represent 58 percent of the sibling population of these homesteads; females represent 42 percent. The population of Nyaheiya is 48 percent male, 52 percent female.

[a]The 62 cattle raiders in the Nyaheiya sample for whom both uterine- and nonuterine-sibling data were available *are* included in this figure.

less than half as many households where their nonuterine siblings grew up—or 32 percent—were in that same situation (see table 7.4).

Coming of age in a household with too few uterine sisters exacts an emotional toll that was described by informants who had turned to cattle raiding as a means of acquiring their bridewealth. Born in 1957, the third son in a household that included four sons and only one daughter, Chacha Gesengi first took up cattle raiding in 1987, at the age of thirty, and remained active for six years until he finally retired from cattle raiding in 1993. Both the household's eldest son and its youngest son served in the Tanzanian army, as their father once had, and they ultimately acquired their own bridewealth cattle with their army pay, but Chacha had no taste for army life, and the remaining brother, the second eldest, was lame in one leg and incapable of leading a physically demanding life. When their lone sister eloped with a man, without benefit of bridewealth, the marital prospects of both Chacha and his brother seemed grim, but ultimately pressure was brought on the runaway couple, bridewealth cattle were finally paid, and those cattle made it possible for Chacha's handicapped brother to take a wife.

That left only Chacha, who claims to have been taunted unrelentingly by other young men for having no more sisters in his household from whom he could derive bridewealth. "They asked me, 'Where are you to get cows to buy your wife?'" he recalled. "They said I was doomed to die without a wife. Such 'jokes,'" he maintained, "made me very much worried, and often I could not sleep at night thinking of ways to get rid of my problem."

As for the village's marriageable young women, "Girls don't tell a man directly," said Chacha, "but you hear rumors. Girls are saying, 'He wants me, but how can he get me when they don't have cows at home?'"

Inspired in part by the example of his peers, penniless like himself, who had succeeded in acquiring wives as a consequence of their involvement in cattle raiding, and also by the escapades of his father's father, who had been a cattle raider in his youth, Chacha threw in his lot with four or five other men who raided other villages for cattle twice a week. On every

TABLE 7.4. Cattle Raiders' Natal Homesteads: Household Demographic Breakdown by Gender (*n* = 122 households)

	More Brothers	More Sisters	Equal Number of Brothers and Sisters	No Children
Cattle raiders' natal	33	4	8	0
households (*n* = 45 households)	(73%)	(9%)	(18%)	(0%)
Cattle raiders' nonnatal	25	29	14	9
households (*n* = 77 households)	(32%)	(38%)	(19%)	(12%)

raid, he carried with him, as talismans, three British army medals that had been awarded to his grandfather in World War II. After five years and "very many" cattle raids, during which two members of his group were killed but swiftly replaced, Chacha married, having acquired the requisite eighteen head of cattle, and a year afterward he retired from cattle raiding, apprehensive over the spreading rumors of his involvement and unnerved by the arrest and imprisonment of a family member.

"Many of the people I associated with," he notes, "many of the people I knew in this business, were men who came from mothers with more sons than daughters."

Although Chacha insists that his case "was not the formula" and that a prior history of family involvement is not a prerequisite to a career in cattle raiding, his references to his grandfather's career call to mind the view often expressed by police and local officials that cattle raiding "runs in families," with young cattle raiders striving to emulate, or being goaded into emulating, the youthful exploits of older kinsmen, most especially their fathers. "I could not have married your mother," one cattle raider quoted his father as having said to him, "if I had not taken Ngoreme cows," the Ngoreme being a people with a close linguistic and cultural affinity to the Kuria (cf. Baker 1935:45, 110). Attempts to obtain compelling data on the past involvement in cattle raiding by the fathers of contemporary cattle raiders were unsuccessful, and it is possible that sons whose fathers were once cattle raiders *may* be more likely than other young men to become cattle raiders themselves. What the data at hand strongly suggest, however, is that, whatever their father's history, young men are highly unlikely to follow in their cattle-raider father's footsteps unless their particular household within his homestead lacks a sufficient number of sisters to enable all the brothers of that household to acquire the bridewealth cattle they will need to marry.

Kurate Juma, an elderly Nyaheiya man who was felled with an arrow and then hacked to death with his own axe in 1994 while out gathering medicinal herbs on Nyaheiya's outskirts, had been, in his younger years, a notorious cattle raider—so notorious, it was said when his body was found, that his enemies in a nearby village had still been lying in wait for him even though he had not stolen a head of cattle in decades. Kurate left behind ten wives and a grand total of thirty-two children—fifteen daughters and seventeen sons—one of whom had been killed during a cattle raid against Nyaheiya only four years earlier, and three of whom had followed in their father's footsteps to become cattle raiders themselves.

Of Kurate's ten wives, four had more sons than daughters, two had more daughters than sons, two had the same number of sons as daughters, and two had as yet had no children at all. Of the four households with more sons than daughters, two do not yet have sons old enough to become cattle raiders, and the same is true of one of the two households with more daughters than sons and one of the two households with sons and daughters in equal number.

Of the four households that remain—two with more sons than daughters, one with more daughters than sons, and one with sons and daughters in equal number—only one of Kurate's households, one of the two households having more sons than daughters *and* having sons old enough to become cattle raiders, produced all three of the sons of Kurate known to have become cattle raiders. They are the three sons of Kurate's first, and oldest, wife (see table 7.5).

One reason why the sons of Kurate's second wife, whose household is the only other household in Kurate's homestead having more sons than daughters *and* having sons old enough to become cattle raiders, have apparently *not* become cattle raiders may be that these sons were born a good deal later—they are, on average, thirteen years younger than their nonuterine brothers who became cattle raiders—and thus were likely born into a much-changed family situation. By then, Kurate had become significantly more affluent than he had been as a younger man, the owner of many cattle, and it may be that he was better able, at this later stage of his life, to assist these younger sons in acquiring their needed bridewealth. Or the explanation may lie simply in temperamental differences. However much a lack of sisters may predispose the young men of a household to engage in cattle raiding, it is, as Chacha Gesengi warned regarding family history, "not the formula."

There are other ways for a young man to acquire the bridewealth cattle he needs for his first marriage other than utilizing the cattle brought into his household by a marrying sister. He may, for example, receive bridewealth cattle from his father, drawing on what is called the "back" of the homestead's herd (*iching'ombe chiomogongo,* the cattle of the back),

TABLE 7.5. The Homestead of Kurate Juma: Breakdown by Gender Ratio of Siblings within Households (*n* = 10 households)

More Sons	More Daughters	Equal Number of Sons and Daughters	No Children
4[a]	2[b]	2[b]	2

[a]Two of these households do not yet have sons old enough to have become cattle raiders. However, all three of Kurate Juma's sons who are known to have become cattle raiders come from one of the two households having sons who *are* old enough to have become cattle raiders.

[b]One of these two households does not yet have sons old enough to have become cattle raiders.

that portion of the homestead's herd that the homestead head has either inherited, principally from his own father, or else acquired through his own efforts—such as through barter or cattle raiding, or by selling crops or mining gold and using the proceeds to buy cattle—and which he, the father, is at liberty to dispose of freely, as he sees fit. All the cattle in a Kuria homestead are the property of the homestead head, but a homestead's back cattle are to be sharply distinguished from the second component of a homestead's herd, the "cattle of the daughters" (*iching'ombe chiabasubaati*), which are the cattle brought into the homestead by its daughters when they marry and in whose use the homestead head is far more restricted.

As a survey of the patterns of cattle ownership in Nyaheiya makes clear, however, the option of acquiring back cattle from a father for use as bridewealth is really nonexistent for the vast majority of Nyaheiya's young men. Although there were about 5,800 head of cattle in Nyaheiya in 1995, cattle custodianship is by no means divided equally among the village's 350 homesteads: only eighty-three (44 percent) of the 190 homesteads surveyed reported keeping any cattle whatsoever in the homestead's cattle enclosure, although the number of surveyed homesteads that may be said to have cattle rises to 103 (54 percent of the total) if one includes homesteads that report having no cattle in the homestead's cattle enclosure but having cattle "put out" with others.

Only a minority of Nyaheiya's homesteads are custodians of anything in the way of what might be termed a permanent herd; the majority of them hold cattle only temporarily, during the relatively brief interval between the time a daughter's marriage brings cattle into the homestead and a son's marriage pays them out again. What this means is that all the young men in the roughly one-half of Nyaheiya's homesteads that have custodianship of no cattle at all, plus some unknown percentage of homesteads that do have custodianship of cattle but have no "back" to their herd, are dependent upon "cattle of the daughters" to marry.

Rights to "cattle of the daughters," however, from which most bridewealth comes, are by no means evenly distributed among a homestead's households, for the female-to-male sibling ratio varies, sometimes widely, from household to household. What sets the sample of sixty-four cattle raiders apart from their fellow villagers is that nearly 77 percent of them come from households with too few uterine sisters to bring in sufficient bridewealth to enable all their uterine brothers to marry, notwithstanding the fact that, in the surveyed homesteads, females constituted 52 percent of the population and males 48 percent.

Rights to the deployment of daughters' cattle as bridewealth are strictly limited to the uterine brothers of the young women whose marriages have brought those cattle into the household. No nonuterine brother from another household within the homestead may lay claim to them, no matter how compelling his need may be. One of the homestead's households may have more daughters than it needs to bring in sufficient bridewealth to enable its sons to marry while another household in the same homestead has too few daughters to meet the bridewealth needs of its sons, but no wife will allow the bridewealth cattle brought in by her daughters to be appropriated for use as bridewealth by her cowives' sons. At best, she may consent to lend her daughters' bridewealth cattle to a cowife's needy son, provided the two wives are on amicable terms and the cowife asked to make the loan deems her cowife's needy son a reliable credit risk.

Such a loan arrangement creates a precarious situation, however, not only for the lending household, which risks never getting its cattle back, but also for the borrowing son and for the new wife he acquires with the borrowed cattle, not only because it puts the needy son under the pressure of repaying the loan, but because, in the event the members of the lending household become impatient with his failure to repay, they are liable to harass his new wife and even, eventually, to appropriate her for one of their own men, saying, in the words of one informant, "You are not his wife anyway, you are our wife, because you were married with our cows." Confronted with this pressure, the harassed wife may flee the homestead altogether, as one woman was known to have done during the course of this fieldwork, out of lack of respect for her deadbeat husband, or because none of the men in the lending household will have her or because she wants no part of them, or merely to avoid the stress and turmoil of an unstable, conflict-ridden situation.

Another strategy available to households with more sons than daughters is that of delaying sons' marriages in order to give the bridewealth cattle brought into the household by its daughters a chance to reproduce and grow, thereby enabling a household with, say, three sons and only two daughters to "stretch" the daughters' cattle so as to enable all three sons to marry. On the other hand, if a wife gives birth to a daughter before having given birth to any sons, her husband, the homestead head, is likely to appropriate the daughter's bridewealth either to acquire another wife for himself or for some other purpose having nothing to do with the marriage of possible future sons, and the same is likely to be true of the bridewealth of succeeding daughters in a household where there are as yet no sons.

A man who has fathered both a son and daughter by the same wife might even go so far as to ignore his son's future needs and appropriate his daughter's bridewealth anyway, although such behavior by a father would be regarded as highly socially irresponsible, akin to an American father's blowing the nest egg intended to send his children to college. The point here is that a household into which three daughters are born followed by three sons is not at all the same household, in terms of bridewealth security for the three sons, as one into which three sons are born followed by three daughters. The ideal is to have children of alternating sexes, tipped numerically in favor of daughters, precisely so that these sorts of problems do not arise (see also Ruel 1959:89).

The birth spacing of the siblings in a household is also a factor, for it affords scant consolation to a quartet of brothers to know that they have four little sisters whose marriages will one day provide them with bridewealth—but not until the brothers are almost 40. And there are instances in which young unmarried women come to live with men "on their own," as it is said, without the consent of their families and without benefit of bridewealth. While it is true that pressure will inevitably be brought by the woman's family, and particularly by her brothers, to pay bridewealth cattle for her, if a woman is determined to remain with a man and he continues to stall on negotiations or to drag out the payment of agreed-upon bridewealth, there is little the woman's family can really do.

As a general rule, then, boys from households with *fewer* sisters than brothers may be said to be more likely than households with *more* sisters than brothers, or than those with an *equal* number of sisters and brothers, to find themselves in the position of having no alternative, if they want to marry, than to acquire their bridewealth cattle on their own, through their own initiative, but a more precise evaluation of the pressures on each son in a given household to acquire his own bridewealth would require a more finely grained investigation than was possible here.

Nor should one discount the possible validity of a belief, encountered even among highly educated, well-traveled Kuria living far from Nya-heiya, that boys who grow up in households with more brothers than sisters exhibit more drive and ambition, are higher achievers generally, than boys who grow up in households with more sisters than brothers, for the simple reason that, being sister-poor, such boys are under far greater pressure to go out and make their own way in the world than their sister-rich peers, who can afford to lie back and wait for the cattle wealth to flow into their households.

The young men in a Kuria household marry in birth order, the eldest son first, the second eldest son second, and so on. A son who moves out of his father's homestead and acquires through his own efforts the bridewealth cattle he needs to marry may marry anytime he wishes, but so long as he remains within his father's homestead, marrying with his father's cattle, whether they be back cattle or daughters' cattle, he must wait to marry in his proper turn.

Absent the prospect of acquiring bridewealth cattle from his family, either through the marriage of his sisters or from the back of his father's herd, a young man is faced with the necessity of obtaining the cattle he needs by the sweat of his own brow. To say that income-producing opportunities are limited for Nyaheiya men is an understatement of the most extreme kind. Educational opportunities for Nyaheiya residents, beyond primary school, are minuscule: in the twelve-year period preceding the onset of this fieldwork, from 1982 to 1994, only one Nyaheiya student had ever attended secondary school; the survey of 190 homesteads turned up no secondary-school graduates; and one of the two Nyaheiya natives encountered in the course of fieldwork who had attended secondary school prior to 1982 but who had not completed it was deeply embittered over his inability to find employment despite his having acquired what amounted to, for a Nyaheiya resident, a fairly advanced education. Furthermore, the Tanzanian army, once a haven of opportunity and advancement without the requirement of an education, is downsizing, and drastically reducing not only the number but also the percentage of Kuria in its ranks, currently down to about 20 percent from about 50 percent at the time of the Tanzania-Uganda War of 1978–79.

In Nyaheiya and the surrounding Nyamongo area generally, employment for wages is all but nonexistent, and the area's erratic lowland rainfall makes agriculture uncertain and unreliable. As one cattle raider put it, "I like farming. But stealing is better than cultivating. Cultivating doesn't get enough money to spend—to buy clothes, for drinking, to make a life."

In the end, it is village geography that dictates the scant and dangerous income-generating opportunities that do exist. In the Irege lowland village of Ekeng'ooro, situated close by the Serengeti National Park, an enterprising young man has two occupations to choose from: wildlife poacher or cattle raider. In Bungurere, Nyantira, and other Irege border-area Tanzanian villages within easy striking distance of Kenya's Masai Mara Game Reserve, young men work as poachers, stage gunpoint holdups of tourist buses in the Masai Mara, or become cattle raiders. In Nyaheiya and the other four Nyamongo villages, however, all blessed by their strategic location in an area studded with gold mines, young men have the option either of "working in the hill," chipping away at the hard gold-bearing rock with short-handled sledgehammers and chisels at the bottom of precariously reinforced mine shafts, or of becoming cattle raiders.

Mining is indisputably the preferred occupation, provided the mines are producing well: 84 percent of the homesteads in the survey sample had at least one male who had at one time or another prospected for gold locally, and 39 percent of the surveyed homesteads were at least partially reliant for cash income on local gold mining at the time the survey was conducted. Both these survey percentages would unquestionably have been higher were it not for the fact that thirty-two of the 190 respondents were the homestead heads' wives, widows, or daughters, only two of whom were engaged in activities related to mining themselves and who often failed to report their husbands' or fathers' ways of earning money.

Half a dozen mining areas, all within two hours' walk of Nyaheiya and some quite a bit closer, have been providing Nyaheiya's residents, as well as those of the other Nyamongo villages, with cash income for more than sixty years, but the mines, now mired in the trough of the boom-to-bust trajectory that is characteristic of indigenous third world mining areas, have now fallen on hard times, and many of the Nyaheiya men who used to work the myriad small mining claims have switched over to cattle raiding, while others continue to eke out whatever they still can from the claims, others work both "jobs," and still others move from cattle raiding to mining and back to cattle raiding again as their mining fortunes wax and wane and as efforts by the police or *Sungusungu* to crack down on cattle raiding, like the one that began in late 1994, take off with a vengeance and then, after administering scores of whippings and sending a few men to prison, run out of steam, their energies spent. "Cattle thieving has stopped now, but it will start again when the *Sungusungu* cools down," one cattle raider said. "They can't stop the stealing," agreed another.

Many of Nyaheiya's young miners, like Makamba Mangure (described later in this chapter), received their baptism of blood as cattle raiders during the prolonged period of warfare between the Nyamongo and Irege clans from 1992 to 1994, when stealing the enemy's livestock, a tactic sanctioned and orchestrated by the elders, received social approbation as an extension of the fighting, and captured animals provided a welcome addition to the otherwise infrequent opportunities to eat meat.

Indeed, stolen cattle are the primary source of butchered beef offered for sale in Nyaheiya, and although all of Nyaheiya's cattle raiders sell the cattle they steal either to local-area butchers in Tanzania or to middlemen buyers in Kenya, many slaughter the smaller stock—the sheep and goats—at home or give them away free to village women.

When the clan fighting ended, some young fighters persevered as cattle raiders because, some said, they found that they could earn money that way "*harakaharaka!*" (Swa., very quickly), faster than they ever could in the mines. Although much is still made by non-Kuria of the seminal force of "tradition" in fostering the careers of today's Kuria cattle raiders ("Stealing cattle. The Kuria like it," explained one Tarime government worker. "It's a tradition now. It's in their blood."), the simple truth is that young men in Tanzania Kurialand steal cattle for the same reason that Willie Sutton is apocryphally claimed to have said he robbed banks: because that's where the money is. The relevance of this statement to the Kuria case is amply demonstrated by the fact that, in the heavily agricultural Kuria highland villages now all but denuded of cattle as a consequence of raiders' depredations, human population increase, and intensification of cash-crop agriculture, housebreaking and petty thievery are on the rise, with perpetrators now resorting to stealing what one highland villager called "silly things," like ploughs and chickens, that up until recently were regarded as not worth taking.

Seventeen (27 percent) of the sixty-four cattle raiders in the sample were eldest sons who were not the only sons, and, of these, fifteen (23 percent) of the sixty-four cattle raiders in the sample were eldest sons in households that had more brothers than sisters. Fourteen of these fifteen had two or more sisters, while one of the fifteen had only one sister; this only sister was not, however, the household's eldest child, which means that her bridewealth was not especially susceptible to being preempted by her father for his own use (see table 7.6).

Even in the total absence of back cattle in these homesteads, these fifteen eldest sons could therefore rest secure in the knowledge that their bridewealth would be assured by a sister's marriage and that only their brothers waiting in line behind them would have a bridewealth problem. If it is in fact lack of bridewealth that so strongly predisposes young men to become cattle raiders, what, then, may be said to have motivated these fifteen eldest sons?

The answer is that there is strong familial pressure on eldest sons, more than on junior sons, not only to amass their own bridewealth so as to enable their sisters' bridewealth to be utilized on behalf of their younger brothers but also to assist their families generally—their uterine siblings, parents, and grandparents—in meeting their diverse financial needs.

Daughter-poor households are *poor* households, not merely because they lack the potential brides needed to bring in the bridewealth cattle to enable the household's sons to marry, but because such households also have *other* needs and wants—clothing, bicycles, building materials, money for school and medical fees—that incoming bridewealth cattle can meet for those families fortunate enough to have daughters whose marriages will provide them. Eldest sons in daughter-poor families turn to cattle raiding not just to make money with which to buy cattle for bridewealth but to fulfill their responsibility as eldest sons to assist their families overall.

Loyalty to family, including siblings, is not limited to eldest sons, of course, as is apparent from the stories of younger brothers who have

TABLE 7.6. The Nyaheiya Cattle Raider Sample: Breakdown by Gender Ratio of the Natal Households of Cattle Raiders Who Are Eldest Sons (*n* = 17 eldest sons)

	More Sons	More Daughters
Eldest son's natal household has	15[a]	2

[a]Of these 15, 14 had two or more uterine sisters; one had one uterine sister only.

donated the lion's share of their cattle-raiding earnings to enable their older uterine brothers to marry in birth order.

Makamba Mangure is one such younger brother. The fourth of six sons in a household of six sons and one daughter, Makamba attended primary school in Nyaheiya, completing Standard 7 at age seventeen. He recalls how his father regaled the boys in the homestead with tales of his own cattle-raiding days, warning them that they would have no other choice but to steal cattle if they wanted to marry because of the heavy preponderance of male offspring in both of his wives' houses.

In 1988, Makamba went to Musoma to learn carpentry, living there two years before returning to Nyaheiya in 1989 and spending the next two years prospecting for gold near Nyangoto until many of the shafts there filled with water, making further mining in the place where he was working impossible. In 1992, with warfare raging between the Nyamongo and Irege, Makamba took part in the fighting and got his first taste of cattle raiding. He remained active in cattle raiding even after the fighting ended because he saw it as the best opportunity available to him for making money.

Marwa, the eldest of his household's six brothers, had moved to Mwanza, Tanzania's second-largest city, permanently as a child to reside with a relative and had married during Makamba's sojourn in Musoma, using the bridewealth cattle brought into the household by Ghati, the brothers' only sister. Five unmarried brothers thus remained in the household, with Makamba now third in line.

The first of these, Sarya, was in frail health and incapable of performing even routine farm chores, let alone meeting the considerably more physically arduous demands made of cattle raiders. Why Gutwa, the next brother in birth order, declined to become a cattle raider is unclear, but a substantial share of Makamba's cattle-raiding earnings have been turned over to his father to finance the purchase of cattle that have enabled the two unmarried older brothers ahead of him to marry. As of the close of the fieldwork period, neither Makamba nor his two younger brothers had yet acquired wives of their own, and the ongoing *Sungusungu* crackdown had imposed at least a temporary halt to Makamba's cattle-raiding activities.

As the fieldwork period drew to a close, however, in early 1996, there were signs of an upsurge in cattle-raiding activity. Whether or not cattle raiding stages a comeback, as it invariably has in the wake of previous attempts to suppress it, market-oriented cattle theft has already exerted a profound impact on the people of Nyaheiya and on the wider area in which they live, an impact that is explored in detail in the following chapter.

CHAPTER 8

Hidden Costs: The Cultural-Ecological Consequences

The Decline of the Cattle Herd

The cattle populations of Tarime District in general and of Nyaheiya in particular have declined drastically since 1978—the year of the onset of the Tanzania-Uganda War—a decline largely attributable, both directly and indirectly, to market-oriented cattle raiding, which has had, and appears likely to continue to have, a profound and devastating impact on Kuria life. The discussion that follows endeavors to document that decline and to delineate that impact.

Accurate statistics regarding almost anything are hard to come by in East Africa, and those regarding cattle populations present particularly thorny problems because pastoralists and agropastoralists are notoriously reluctant to reveal the exact number of cattle they own, about as reluctant as Americans might be to freely disclose the contents of their tax returns. Although there is general agreement, among both Kuria and non-Kuria, that a decline has occurred in the district cattle herd since 1978, no one knows how many head of cattle there are in Tarime District now or how many there ever were in any particular past year. Nonetheless, a compelling case can be made for the general fact of decline, even though the numbers we derive will never be precise ones. For Nyaheiya specifically, the shape of that decline can be roughly quantified through an analysis of cattle censuses, police livestock-theft reports, and changes in bridewealth payments through time.

Cattle Censuses

Warning that the figures are "crude and shaky," Tobisson cites the following cattle-population estimates for Tarime District made available to her by the Livestock Development Office at Tarime town (1986:197 n. 10):

    1945:   216,000
    1948:   236,000
    1958:   315,000

These figures reflect a steady, stable growth rate of the Tarime (then North Mara) herd during this 1945 to 1958 period of just under 3 percent per year. But over the course of the next twenty years, from 1958 to 1978, that rate, as measured by the national livestock census of 1978, the first of two such censuses conducted by the government of Tanzania since independence, fell sharply, to under 0.7 percent per year, the chief culprits most likely being the epizootics of rinderpest (*endoroe*) and contagious bovine pleuropneumonia (CBPP) (*ekehaha*) that ravaged the area until 1974–75, when the last cases were finally eradicated by a series of annual vaccination programs, not to reappear until the resurgence of rinderpest in 1985, and then of CBPP in 1989. Nonetheless, the size of the Tarime herd had increased since 1958, according to the 1978 census, to a total of 360,766 head.

By the time Tanzania conducted its second livestock census, in 1984, however, the size of the district's herd had plummeted, according to this latest census, to 305,858 head—a decline of slightly more than 15 percent in only six years' time—despite the fact that no outbreaks of bovine epidemics are reported as having occurred during this period. Figure 8.1 charts the growth and decline of the Tarime District cattle herd from 1945 to 1984 as measured by these cattle censuses.

In the cattle-rich lowland villages of the Nyamongo clan, which include Nyaheiya, the 1978 through 1984 decline was far more devastating: together, these villages lost slightly less than 39 percent of their cattle; Nyaheiya alone lost 61 percent. These losses are both the direct and indirect effect of the technological modernization and consequent escalation of cattle raiding that occurred in the immediate aftermath of the Tanzania-Uganda War of 1978–79 (see chap. 5).

Nyaheiya was not officially designated a village until 1974, and the two national livestock censuses of 1978 and 1984 included the first formal attempts to provide a count of the village's cattle:

1978:   11,656
1984:   4,537

The six-year period separating these two counts had borne witness to terrible violence in Nyaheiya, with the Nyamongo heavily outnumbered and outgunned by the Irege, whose representation in the army had been much greater than theirs and who had therefore succeeded in smuggling more military weaponry home from the war. Once on excellent terms with their Irege neighbors, to the point where Nyamongo and Irege worked, pastured their cattle, and attended primary school in Nyaheiya side by side, the people of Nyaheiya forcibly expelled the Irege from their village

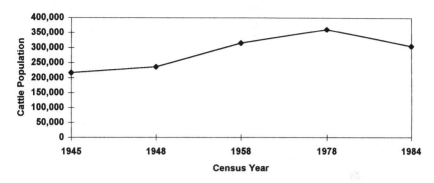

FIG. 8.1. The Tarime District cattle herd, 1945–84 (as measured by cattle censuses)

in 1981, as the new, modernized cattle raiding swept the area and livestock losses escalated out of control (see chap. 5).

Since then, the Nyaheiya village authorities have, on their own, carried out their own village livestock counts on three separate occasions, in 1990, 1994, and 1995. According to these figures, which appear below, the village cattle herd grew by slightly more than 3 percent per year between 1984 and 1990 to a total of 5,483 head—a gain that would most certainly have been greater had it not been for the rinderpest outbreak of 1985 and the CBPP outbreak of 1989. But in the course of the ensuing four years, from 1990 to 1994, again according to the village census figures, Nyaheiya's cattle population plummeted again, by nearly 31 percent, to a total of 3,787 head, a decline attributable to relentless cattle-raiding pressure and to yet another CBPP outbreak, in 1992. Then, in one single year, from 1994 to 1995, Nyaheiya's cattle herd fell yet again, according to the Nyaheiya census counts, this time by 24 percent, to 2,880 head, the lowest village herd total ever recorded in Nyaheiya. The reasons were threefold: a further outbreak of CBPP; the need of owners to sell cattle to buy food in the wake of a year of low, and ill-timed, rainfall; and escalating cattle raiding. Indeed, it was the nonstop cattle raiding throughout Tarime District in 1994—Nyaheiya alone was raided on an average of once every six days during the early months of this fieldwork—that ignited the *Sungusungu* crackdown on cattle raiding in the final months of 1994 (see chap. 6).

1990:	5,483
1994:	3,787
1995:	2,880

With the exception of the 1990 census, which registered an upturn from the calamitous 1984 count amounting to a herd-growth rate of just under 3.3 percent per year, these five censuses of Nyaheiya's cattle document—or would seem to document—the inexorable decline of the Nyaheiya cattle herd throughout the seventeen-year-long period from 1978, the year the Tanzania-Uganda War began, to 1995, a decline of just over 75 percent. Figure 8.2 charts the decline of the Nyaheiya village cattle herd from 1978 to 1995 as measured by these cattle censuses.

Although the size of the Nyaheiya cattle herd has most certainly declined since 1978, however, the census figures purporting to document that decline are inaccurate. To better understand the import of these figures, it is useful to understand the different ways in which these various census counts were carried out.

For each of the two countrywide counts (1978 and 1984), a national livestock-census day was formally announced, and, approximately two to three weeks in advance of that date, district livestock officials drove out to the villages to consult with village officials and to examine the lists of livestock holders and their holdings that each village maintains.

Then, on the formally announced census day, the district livestock-office team assigned to each village—accompanied in their rounds by the appropriate *balozi* (Swa., ten-cell leader)—began conducting what one former livestock-census taker called a "systematic" census of the village livestock, paying a call on every homestead in the early daylight hours to count the livestock in every homestead and to compare those counts with those provided by the village, a process that took several weeks to complete.

The orderly, "systematic" way in which the census was carried out meant that each *balozi,* and through him each livestock holder, knew in advance which homesteads were scheduled to be censused on any given day. The dangers inherent in such a system are obvious, as witnessed by one of Tobisson's informants recalling government cattle counts carried out during the colonial era, when taxes were imposed on cattle holders based on the number of cattle in their corrals:

> We were always a day ahead of them [government officials] and could reduce our herds to nil over night. Government people travelled in a roundabout way, so we had plenty of time to get the message and let our cattle escape through the bush. When my *oboori* [cattle-enclosure] was empty, Itembe and Waerema were rich men. The next week it was their turn to be poor, while my *oboori* was almost bursting. (Tobisson 1986:27–28)

Although there were no cattle taxes in effect in Tanzania in 1978 and 1984, pastoralists still prefer to keep the size of their holdings to themselves: because their memories of colonial-era cattle taxation remain fresh;

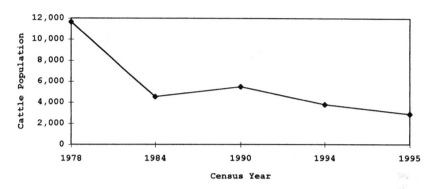

FIG. 8.2. The Nyaheiya village cattle herd, 1978–95 (as measured by cattle censuses)

because they know that their government can impose cattle taxes at any time; because for a man to reveal the precise extent of his wealth makes him more vulnerable to the envy, resentment, and even malicious intentions of others.

One livestock official who played a role in the 1978 count, albeit in an altogether different district, claimed that the discrepancy between the number of cattle in a holder's corral and the number recorded in the official village lists often resulted from the holder's having included only fully grown, adult animals in his report to the village, omitting any mention of calves. Confronted with these omissions in the course of the census, said this official, many paid modest bribes to census enumerators to overlook the "misunderstanding" and assure the recording of lower-than-accurate counts. Or perhaps it was the enumerators themselves who took the initiative and demanded the payments by threatening to report the discrepancies. Whatever the true story may have been, the official estimated the undercount in the area where he worked in 1978 at somewhere between 20 and 30 percent.

The censuses carried out by the individual villages are conducted more haphazardly than the national counts. In Nyaheiya, the chairman's office maintains active, ongoing lists of livestock holders and their holdings—and holders, *balozi,* and the various *wakuu wa vitongoji* (Swa., neighborhood heads) are advised to help keep the lists current by keeping the chairman's office apprised of herd-count changes as they occur. But the record keeping is chaotic, with cattle continually changing hands through sale or barter or payment of bridewealth, with animals being born or dying of disease, and with still others being slaughtered to celebrate a wedding, circumcision, or other special occasion, or being taken by cattle raiders.

In some years but not others—although village officials now say they plan to conduct a new count every year—Nyaheiya conducts a livestock census, with the ten-cell leaders and neighborhood heads authorized to carry out the counts. The bribery of these officials is the village norm, with cattle holders generally underreporting their herd counts by half. Indeed, a careful count conducted in the wake of the 1995 census, which had reported a village total of 2,880 head of cattle, produced a total of 5,834 head of cattle, slightly more than double the official village count. This served to substantiate the estimates of informants, who had independently stated the size of the Nyaheiya cattle herd in that year to be somewhere between 5,000 and 6,000 head.

The consistency (or lack thereof) with which herd sizes are underreported from census to census is also a problem when endeavoring to evaluate the various census counts, for the gap between fact and fiction may safely be presumed to have widened beginning with the 1994 census, which was the first village census to be conducted following the inauguration, in 1992, of an annual cattle tax of Tsh 100 per head by the Tarime District Council, which gave all of the district's cattle holders a much stronger incentive than they had had previously to underreport the size of their herds.

A truer picture of Nyaheiya's herd decline than that contained in the cattle-census counts would therefore probably look something like this: Nyaheiya's cattle holders probably underreported their cattle holdings on the national livestock censuses of 1978 and 1984, but probably to the *same* extent in both of those years, and probably to a *lesser* extent than they did after the imposition of the tax in 1992. If we assume that the livestock official who participated in the 1978 census is correct in his estimate, the undercounts in these pretax years were probably on the order of 20 to 30 percent.

There were no bovine disease outbreaks during the years 1978 to 1984, yet the village herd size plummeted drastically, clearly as a consequence of the newly modernized postwar cattle raiding of that period. When Nyaheiya carried out its own first village census, in 1990, its cattle holders had no greater incentive to underreport the true size of their holdings than they had had at the time of the national counts of 1978 and 1984. Whatever the true village herd size may have been in 1990, therefore, it probably still reflected the same *percentage* of total increase over the six-year period from 1984 to 1990 that is reflected in the census figures: about 22 percent overall, equivalent to an annual growth rate of just under 3.3 percent per year. This is an altogether respectable growth rate, particularly given the resurgence of rinderpest in 1985 and then of CBPP four years later, in 1989. No matter what the impact of cattle raiding may have been during these years immediately following the Field Force crackdown of

1986 (see chap. 5), it was clearly not sufficient to reverse herd growth, although it obviously had the effect of reducing it.

If informants are to be believed, the 1994 village census total of 3,787 is bogus, with the real count being double that number, or about 7,574. The annual district cattle tax had been imposed two years earlier, and, lacking a more up-to-date village census, people had found themselves compelled to pay their cattle taxes for two years running—in 1992 and again in 1993—based on the count that had been taken in 1990, when the village cattle population was larger than what it had shrunk to by 1992 and 1993, whether one chooses to accept the official village census figures as gospel or not.

If the reported 1990 count of 5,483 had actually been accurate, and if the reported 1994 count of 3,787 really represented only *half* the herd—putting the *actual* herd count for 1994 at 7,574, in keeping with informants' statements—that would mean that the Nyaheiya herd would have grown by 38 percent during the four-year period from 1990 to 1994, an annual growth rate of nearly 8.5 percent that is unlikely to be accurate. But if we assume, in accordance with the views expressed by the livestock official with respect to the 1978 count, that pretax (i.e., pre-1992) herd counts reflected underreporting of between 20 and 30 percent—let us here split the difference and say 25 percent—then the true size of the Nyaheiya herd in 1990 was not 5,483 but, rather, 7,311. If that is so, then an average annual herd-growth rate of 0.8 percent would have produced a 1994 total of 7,548 head of cattle, very close to the count of 7,574—which is exactly double the officially reported count of 3,787—that we have postulated for 1994. But why would there have been such a meager herd growth rate between 1990 and 1994? Because the number of cattle raids perpetrated by cattle raiders against Nyaheiya escalated dramatically during those four years.

The 1995 Nyaheiya herd count of 2,880 is most definitely bogus, a true count of 5,834 having been carried out in the course of fieldwork in the wake of the village census for that year. This true count represents a decline in the Nyaheiya cattle population of just under 23 percent from the count of 7,574—double the official count of 3,787—that we have postulated for 1994. From a cattle holder's point of view, 1994 was a terrible year: a year when CBPP struck the herds, when crop failure made it necessary to sell cattle in order to buy food, and when cattle raiders struck with more frequency and severity than they had in any year since the harsh Field Force crackdown of 1986.

In 1994, the number of cattle raids carried out against Nyaheiya increased by 47 percent over 1993 and by 178 percent over 1992. For the first time since the 1980s, herd growth had been reversed. Small wonder, then, that 1994 ushered in the *Sungusungu* crackdown on cattle raiding that began in the closing months of that year (see chap. 6). Table 8.1 tabulates the figures germane to this discussion of the decline of the Nyaheiya cattle herd between 1978 and 1995.

Bridewealth

Whatever herd-size numbers we choose to employ here, it remains inescapable that a cattle-population decline of serious magnitude is under way in the heart of one of the great cattle-growing regions of Africa. Further evidence of this decline is manifest in the inexorable decline in average bridewealth fetched and paid in Nyaheiya over the course of this same 1978 through 1995 period, for wherever bridewealth is determined by negotiation, as it is among the Kuria—as opposed to being a fixed, standard sum, as it is, for example, among both the Maasai and the Arusha (Goldschmidt 1974:326)—bridewealth falls as cattle population falls (Ruel 1959:171), albeit not necessarily in a straightforward, linear fashion.

In the homestead survey, respondents were asked to provide the names of the homestead head's wives, the years he married them, and the bridewealth that he paid for each one; the names of the homestead head's married sons, the years they married their first wives, and the bridewealth that was paid for each one; and the names of the homestead head's married daughters, the years they were married, and the bridewealth that had been fetched for each one. The result was a list of names, marriage years, and bridewealth figures for 389 marriages occurring between 1930 and 1995. Table 8.2 provides year-by-year bridewealth averages, based on the survey data, from 1974 through 1995.

A special problem exists with respect to the average bridewealth paid or fetched in 1995. It is regarded as a mark of affluence to have paid a high bridewealth, and men will sometimes exaggerate the amount they paid for

TABLE 8.1.   Decline of the Nyaheiya Cattle Herd, 1978–95

Year	Cattle Censuses	Estimates Based on Fieldwork
1978	11,656[a]	15,541[c]
1984	4,537[a]	6,049[c]
1990	5,483[b]	7,311[c]
1992	Tarime District cattle tax imposed	
1994	3,787[b]	7,574[d]
1995	2,880[b]	5,834[e]

[a]National livestock census
[b]Nyaheiya village census
[c]Assumes census underreporting of 25%
[d]Based on informants' reports
[e]Fieldwork count

a wife, although they are far more likely to do so when speaking of an event that occurred just recently than when they are recalling one that occurred even one year ago. There was a large drop in the Nyaheiya cattle population between 1994 and 1995, and many people were ashamed of how much they had lost, especially when answering questions put to them by a foreigner. The homestead survey, which was carried out in 1995 and into the beginning of 1996, recorded a 1995 bridewealth average of 12.3, a drop of 11 percent from the previous year but almost certainly a product of face-saving inflation. Many, many people who expressed themselves on this subject outside the context of responding to the survey insisted that prospective grooms in 1995 were paying between 8 and 11 head of cattle.

What is even more important is that bridewealth averages tend, unfortunately, to obscure the intricacies and variability of a transaction

TABLE 8.2.   Average Bridewealth in Nyaheiya, 1974–95 (total number of marriages = 329)

Year	Average Bridewealth
1974	29.3
1975	28.7
1976	25.0
1977	31.0
1978	24.9
1979	26.5
1980	27.1[a]
1981	23.0
1982	24.1
1983	24.5
1984	21.0[b]
1985	20.1
1986	19.8
1987	18.0
1988	17.5
1989	18.1
1990	15.6[a]
1991	12.8
1992	15.7
1993	13.7
1994	13.8[c]
1995	12.3

[a]A single instance of bridewealth paid in cash by a Nyaheiya man for a non-Kuria wife during this year was not included in this average.

[b]Two instances of bridewealth paid in cash by Nyaheiya men for non-Kuria wives during this year were not included in this average.

[c]A single instance of bridewealth paid in cash plus cattle by a Nyaheiya man for a Kuria wife who was not from Nyaheiya was not included in this average.

that is actually exceedingly complex, for, notwithstanding what the going bridewealth may be said to be at any given moment in time, the amount actually agreed upon between the prospective groom's family and that of the bride is influenced by a wide array of factors. Marriage and bridewealth were a constant topic of conversation in Nyaheiya, and villagers were invariably in close agreement regarding the fairly narrow range of what might be called the current "standard" bridewealth amounts, but a wide range of considerations would affect the bridewealth paid in the case of any one particular marriage, often producing deviations, in either direction, quite beyond these norms.

Among the most important considerations is what was frequently referred to as "the condition of life the daughter is going to face after marrying," with the fathers of prospective brides insisting on higher bridewealth for daughters whose married lives seem likely to be especially insecure economically, on the theory that it is these brides' fathers who are likely to be called upon to come to the aid of their daughters if and when serious economic problems arise for them in their marital homesteads.

But bridewealth is also affected by a host of other factors.

A father with a marriageable daughter living at home who knows that his daughter's suitor is in love with her and is determined to have her is in a position to command a higher-than-average bridewealth, provided he knows that his daughter is cool toward the man. If the love feelings between daughter and suitor are reciprocal, however, and there is a real danger that the daughter will elope with him if a bargain is not struck, a prudent father will hasten to make the best deal he can.

When Gutugwa Mwita was approached by the family of twenty-year-old Mnanka Maswi to begin negotiations for the hand of Gutugwa's fourteen-year-old daughter Robi, in 1994, Gutugwa was deeply concerned with the would-be groom's reputation for being a hard drinker with an exceptionally nasty temper. But when Gutugwa confided his concerns to Robi, and she made it clear that she loved Mnanka and was determined to marry him nonetheless, Gutugwa felt that his only option was to hammer out the best deal he could, ultimately accepting a dozen head of cattle in lieu of the fourteen or fifteen he might have gotten had his daughter's feelings been different. Had Robi actually eloped with Mnanka and taken up residence with him without formally marrying him, Marwa's negotiating hand would have been weakened considerably, perhaps even to the point of obliging him to settle for a bridewealth payable on the installment plan, a substantial portion of which he might never have been able to collect at all.

Sarya Saiya had three wives in his homestead, two of whom—his first and third wives—he had already paid bridewealth for; the other, Matinde, had left her father's homestead in a fairly distant village and come to live with him "by herself," that is, without benefit of bridewealth. Eventually, her family brought pressure to bear on Sarya and a bridewealth amount was agreed upon, but Sarya never paid even a single installment of it, and, in late 1995, some two or three years later, her brothers arrived in Nyaheiya and took their sister home with them. What must have especially incensed the brothers was that Sarya had already paid the full bridewealth for his third wife, born and raised in Nyaheiya, without having tendered even a partial payment for their sister, who had been living with him longer. Within a month, however, Matinde was back in Nyaheiya living with Sarya again, her bridewealth still having not been paid.

Extremely low bridewealth may also be fetched by young women with physical handicaps or health problems likely to impair their productivity as workers, such as the epileptic who was married for only five head of cattle in 1993, a year when the average bridewealth paid in Nyaheiya was 13.7; similarly low bridewealth is likely to be fetched by prospective wives with a reputation for disobeying their parents or of being disinclined to hard work, and by women who are newly eligible because of previous, "broken" marriages, having been returned to their natal families by dissatisfied husbands demanding bridewealth refunds on the claim that the wives had committed adultery or lacked the necessary "discipline" for hard work.

Low bridewealth amounts are also paid for wives recruited from other tribes—such as the Luo, who share Tarime District with the Kuria—whose bridewealth is invariably lower than that of the Kuria. Writing in 1986, Tobisson remarked:

> The increase in Kuria bridewealth and in the rate of polygamous marriage over the past few decades has continued to make the marriage of non-Kuria women an attractive alternative. (1986:118n. 1)

However, this is definitely not the case with Nyaheiya men: of the 333 bridewealth figures tallied from responses to the homestead survey for marriages contracted between 1974 and 1995 (i.e., the 329 marriages, entailing payment of bridewealth in cattle only, whose bridewealth averages appeared in table 8.2, plus the four additional marriages, footnoted but *not* included in its averages, entailing payment of bridewealth either wholly or partially in cash), only four of them, amounting to a scant 1.2 percent of the total, involved marriages of Kuria males to non-Kuria females.

The men of Nyaheiya not only do not regard marriage to non-Kuria women as an "attractive alternative" (more than one informant commented that a non-Kuria wife hardly qualifies as a wife at all), they also are not rushing off to take brides from other area villages (even other *Nyamongo* villages). This is true in spite of the fact that, with the standard bridewealth in each Kurialand village varying in rough proportion to its cattle population, vastly less expensive Kuria brides are available only a stone's throw away (see table 8.3).

Kerende, Kewanja, and Nyangoto are all Nyamongo-clan villages located within a two-and-a-half-hour walk from Nyaheiya, and Nyaheiya people visit these places frequently. The bridewealth amounts prevailing in these three villages are all lower—in the case of Kewanja and Nyangoto, very substantially lower—than either the 1995 average Nyaheiya bridewealth of 12.3 reported on the homestead survey or the figure of 9.5 arrived at by averaging the range of estimates (i.e., from 8 to 11) provided by informants who were not included in the homestead survey. Nonetheless, a high bridewealth is good, Nyaheiya men say, because it promotes marital stability, making it more difficult for a disaffected bride to run back home to her natal homestead and prevail upon her father to refund her bridewealth.

Nyaheiya men are also quick to confess that young women living in the comparably cattle-poor, therefore low-bridewealth, Nyamongo villages whose economies are dependent mainly upon mining have little enthusiasm for marrying Nyaheiya men. These women much prefer the prospect of helping a husband tend a small shop, bar, or restaurant that caters to the miners to that of marrying into Nyaheiya, with its heavy homestead workload of cultivating crops, fetching water and firewood, and herding cattle. Many of them, particularly at Nyangoto, which much more closely resembles a small town than a village, have achieved a high degree of independence for women in this part of Africa, earning money by picking through debris from the mine shafts for traces of overlooked gold or by selling food, products, and services to miners. Some Nyangoto women, it is said, have no interest in marrying at all.

For Nyaheiya wife seekers, marrying at home confers the added

TABLE 8.3.   Prevailing Bridewealth in a Sampling of Area Kuria Villages in 1995[a]

Village	Bridewealth
Gibaso	10
Matongo	8
Kerende	9
Genkuru	5
Nyangoto	3
Kewanja	3
Itiryo	11
Nyaheiya	9.5

[a]These bridewealth figures are based on informants' reports.

advantage that it is easier for them to acquire accurate intelligence regarding potential spouses in Nyaheiya than on young women residing even a short distance away. This poignant lesson was learned the hard way by a Nyaheiya man, Maswi Mihogo, who took a fancy to a woman residing in her father's homestead in a nearby Irege village, unaware that she was already married to a husband in prison for cattle raiding and that she had returned to live in her natal homestead only to await his release. Maswi's suspicions were also evidently not aroused by the bargain-basement bridewealth that her swindling father asked for her, which ought to have set off alarm bells, but didn't. A wedding celebration was held in Nyaheiya, and the new "wife" was living in Maswi's homestead at the time it came to be included, entirely by chance, in the homestead survey—but she fled her new marital homestead shortly afterward, as soon as her real husband was let out of prison.

For these and perhaps also other reasons, the vast majority of Nyaheiya men take Nyaheiya brides. Bridewealth is still comparatively high in Nyaheiya, as Kuria bridewealth goes, but it has declined drastically in the last twenty years or so, from an average of 29.3 head of cattle in 1974 to 12.3 (if one employs the homestead survey average) in 1995, a decline of nearly 58 percent. If one employs the 1995 bridewealth average of 9.5 reported by nonsurvey informants, the decline from 1974 to 1995 has been even steeper: nearly 68 percent.

Figure 8.3 charts the decline in Nyaheiya's bridewealth from 1974 through 1995 as measured by responses to the homestead survey. The 1995 bridewealth average recorded on the graph is the survey average of 12.3.

Police Reports

Cattle raiding is a complex phenomenon, and it adversely affects cattle population in both direct and indirect ways. The most obvious, of course, is that the animals are stolen from their homesteads and never heard from again, sold to local-area butchers in Tanzania or to buyers in Kenya, with many of these latter buyers trucking their animals to meat-packing factories in Nairobi, where they are either slaughtered to meet the demands of domestic butcher shops and tanneries or else shipped (in the form of live animals or as canned beef) to foreign destinations.

We will never know how many head of cattle and other livestock have been stolen from the people of Nyaheiya since it was officially declared a village in 1974. Police reluctance to reveal data concerning crime is one reason—crime statistics have a status similar to that of military secrets in Tanzania, and cattle theft is an extremely touchy subject throughout Mara Region—and sloppy record keeping is another. The district's crime records are said to be routinely destroyed by the Tarime District police

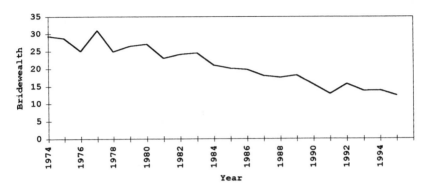

FIG. 8.3. Bridewealth in Nyaheiya, 1974–95

headquarters every five years, but a letter provided by the Officer Commanding District (OCD) of Tarime, the district's highest-ranking police
official, in connection with this research asserts that in the five-and-a-half-
year period from January 1990 to June 1995, 1,155 cases of cattle theft
were reported to district police, an average of 210 thefts per year. These
thefts are said to have involved 10,930 head of cattle, 315 of which were
recovered (a recovery rate of 2.9 percent), leaving a net loss of 10,615 head.
The document claims that a total of 181 arrests and prosecutions were carried out during that same period.

On the homestead survey, respondents representing 34 percent of the
entire homestead sample—but representing 77 percent of the homesteads
that reported having cattle in their cattle corral at the time they were surveyed—claimed that cattle raiders had made one or more attempts to steal
cattle from their homesteads sometime during the course of the past ten
years. Altogether, these respondents reported having been the victims of a
total of 110 such attempts, 71 (65 percent) of which had been successful, that
is, the cattle raiders had gotten away with one or more cows. This reported
cattle-theft "success" rate corresponds almost perfectly with the interview
testimony of the cattle raiders themselves, who claimed that one out of every
three raids was unsuccessful. Projecting these survey percentages onto the
entire village of Nyaheiya suggests that the village suffered a total of 203
attempted thefts in the past ten years, 131 of which were successful.

Villagers generally do not bother to report unsuccessful attempts to
the police, although there have been a few rare exceptions to this. The vast
majority of raids have always taken place at night, although the frequency
of daylight raids was higher in the 1980s, when readier access on the part

of cattle raiders to military-style weaponry made more audacious daylight raiding a more viable option than it is today.

When a raid occurs, and a cry of alarm (*ikuurate*) is sounded, men grab their weapons and race to cut off the escape routes leading out of the village. If that tactic fails, they follow the tracks of the stolen cattle with the aid of moonlight and flashlights, hoping to overtake the cattle raiders and recover their livestock. If they succeed, they return home with triumphant cries. If they fail, someone will report the incident to the local police post, usually the following day. Police records of 99 cases of livestock theft reported by the people of Nyaheiya to the police during the ten-year period from 1986 through 1995 still survive. Of the 120 months covered by these records, parts of three separate years, about twenty-four months' worth—or 20 percent of the entire ten-year run—are missing, but if we hazard the risky assumption that the 99 cases that we do have, altogether representing ninety-six months of reporting, accurately represent the frequency of reported thefts for the twenty-four months that are missing, we end up with a total of 124 (123.8 rounded) livestock-theft reports, astoundingly close to the total of 131 successful thefts for the ten-year period projected for Nyaheiya on the basis of the homestead survey.

Of the 99 intact cases, 8 involved livestock other than cattle; for one case, the number of cattle reported stolen was not legible; and for two cases the number of cattle reported stolen was legible but the number of cattle finally recovered was not. Deleting these eleven cases from the sample leaves us with 88 intact cases. In these 88 cases, a total of 2,699 cattle were reported stolen and 190 were recovered, leaving the total of unrecovered cattle at 2,509—an average of 28.5 head of cattle not recovered for each of the 88 thefts.

If we were justified in assuming that the number of cattle stolen during the missing twenty-four months was proportional to the number stolen during the ninety-six months for which data are available, we would conclude that the people of Nyaheiya lost 3,136 head of cattle—an average of 314 (313.6 rounded) head of cattle per year—during the ten-year period from 1986 through 1995. In and of itself, a loss of this magnitude—even in the complete absence of bovine diseases, in the total absence of drought—would have been sufficient to cause a steep decline in the size of the Nyaheiya cattle herd. We cannot make this assumption, however, because the theft-loss averages vary widely from year to year—from an average of 71.2 cattle lost per theft in 1986, when 13 thefts were reported, to the two cattle lost in the single theft in 1987 for which a record still survives—and the data that have survived are tilted in favor of the high-theft-loss years.

Earlier, we postulated that the 1984 census count of 4,537 head of cattle for the village of Nyaheiya represented an undercount of 25 percent and that the real size of Nyaheiya's cattle herd in that year was therefore

6,049 head. Assuming a steady annual growth rate of 3 percent, that herd would have numbered 8,373 head (8,373.2 rounded) in 1995. Were we to factor in a theft rate of even 200 head of cattle per year, however, the effect of this theft depletion would be to reduce that 1995 herd count to 5,812 (5,811.7 rounded) head. In fact, the *true* number of cattle in Nyaheiya in 1995 was extremely close to that: it was 5,834 head.

Eight of the years for which police records still exist are "intact" years, in the sense that there appear to be no gaps within those years for which theft reports are missing. Figure 8.4 charts the number of livestock-theft reports made during those years by people from all the villages of Kemambo ward, including Nyaheiya, as well as the number of livestock-theft reports filed in those years by the people of Nyaheiya alone. Figure 8.5 charts the net cattle-theft losses—the number of cattle reported to the police as stolen minus the number recovered—during those same "intact" years, both for the people of Kemambo ward, including Nyaheiya, and also for the people of Nyaheiya alone.

A cautionary note is in order, however, because cattle-theft victims have been known to deliberately inflate their reported losses in hopes of eventually receiving compensation in excess of the losses they have actually suffered, although there is no indication of victims having gone so far as to report wholly fictitious thefts.

In 1974, a directive issued by then-president Julius K. Nyerere ordered that a fine of ten head of cattle be imposed on every homestead in a village where the tracks of stolen cattle were found to terminate if the villagers failed to name the thieves and surrender the stolen cattle. This directive notwithstanding, the payment of compensation to theft victims has been notoriously sporadic and undependable, so much so that Anacleti, writing in 1979, flatly bemoaned the fact that "those measures of seizing ten head of cattle [from each corral] . . . have not been pursued" (1979:14, my translation; brackets in original).

More than twenty years later, this is still the case, although it does remain official policy that any village where the tracks of stolen cattle stop must either surrender the thieves to the authorities so that the stolen livestock may be recovered from them or else face confiscation of a sufficient number of cattle from the village at large to fully compensate the victims. To guard against inflated claims, officials say, a victim's village cattle records are reviewed to establish whether he actually had a sufficient number of cattle in his possession to make his theft claim credible. Since villagers routinely understate their cattle holdings to reduce their tax liability, such a procedure would seemingly limit the ability of cattle holders to claim compensation even for real losses.

Nevertheless, an unknown number of inflated losses are reported.

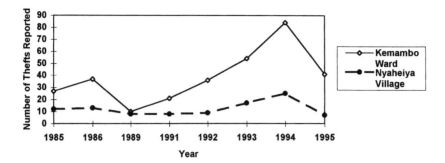

FIG. 8.4.   Police livestock theft reports for intact reporting years

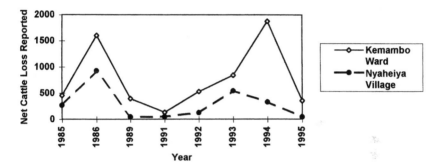

FIG. 8.5.   Net cattle losses for Kemambo ward and Nyaheiya village for intact reporting years

When, during the course of fieldwork, eleven sheep were stolen from a Nyaheiya man, the Nyaheiya *Sungusungu* made strenuous attempts to recover them, hauling in five suspects, whipping and interrogating them over the course of two days until finally three of them confessed. A contingent of *Sungusungu* were dispatched to the Irege village where the sheep had been passed to accomplices, then on to another Irege village, in Kenya, where it was found they had already been sold at the weekly market to an outside buyer. The *Sungusungu* contingent returned to Nyaheiya in frustration and confiscated a few of the cattle raiders' paltry possessions to help defray their own costs. When the theft was reported to the police, however, the number of sheep reported stolen was put at twenty-three.

These events unfolded during a period, however, when victims, their hopes for official forms of compensation heightened by the law-and-order climate of the forceful *Sungusungu* crackdown, may have become newly emboldened to advance exaggerated claims. Weighing against the possibility that a large proportion of all theft reports are wildly exaggerated, however, is the fact that bridewealth in Nyaheiya has declined precipitously in the ten-year period from 1986 through 1995, from an average of 19.8 head of cattle in 1986 to 12.3 (if one employs the homestead survey average) in 1995, a decline of nearly 38 percent. If one employs the 1995 bridewealth average of 9.5 reported by nonsurvey informants, the decline from 1986 through 1995 has been even more dramatic: 52 percent.

There are only two plausible explanations for a bridewealth decline of this magnitude, herd decline being the first, the second being that average bridewealth has declined merely as the village's human population has risen, in order to enable the larger number of wife-seekers to make marriages utilizing a village cattle population that has failed to keep pace with the growth of the human population. Militating strongly against this second interpretation, however, is the fact that Nyaheiya's human population has increased merely by about half, from approximately 1,500 people at the time of the village's founding, in 1974, to an estimated 2,232 people, based on data collected as part of the homestead survey, in 1995 and 1996. If, in keeping with the magnitude of that human population increase, average bridewealth in Nyaheiya had fallen by about one-third during that period, we could reasonably attribute that decline to human population growth. In actuality, however, average bridewealth fell from an average of 29.3 in 1974 to 12.3 (if one employs the homestead survey average) in 1995, a decline of nearly 58 percent. If, alternatively, one employs the 1995 bridewealth average of 9.5 reported by nonsurvey informants, the decline from 1974 through 1995 has been even more dramatic: nearly 68 percent.

In addition, it must be noted that, for victims, every livestock loss is significant: even the loss of a single calf, the least expensive category of cattle, represented, by early 1996, a loss equivalent to somewhere between 75 and 80 percent of Tanzania's estimated GNP per capita for 1993 of U.S.$90.00 (World Bank 1995:657). A good-sized ox was worth two-and-a-half times that.

Indirect Causes of Herd Decline

Cattle raiding is depleting the Nyaheiya cattle herd in other, more indirect ways, however, beyond the brute numbers of animals actually taken by cattle raiders and the loss of the offspring that those animals would have produced for their owners had they not been taken. Herd reduction driven by cattle raiding is also occurring for the following reasons.

(*a*) Ever since 1979, when the Tanzania-Uganda War ended and cattle raiding escalated, many cattle holders, in Nyaheiya and other villages, have adopted the strategy of keeping fewer cattle, selling off many of their beasts for cash or investing them in the acquisition of additional wives. In the aftermath of the war, noted one informant, "cows were seen as nothing." What was the sense of holding onto them, he argued, if they might be stolen at any time?

(*b*) Cattle holders and herders take the frequent precaution of grazing their livestock close to home, so that the animals may be returned to their corrals hurriedly at the first sign of trouble. This has the effect of depriving the animals of the more plentiful, more highly nutritious grasses in the larger, lusher pasturelands further away from the village, causing the mortality of the herds to rise.

(*c*) Livestock holders make the decision to move their herds, and sometimes their entire families, out of Nyaheiya and Tarime District to other parts of Tanzania, farther from the Kenya border, where cattle raiding is less prevalent.

Werema Marwa was one such emigrant. Born in 1960, he was relocated to Nyaheiya by *ujamaa* (Tanzania's program of forced villagization) in 1974 and lived in the homestead of his father's brother. In 1986, after 141 head of cattle were taken from them in a single cattle raid, the men tracked them to the Irege village of Masanga and lost them forever when they disappeared into Kenya, despite their repeated efforts to prod the bureaucracies of both countries into helping recover them.

For the next ten years, they staved off further thefts by sleeping in shifts, seeing to it that one man in the homestead was always awake to maintain a vigil over the cattle. Finally, in 1994, confiding that he was "tired of being a watchman," Werema let the family's rebuilt cattle herd out of its corral and, accompanied by his uncle and his uncle's sons, quietly slipped out of Nyaheiya in the predawn hours to resettle in a mixed village of Kuria and other peoples in another district, far from the Kenya border. A month later, the men returned to Nyaheiya to claim their wives and children—and then they were gone.

Moving livestock from one district to another entails the acquisition of a Livestock Movement Permit, available either at the government livestock office in Tarime or from livestock officers working in the field, and payment of a Tsh 200-per-head vaccination fee for cattle, Tsh 100 per head for sheep and goats. Both during and after these emigrations, the animals are subjected to significantly heightened mortality as a consequence of the stresses of the long journeys and the unaccustomed grasses and pathogens they encounter in their new environment. Pascal F. Mujuni, the regional veterinary officer for Mara Region, claims that cattle mortality consequent upon emigration may run as high as 30 percent (pers. comm.).

Unless the projected journey is a short one, such as to an adjacent district, most people do tend to acquire these permits despite the vaccination cost, because the cost to a herder of bribing a policeman who catches him moving livestock without a permit is liable to be a good deal higher than the legal fee. Livestock officers informally estimate that half to three-quarters of those moving livestock between districts actually go to the trouble and expense of obtaining valid permits, which record the name of the livestock holder, the animals' villages of origin and destination, and the numbers of cattle, sheep, and goats to be moved.

There are no reliable statistics regarding the numbers of livestock that have emigrated from Tarime District, however, because: (1) livestock officers in the field may issue permits and then pocket the vaccination fees, so that no record of the permits having been issued ever reaches Tarime; and (2) the lack of procedures and facilities for the storage of documents has resulted in the loss and destruction of many of these permit records. Seven months after Werema Marwa obtained his permit at Tarime, no record of it was to be found in livestock office files.

For the permits for which records were available, figure 8.6 charts the number of permits issued each year from 1983 to 1994, while figure 8.7 charts the number of cattle recorded by those permits as having emigrated from Tarime District in each of those same years.

(d)   Quite apart from this legal transfer of livestock, the promiscuous, unregulated movement of livestock by cattle raiders from one area to another, and particularly across the international border to Kenya, immeasurably facilitates the spread of such deadly bovine diseases as contagious bovine pleuropneumonia (CBPP), whose spread across East African borders has been explicitly linked to cattle theft by the UN Food and Agriculture Organisation (FAO) (Chintowa 1995:3). In the one-year period from mid-1994 to mid-1995 alone, Tanzania is said to have lost 15,000 head of cattle to CBPP, at a conservatively estimated cost of U.S.$1.5 million (Chintowa 1995:1).

In Nyaheiya and the other Kuria villages, this steady, unauthorized movement of cattle only serves to exacerbate an already serious threat to livestock holders posed by inadequately funded vaccination programs, an appalling shortage of working cattle dips, and inadequate access generally to veterinary resources.

(e)   Because it is the heavier, hence more valuable, animals—the steers, bulls, and oxen—that are the prime targets of cattle raiders, villagers find themselves increasingly compelled to utilize smaller, female animals—cows—both for ploughing and for hauling loads. "Reproduction is a luxury for a cow," notes regional veterinarian Mujuni, and so, although cows used for traction are said to begin reproducing earlier than cows not used for traction, they also have a shorter reproductive life and bear fewer calves overall.

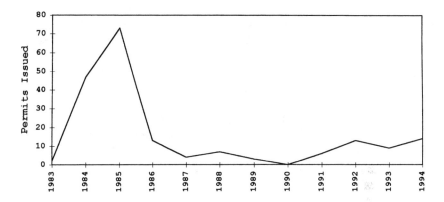

FIG. 8.6.　Tarime District livestock movement permits issued, 1983–94

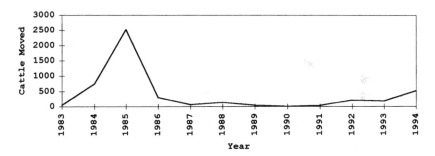

FIG. 8.7.　Cattle emigration from Tarime District, 1983–94

Cultural-Ecological Consequences

Decline of Food Production

On the homestead survey, when asked, "Is your land sufficient for supporting your family?" 89 percent of the respondents answered in the affirmative, and those few who answered negatively said they would resolve their shortage by applying to the village government for an additional allotment of land. There is a great deal of open, unoccupied arable land in Nyaheiya, enough to accommodate population growth for some time to come.

Yet, on the same survey, when respondents were asked to provide a listing of the foodstuffs they purchased, how often they purchased them

and in what amounts, and how much they paid for them, many respondents, in addition to enumerating such items as sugar, rice, tea leaves, and
salt, also reported buying sackfuls of millet, maize, and cassava, the very
things they had claimed, in response to other questions on the survey, that
they were growing in their fields.

Informants offered several explanations for this seeming incongruity.
The people of Nyaheiya do not like to cultivate, some said. They prefer to
mine for gold instead and to use the money they earn to buy their food.
Not true, claimed others, the people of Nyaheiya love farming, but 1994
was a year of insufficient rainfall, and in years of drought people have no
alternative but to buy their food. When it was pointed out to them that the
survey had been conducted mainly in 1995, not in 1994, and that 1995 had
been a *good* year for farming, it was suggested that the survey question had
been ambiguous—that people distinguish between basic "food," like
maize and millet, and other sorts of comestibles, like salt and sugar, that
they do not regard as "food," and that, in any event, it is a bitter experience for people when they are forced to *buy* "food," as a consequence of
which, no matter when they are asked about it, they are likely to recall that
experience and to answer in accordance with the last time they did it.

Perhaps this is true. There are no statistics available on the status of
food production in Nyaheiya. But according to figures provided by the district government agriculture office in Tarime, the number of hectares of
land under food-crop production (maize, sorghum, finger millet, cassava,
sweet potatoes, and bananas) in Tarime District as a whole has declined
steeply in the 1990s—from 61,093 hectares in 1990/91 to 40,914 hectares in
1994/95—and actual food production has declined along with it, from
112,411 tons to 41,480 tons during that same period—all in the face of a
steady human population increase. Hectarage devoted to cash crops (coffee, cotton) has apparently also plummeted, from 8,791 hectares in 1990/91
to 575 hectares in 1994/95, as has actual cash-crop production itself, from
2,864 tons to 1,427 tons during that same period (see table 8.4).[1]

Ploughing with oxen is the primary method of cultivation in Tarime
District, with Kuria farmers frequently employing mixed ploughing teams
of both steers and oxen (see also Ruel 1959:20). Eighty-five percent of the
district's cultivation is carried out in this manner, according to the agriculture office, with the remainder accomplished either by tractor (10 percent)
or by hand-hoeing (5 percent).

---

1. With respect to cash-crop production particularly, the district government figures
are highly, even bizarrely, anomalous—as if no rational relationship existed at all between
the number of hectares of land in production and the number of tons of cash crops produced
on it. Nonetheless, food production, which most concerns us here, displays a thoroughly
credible and dramatic decline, not only in the amount of food being produced but also in the
efficiency, relative to the amount of land being used to grow it, with which it is produced.

In Nyaheiya, there are no tractors, and ploughing with oxen is the norm. At the minimum, in the opinion of agriculture office personnel, each homestead should be equipped with its own "working plough," defined as a plough with a team of four oxen to pull it. At the time that Ruel wrote his Kuria field report in 1959, he was able to state that "the majority of homestead heads now possess their own plough and have a ploughing team" (1959:7), and Tobisson, who did her fieldwork twenty years later, reports that "the number of ploughs has continued to increase steadily" in the Tarime area since 1936 (1986:25).

But in 1995, having estimated the number of homesteads in the district at 51,049, the agriculture office reported only 17,778 ploughs in "good working condition" in the district—that is, only 34.8 percent of the homesteads had ploughs—an acknowledged shortfall of more than 33,000 ploughs. And the agriculture office does not report whether all of those ploughs had oxen to pull them. The number of ploughs in Tarime District has thus increased by 18.5 percent since 1959, when North Mara is said to have had 15,000 ploughs (Kjerland 1995:233), while human population has more than tripled.

Furthermore, the number of homesteads estimated for the district—51,049—is almost certainly too low. Tarime District's population in 1994 was an estimated 398,827. If the average population per homestead is the same in Tarime District as a whole as it is in the homesteads in the Nyaheiya survey sample (6.4 persons per homestead) then the total number of homesteads in Tarime District is actually on the order of 62,317—which would mean that only 28.5 percent of the district's homesteads have ploughs in good working condition, a shortfall of 44,539 ploughs.

Nyaheiya appears to be better off in this regard than the Tarime District average, with 43 percent of homesteads in the survey sample reporting that they have both a plough and oxen to pull it, although this percentage still falls short of Ruel's "majority." Of that sample, those homesteads that said they lack a working plough reported either that they borrow what they

TABLE 8.4. Hectarage of Land under Agricultural Production and Tonnage of Crops Produced in Tarime District, 1990–95

Fiscal Year	Food Crops		Cash Crops	
	Hectares	Production in Tons	Hectares	Production in Tons
1990/91	61,093	112,411	8,791	2,864
1991/92	45,512	93,189	3,174	3,639
1992/93	33,969	45,595	3,073	1,503
1993/94	[?]	59,317	826	4,880
1994/95	40,914	41,480	575	1,427

Source: Figures courtesy Government Agriculture Office, Tarime.

need (20 percent), rent what they need (9 percent), join together with someone who has what they need to help each other (15 percent), utilize traditional work groups (3 percent), or practice some combination of the above (6 percent). The remaining homesteads either failed to respond to the question (2 percent) or said only that the question did not apply to them despite their *not* having a working plough (2 percent), probably because they habitually buy all their food or cultivate exclusively by hoe.

Whatever the work regime, however, the need to share working ploughs or to borrow or rent them can only serve to diminish the hectarage of land under production and the total amount of food that is produced. There are optimal times for sowing, for weeding, for ploughing, and when homesteads are forced to share either plough animals or equipment, some inevitably find themselves in the position of being unable to cultivate their land at the optimal times and/or to the maximum extent. If sufficient numbers of steers and oxen are unavailable for any reason, they must be replaced by cows, which are not as strong as steers and oxen, tire sooner, and cannot plough as much land within the requisite amounts of time. What is happening in Tarime District today is that many people are reverting to hoe cultivation, with a consequent decline in the amount of land under production as well as a decline in the quantity of food being produced (see Ruel 1959:170–71, but cf. Tobisson 1986:76). Figure 8.8 charts the decline in hectarage under food production in Tarime District, according to the district government figures, from fiscal year 1990/91 to fiscal year 1994/95 (no hectarage figure was provided, however, for fiscal year 1993/94), as well as the decline in food production, in tons, in Tarime District during that same period. Figure 8.9 does the same for cash-crop production, both in terms of hectares of land under production and tons of cash crops produced (for cash crops, a hectarage figure *was* provided for 1993/94).

Even in the total absence of cattle raiding, agriculture in the lowlands is a precarious enterprise. Year-to-year rainfall is erratic and undependable (see fig. 8.10), and lowland soils are not as fertile as highland soils. According to the district agriculture office, ideal lowland rainfall, needed to produce bumper harvests, is from 900 mm to 1,000 mm per year; average rainfall, needed to produce average harvests, is 850 mm to 900 mm per year; and "critical" rainfall, accompanied by food shortage, is 650 mm to 850 mm per year.

Rainfall measurements taken at the Mennonite Mission in lowland Shirati, which serves as a reasonable proxy for Nyaheiya and its sister lowland villages, suggest that Nyaheiya had ideal rainfall during 1990 and 1991, and then plummeted deep into the critical range over the course of the next three years.

By contrast, the Tarime highlands, agriculturally the richest, most

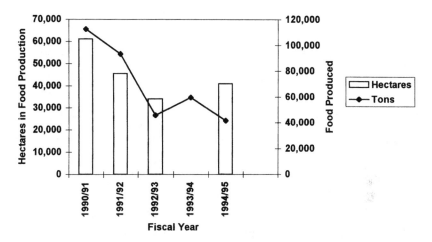

FIG. 8.8. Hectarage in food production and tons of food produced in Tarime District from fiscal year 1990/91 to fiscal year 1994/95

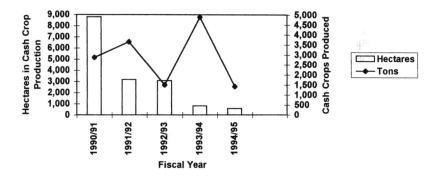

FIG. 8.9. Hectarage in cash-crop production and tons of cash crops produced in Tarime District from fiscal year 1990/91 to fiscal year 1994/95

productive area of Tarime District, enjoyed average or slightly less-than-average rainfall during 1990, 1991, and 1992, plummeted into the critical range in 1993, and then experienced ideal rainfall in 1994. Tarime District's precipitous agricultural decline thus cannot be attributed to a lack of rainfall. But many highland farmers keep their oxen "put out" in the lowlands with stock associates, recalling them to the highlands for ploughing at the appropriate times. When a highlander's oxen are lost to a cattle raid in the lowlands, he can either share oxen belonging to other farmers

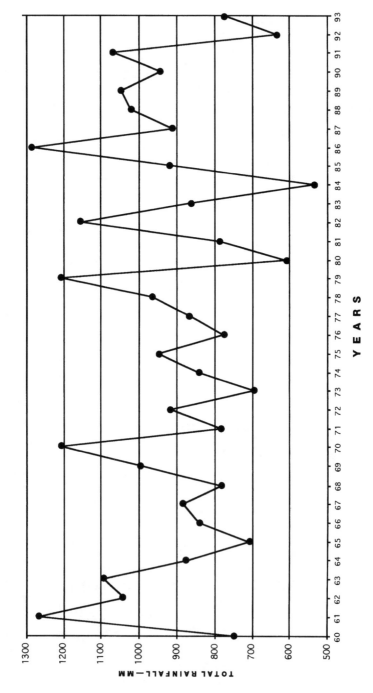

FIG. 8.10. Lowland rainfall measurements recorded at Shirati, Tanzania, 1960–93. (Data courtesy of the Mennonite Mission, Shirati.)

or revert to the hoe: either way, he cultivates less land and reaps fewer crops.

The salient point here is not that the loss of plough oxen, wholly divorced from other factors, has devastated agriculture throughout Tarime District, but that the loss of plough animals acts in synergy with other factors, recurrent drought among them, to produce devastating effects in an environment that is always a high-risk one for agriculture.

Cattle are also important sources of food, of course, and the decline of the cattle herd therefore also means that there is less milk, beef, and cow's blood available to fulfill people's nutritional needs.

Spread of Bovine Diseases

As cattle migrate, whether set in motion directly, by cattle raiders moving them cross-country within Tanzania and/or across the Kenya border to markets and buyers, or indirectly, by frightening owners into seeking safer venues for their livestock in other districts, their migration serves to intensify the spread of bovine diseases, such as rinderpest and CBPP, causing infertility and death among cattle and reducing ox power and the availability of manure for agriculture and other uses (Chintowa 1995:2).

The Tanzanian government's response to such outbreaks has been to order widespread quarantines of its cattle markets, forbidding the sale or movement of cattle between districts and regions. This in turn has the effect of damping down the legal cattle trade, already strangling in bureaucratic restrictions, and of making legal beef even more difficult and expensive to obtain, thereby expanding even further the scope of the illicit market in cattle and intensifying the cycle of violence and livestock decline.

Over the past six to ten years, as a consequence of cattle raiding, the phenomenon has arisen, wholly new to Tarime District, of the district's butchers being unable to supply their customers' demands for beef by buying and slaughtering only cattle reared within the district. At Magena, Tanzania, site of a major area cattle market located about twelve kilometers from the town of Sirari, at the Tanzania/Kenya border, livestock sellers have been bringing cattle from neighboring areas of Tanzania—for example, Bariadi District, in Shinyanga Region, and Magu District, in Mwanza Region—to capitalize on the Tarime District demand.

For much of the fieldwork period, however, the Magena market was closed due to the government's imposition of a CBPP quarantine barring the importation of livestock from outside the region. With a kind of vicious inevitability, cattle raiding promotes and intensifies the spread of bovine diseases; and quarantines, designed to stem these outbreaks, have the effect of stifling the legal livestock trade and thus of fueling the illicit one.

Lack of adequate funding for livestock vaccination programs only serves to make matters worse: Tarime District's 1994/95 rinderpest/CBPP vaccination program, for example, was carried out in fits and starts, as livestock officers implemented the program in a number of villages, only to be forced to suspend operations while they waited to receive further funds for vaccines. In the meantime, with the year's vaccination program still incomplete, the government abruptly doubled the first-time-ever CBPP vaccination charge that had been imposed at the onset of the program from Tsh 25 per head to Tsh 50 per head.

The uneasy historical relationship, dating back to colonial times, between the Kuria and vaccination programs does nothing to help matters. The belief is widespread among Kuria people that British colonial officials deliberately laced a percentage of their rinderpest vaccines with poison as a surreptitious, heinous means of destocking the range (see also Tobisson 1986:28). Whether it is actually true that deliberate poisoning occurred, which seems dubious (Kjerland 1995:87 n. 110), or whether cattle already infected with rinderpest prior to being vaccinated simply died of the disease that would have killed them anyway, or, alternatively, if the cattle deaths were the unintended consequence of the much less reliable vaccine quality-control of those days, the fact remains that Kuria cattle holders in Tarime and adjacent Serengeti districts typically bring forward only an unknown fraction of their cattle herd to be vaccinated—a fraction sometimes estimated at 50 percent—including those animals that are already sick.

This level of vaccination "coverage" contrasts sharply, according to regional veterinarian Mujuni, with what he says occurs in Bunda and Musoma districts, inhabited by a varied mix of peoples, including Kuria, who are believed to bring out their cattle to be vaccinated at a much higher rate, perhaps as high as 80 percent—but since no one at or above the district level knows how many cattle there really are in any village or district, it is impossible to know what percentage of them are actually being vaccinated. Livestock veterinarians insist, however, that continuing immunity to CBPP requires that every animal be vaccinated whenever vaccinations are given, and they would like to see the vaccination frequency doubled to twice a year.

Regrettably, no vaccination statistics are available for Tarime District before 1986/87, and there are no statistics whatsoever for individual villages that might help to further substantiate the decline of the Nyaheiya herd or to trace its trajectory. Due to a shortage of space and resources, such vaccination reports as are kept at Tarime are periodically transferred from its district livestock office to the government hospital, where they are rolled into paper cones for the dispensing of patients' drugs.

In 1986/87, just two to three years after the national livestock census of 1984 reported that Tarime District had a total of 305,858 head of cattle—at a time when there was no vaccination fee—156,510 head of cattle were vaccinated for rinderpest in the district, a turnout equivalent to just over half (51.2 percent) of the district's official 1984 census total. But cattle raiding had skyrocketed during this two- to three-year period, so had cattle emigration, and rinderpest had reared its ugly head again. On the plus side of the ledger, the 1984 census count was probably an undercount. Given all these factors, it is simply not possible to determine how many cattle there were in the district at that time or what percentage of the district herd was vaccinated.

Loss of Wealth

In pastoral and agropastoral environments, livestock—particularly cattle—are not only an indispensable means of subsistence, they are also the primary, often the only, mode of wealth accumulation (Tanner 1966:37; Christiansson and Tobisson 1988:15, cited in Kjerland 1995:32). It costs next to nothing to keep and raise them—the grass is free, the water is free, the labor needed to herd and maintain them is free—except for payment (since 1992) of the district cattle tax and the cost (since 1994) of periodic vaccinations for CBPP. Cattle holders do have other basic veterinary needs, but local people often ignore them simply because they cannot afford to meet them.

Cattle reproduce, a cow typically birthing a new calf every year, and they are a far better investment than Tanzanian bank accounts, which, during the fieldwork period, were being hammered by an annual inflation rate of about 36 percent. Among the Kuria and, indeed, in any kin-based society, where people are under extraordinary social pressure to share what little they have and where a few coins jingling in a man's pocket or tied into a knot in a woman's *kanga* (Swa., the two-piece cloth garment worn by women) are bound to have many claimants, wealth is extraordinarily difficult to accumulate unless it is invested in things that are by their nature indivisible and therefore unshareable, such as livestock, wives, a brick or cement house. Of these things, only one—livestock—can be readily converted to cash.

Very few people in Kurialand today are able to go through life without having at least a little money for clothing, medical expenses, school fees, taxes, bribes to officials, plastic water buckets and other sundries, kerosene, grinding-mill fees, and such miscellaneous staples as cooking oil, matches, and salt. In the homestead survey, 56.9 percent of those respondents who said they possessed cattle (i.e., that they possessed a cattle "herd," of whatever size) said that they had sold at least one head of cattle for cash in the previous twelve months, which means that 30.5 percent of the entire homestead sample did so. Cows also give milk: in the homestead survey, 78.3 percent of the homesteads that reported that they had cattle in their own corral also reported that they sold milk to earn cash income.

Cattle and other livestock can also be used to obtain financial and other help even when they are not sold: If you will help me now, a homestead head can say, I will give you my next calf.

To one degree or other, all Kuria are enmeshed in the world capitalist web. Cattle constitute their primary means of accumulating wealth, their principal repositories of value. As that cattle "fund" is inexorably drained away by cattle raiding and its correlates, the Kuria's hold on survival in an already harsh natural and economic environment becomes increasingly tenuous.

Impact on Development

Tanzanian government officials at both the regional and district levels have described cattle theft as the principal obstacle to the development of Tarime District as well as of Mara Region, of which the district is part. The continuing decline of the area's cattle wealth means that less and less wealth is even potentially available for building better houses, starting small businesses, and educating children. However bleak the economic landscape looks now, the people of Nyaheiya seem convinced that their children's ability to seize future opportunities will depend on access to education beyond primary school.

On the homestead survey, respondents were asked to give their estimation of the value of an education for a boy, and for a girl, growing up in Nyaheiya today. The survey sample presents a statistically representative profile of Nyaheiya's 350 *homesteads* and *not* of the estimated 2,232 individuals who make up its entire population. Nonetheless, 93 percent of the respondents who answered the question, and 89.5 percent of all the survey respondents, rated education for a boy as "essential to a good life," while 47 percent of those who answered the question, and 45.3 percent of all the survey respondents, said the same for a girl. Approximately one-third of the respondents (33.9 percent of those who answered the question, and 32.6 percent of all the survey respondents) said they regarded education for a girl as "a waste of time and money," stressing mainly, in response to a follow-up question, the need widely felt by villagers for girls to marry early in order to bring bridewealth cattle into their households.

The steady diminution of Nyaheiya's cattle wealth reduces the possibility of its being utilized in innovative productive ways, and this, in turn, lessens the likelihood of the area's being able to generate tax revenues that will incline the national government in Dar es Salaam to invest even meagerly in the area's roads and other infrastructure, law enforcement, and social services. As things stand, state power and influence are scarcely man-ifested here except at times when the state's ability to maintain order is directly threatened, such as occurred when cattle raiders acquired military weaponry in the aftermath of the Tanzania-Uganda War (see chap. 5).

As one Kuria, a Catholic seminarian who was not from Nyaheiya, put it, "If thieves went to Kilimanjaro and stole Chagga coffee," an impor-tant crop from which the national government derives large tax revenues, "the army would go after them *harakaharaka* [Swa., very quickly]. But here a hundred people could be killed and in Dar es Salaam it would not even be in a newspaper."

The unending violence that is an integral part of cattle raiding exerts its own baleful effects. On the homestead survey, respondents reported a total of eleven deaths—seven of homestead members and four of cattle raiders—in connection with cattle raids on their respective homesteads from 1980 onward, a number that suggests a figure of slightly more than twenty cattle-raiding-related deaths for the village at large. There are no figures to document the present and ongoing carnage districtwide, but in adjacent Serengeti District, in the year 1986, Fr. Brian Barrons, a Mary-knoll Catholic missionary who spent eight years among the Kuria, main-tained a tally of all cattle-raiding-related deaths in the district—those of police, of cattle raiders, and of innocent civilians—and came up with a death toll for that year of nearly two hundred names (1995: pers. comm.). Christiansson and Tobisson, who were doing research in the area in 1986, report one hundred cattle-raiding-related deaths for the first eight months of that year (Christiansson and Tobisson 1988:3, cited in Kjerland 1995:66), a figure roughly consistent with Barrons's.

In chapter 7, we learned that of sixty-four Nyaheiya cattle raiders for whom uterine-sibling data were available, forty-nine—or nearly 77 per-cent—of them grew up in households having fewer female uterine siblings than male uterine siblings, and from this finding one might be tempted to conclude that it is the Kuria's high bridewealth that is the root cause of cattle raiding.

From Tanzanian officialdom today, one tends to hear a different view: that cattle raiding is "a business," illegal but otherwise much like any other business, and that young men lacking traditional sources of bridewealth are no more likely to engage in it than young men who are for-tunate enough to have many sisters. "A thief is a thief" is a refrain that is very often heard. Tarime District's top police official put it this way: "Looking at its current causes, cattle theft is more or less the same as such other offences like burlglars [*sic*], house breakings, or armed robberies" (1995: pers. comm.).

Each of these views is partly true. Reconciling them will be among the tasks of the following chapter.

CHAPTER 9

Ways of Seeing Cattle: "Now Everything Is Getting Stolen"

Every Kuria alive today, past early childhood, is well aware that cattle and other livestock can be readily exchanged for cash money and that that money can, in turn, be used to purchase food, clothing, medical services, and a whole host of fine things. Many Kuria, however—maybe all Kuria—also have other, competing ways of perceiving their livestock: as bridewealth, as milk and meat, as plough animals, as a means of fostering social relationships and garnering prestige, and as objects of ritual. And they are all but certain to assign a vastly different hierarchy of value to these other ways than, say, those who operate cattle ranches in the United States. In Nyaheiya today, all cattle holders occasionally sell cattle for cash, albeit usually reluctantly, but individuals still differ in the frequency with which they do this, in their precise motives for doing it, in how they dispose of the money.

In his study of changes in East African cattle husbandry during the colonial period, Murmann defines "market oriented cattle husbandry" as a situation in which

> there is *deliberately* produced a surplus of cattle products, either meat in the form of live or slaughtered animals, or milk, which is sold for cash. The sale does not have to take place at a specific livestock market or at a dairy, but can be to a traveling buyer or directly to the consumers. . . .
>
> When the cattle products are marketed, cattle keeping becomes market oriented or commercialized. (1974:8, my emphasis)

Market orientation, by this definition, would appear to hinge on intent: cattle husbandry is market oriented if cattle owners raise them "deliberately" for that purpose. In Nyaheiya, however, as we have seen, the situation is considerably less tidy: cattle are being raised for market sale, all right, but *not* deliberately. The "primary producers" perceive their cattle primarily in a nonmarket way, while the cattle raiders slyly scoping out their cattle corrals view those same animals as cash on the hoof—as commodities—although they, too, have other, noncommodity ways of perceiving cattle in general. What is at once interesting and important about what is going on in Nyaheiya today is that different people are viewing cattle in different ways and acting differently in accordance with their different ways of seeing them.

In Kenya, the arrival of the cash market set in train a specific congeries of processes and events, including the privatization of land; agricultural intensification and, with it, the squeezing out of the cattle herds; the declining social and economic importance of cattle and the emergence of avenues of investment other than in cattle; the monetization and privatization of bridewealth payments; and, for many, the complete commoditization, or commercialization, of cattle, in which cattle are viewed solely as commodities by both producers and consumers.

This scenario is not strictly applicable to the Nyaheiya case, however, because there is no land shortage in Nyaheiya and cattle are *not* being squeezed off the land. The scenario retains some of its descriptive and theoretical usefulness, however, so long as we apply MacGaffey's admonition that "African economies need to be considered in multi-country regional studies as well as in studies of individual nations" (1991:7).

In a passage relating to the smuggling of food crops out of Zaire (now the Democratic Republic of the Congo) to take advantage of the higher prices available in neighboring countries, she writes:

> These flows of unrecorded transborder trade . . . are defined as smuggling because they illegally cross national borders and evade tariffs, customs dues or regulations, but they are more appropriately seen as part of trade circuits within natural geographical regions. (MacGaffey 1991:19)

Such a regional perspective is definitely applicable to our study area, for, as was discussed in chapter 4, the "island-like circumstances" of Tarime District (formerly North Mara) "have caused the entire history of North Mara to be greatly influenced by the neighboring country of Kenya" (Anacleti 1979:2, my translation). What this means in terms of the illicit cattle trade and the commoditization of cattle in Tanzania is that land scarcity brought about by privatization and agricultural intensification has indeed played a seminal role in the phenomena under discussion here, but the land shortage in question is a *Kenya* land shortage whose reverberations are being felt well beyond Kenya's borders owing to the fact that northern Tanzania is part of the same "natural geographical region" as Kenya and thus falls within Kenya's sphere of economic influence.

International trade is made possible by—and is thus the product of—

the production-system differences of the trading partners. These differences are especially susceptible to exploitation by people living in proximity to international borders, especially when those borders are essentially unregulated, the officials charged with policing them corrupt. Make a few simple word changes—Kuria for Igbo, Ksh for CFA, and Tsh for naira— in a passage by MacGaffey describing the transborder smuggling trade between Cameroon and Nigeria, and that passage becomes an equally valid statement about the Kuria illicit cattle trade:

> An important factor in the success of this trade is that numerous Igbo people live on both sides of the border and have been active in organizing this commerce. Another factor is the strength of the CFA franc compared with the Nigerian naira, which has resulted in the development of a lively parallel money market on the frontier. Some 30,000 people [this number is *not* applicable to the Kuria case] are estimated to be involved in this illicit transborder trade, most of them young men with a low level of education. (1991:22–23)

The British settled in Kenya in large numbers, appropriated large tracts of arable land there, and left behind them when they left, at independence, an economy and infrastructure far superior to Tanzania's. Tanzania's decision to pursue a socialist path after 1961, while Kenya followed a capitalist one, only widened the economic rift between the two countries even further. Today, Kenya is a richer country than Tanzania; its currency has a higher value than Tanzania's; innumerable commodities used by the people of Tanzania, particularly those of northern Tanzania, come from Kenya; and the people of Kenya are by virtually every measure more affluent than their Tanzanian counterparts—but not in cattle.

For third world people generally, beef is a luxury food. The Kuria have a noun, *oboteehu,* that means "a longing for meat," a longing that arises especially from not having had meat for a long time. As people become more affluent, they want—they expect—to eat more meat. In Kenya, the demand is there, and it is growing fast (Evangelou 1984), but the diversion of land for agriculture has effectively driven out the cattle needed to satisfy it.

Tanzania has the cattle, but the pastoral peoples who own them do not want to sell them—cannot afford to sell them—because they rely on those cattle for other things: for milk, blood, and beef; traction for ploughing; bridewealth and ritual sacrifice; emergency cash; "interest" on their pastoralist investment in the form of calves; and for the prestige that cattle still confer on their owners. The Tanzanian government sees no national economic interest in safeguarding either these cattle or the lives of their owners, and it has drowned what nascent legitimate livestock trade there is in a river of red tape. Market forces are sucking Kuria cattle out of Tanzania and into Kenya.

"The centrality of livestock in the pre-colonial economy of both nomadic pastoralists and sedentary pastoralists," writes Kitching,

> derived (a) from its multifarious use values and (b) from its being the only product which served both as a measure of wealth and medium of exchange. (1980:206)

In the precolonial situation, a man who possessed many cattle was affluent by any reasonable definition of the term: the animals themselves, and the wives, children, and affines he was able to acquire by deploying those animals as bridewealth, assured them all of a larger and more dependable food supply, survival insurance against famine and drought, safe passage through enemy areas, allies in the event of interclan warfare or intraclan disputes, enhanced security in old age—in short, a safer, more secure life than was available to those who had less.

Much has changed since precolonial times, but not that, not the utterly rational desire to acquire cattle and other forms of livestock. For the people of Nyaheiya, livestock remains the most profitable investment of their time and energies; their most reliable hedge against runaway money inflation; "collateral" with which to secure favors and a fund with which to meet obligations; milk for protein-needy children; money for food, school fees, taxes, health care, and other emergencies; insurance against famine and drought; security in old age. The list goes on.

What has indisputably changed since precolonial times is that the arrival of the cash market has opened a window onto a wider world for the Kuria, creating widening wants in the form of a delectable array of things to buy. As Murmann remarks:

> The African farmers were obliged [under colonialism] to provide money in order to meet the tax demands; however, it was primarily the desire to acquire consumer goods which in the long run was the main motivation for them to practise market oriented farming, both in the agricultural and the cattle sector. (1974:105)

To imagine that high bridewealth is the engine behind cattle raiding in these new circumstances is mainly—albeit not entirely—to miss the point. Bridewealth, after all, has been declining drastically in Nyaheiya for nearly the past two decades, mirroring the steady decline of the village's cattle herd. But cattle raiding has *not* declined in that time, because cattle raiding is driven, on the supply end, mainly by the desire of young men to acquire wealth (*oboome*), or, as many of Nyaheiya's cattle raiders phrased it, *kufanya starehe* (Swa.), "to take life easy" or "to live the good life." As Ruel noted decades ago,

> One of the major factors in cattle-theft is undoubtedly the high rate of bridewealth, but there are other factors besides this. Most of the values of "wealth" (*oboome*) in Kuria society are associated with cattle, so that in one sense the acquisition of cattle is an end in itself. When asked, Renchoka [clan] elders named "wealth" as a reason equal in force to "marriage" (i.e. the need to marry) for the extent of cattle-theft. (1959:177)

If, as is argued here, however, *kufanya starehe* is really a more significant factor in cattle raiding today than the need for bridewealth, what does it mean that—as detailed in chapter 7—more than three-quarters of the respondents in a sample of sixty-four cattle raiders grew up in mother-centered households having more uterine male siblings than uterine female siblings? It means that, in the Kuria world, young men who have had the misfortune to be born into households with too few sisters are poor.

Unlike our own society, where poverty and deprivation correlate strongly with class, among the Kuria, whether a boy grows up with good prospects or poor prospects is a demographic crapshoot: absent a father with a sizable back to his herd (the portion of the family herd that his father, the homestead head, can dispose of freely, as he sees fit), a young male's future is likely to be heavily influenced, for good or ill, by the ratio of girl children to boy children that his own mother has. For a Kuria boy, having innumerable nonuterine sisters, the female offspring of his father's other wives, counts for next to nothing: only the bridewealth cattle brought into a mother-centered household by one's own uterine sisters serve to swell the coffers of household wealth.

Economically as well as socially, marriage is paramount for Kuria of both sexes, and the father of a marriageable young woman does not even want his daughter *talking* to a young admirer whose family does not have cattle at home. There are no jobs in the Nyamongo area. Agriculture is tenuous, the cash payoffs unreliable and slow in coming. The local gold mines are producing poorly these days, but the beef shortage in Kenya means that the cattle market is riding high. Periodic warfare between clans, arising from ongoing conflict over access to strategic resources, serves to intensify and sustain interclan enmities as well as serving as a training ground for a life in cattle raiding. And then there is often one's own father, reminiscing about his own young manhood: "If I had not taken cows," he reminds his offspring, "I would not have been able to marry your mother."

In her book on Zaire's informal economy, MacGaffey observes that "people take advantage of any available opportunity" (1991:157), but it would be more precise to say that people will tend to take advantage first of the *best* opportunity, the one that yields the largest amount of payout for the least amount of work. That is why, by their own candid admission, so many of the cattle raiders interviewed for this study abandoned gold mining in favor of cattle raiding: not because earning income from gold mining had become impossible, or because they or their families were threatened with starvation, but because they found that through cattle raiding they could make money "*harakaharaka*" (Swa., very quickly).

It is often said, in our own society, that the children of the middle class are generally more ambitious and highly motivated than their counterparts among the very rich because the former must find a way to make their own way in the world—"If I hadn't gotten a job waiting on tables when I was your age, I wouldn't have been able to go to college!"—while the children of wealthy families can afford to sit back and wait for the benefits of inherited affluence to come to them.

For a Kuria young man, being sister-poor means that unless he relishes the idea of being relegated to society's margins, he had better get out there and do whatever he has to do to meet his own cattle needs. Of course, cattle raiding is risky business. Young men die doing it. For sister-rich young men for whom marriage is virtually a birthright, it is evidently less often worth the risk. Not quite one-quarter of the young men in the Nyaheiya cattle-raider sample were in that more fortunate situation yet chose to become involved in cattle raiding in spite of it.

While some of the cattle raiders interviewed for this study used their proceeds from cattle raiding to acquire their first wife and then withdrew from the trade, and some others abandoned cattle raiding after seeing one of their comrades killed in the course of carrying out a raid, still others kept on with it, acquiring additional wives, buying clothing for themselves and their families, helping their uterine brothers acquire their own bridewealth, using their earnings from cattle raiding to purchase cattle for their own herds.

Not one of those cattle raiders who were interviewed, however, had amassed savings and used them to start a small business or to build a permanent, nontraditional house. The main reason is that, excepting wives and cattle, there simply are no investment avenues open to the people of Nyaheiya capable of yielding a reliable return. Another reason is that there are strong social disincentives in Nyaheiya to accumulating money or to displaying money-wealth in "permanent," ostentatious ways. Cattle wealth circulates, in the form of bridewealth, to every household that has daughters, and it is therefore seen as being "shared," in some sense, by the community at large. Even the poorest man, after all, can dream of becoming a winner in the lottery of having daughters.

Money-wealth, however, becomes "frozen" in the things that money buys—fancy houses, for example, do *not* circulate—and thus fuels the fires of envy and hatred. The belief, widespread in Nyaheiya, that anyone who becomes money-rich (as opposed to cattle-rich) will die at the hands of sorcerers—called *abaturutumbi* (sing., *umuturutumbi*)—who ride hyenas like motorcycles and dance naked outside their victims' homesteads in the dead of night, expresses this common resentment toward those individuals who have heinously withdrawn from the socially sanctioned system of sharing and locked their wealth away in impartible forms, rendering the status quo permanent, institutionalizing inequality.

All this, coupled with the extreme pressure to share whatever one has with others—right now, today, before it can be accumulated—and the evident need for the members of cattle-raiding groups to continually reinforce and celebrate a kind of soldierly camaraderie, to invest in their own solidarity with one another, explains why a good deal of the income earned by cattle raiders is "invested" in beer drinking and just pissed away.

Unlike the situation that prevailed in precolonial times, however, when the offtake from cattle raiding was tolerable for society as a whole, albeit considerably less tolerable for the unfortunate individual cattle holders who happened to be victimized, cattle raiding today is no longer a sustainable activity, and the area's cattle are heading off to market faster than they can reproduce themselves. Barring drastic change, there will still be open land in Nyaheiya in the foreseeable future but no longer any cattle left to graze on it. The young men will still be there, however, and there will likely be more of them.

"The youths are the fire and the elders are the water," goes a Kuria saying, but in Nyaheiya today, no one—not the elders, not the *Sungusungu,* sure as hell not the police force—has whatever it would take to quench the blaze. With the village cattle herd dwindling, with families painfully aware that their neighbors' sons are conspiring with outsiders to steal their cattle, cattle raiding—once a mechanism for demonstrating the mettle of new warriors and enlarging the community cattle herd—has now become transformed into something else.

Any observer with two eyes in his face can see where all this is going. In the crowded villages of the Tarime highlands, all but denuded of cattle, housebreakings are on the rise—even though there is scarcely anything inside the houses worth taking. In Tarime town, housebreakings are already commonplace, and it is unsafe to walk the streets after 10:00 P.M.

In Nyaheiya, throughout the fieldwork period, the violence and costliness of cattle raiding were villagers' primary "crime" concerns, but small shopkeepers lived in fear of nighttime break-ins, and petty thievery, neighbor against neighbor, was an endemic part of village life. Plastic water buckets, the occasional radio, even a clutch of baby chicks—these and other possessions, left untended—even inside a hut with a small padlock on its door—not infrequently disappeared.

Now, by temporarily pinching off a primary source of cash income, the *Sungusungu* crackdown on cattle raiding is aggravating intravillage tensions as much as cattle raiding ever did.

Dear Michael,

. . . . Today we have many thieves here in Nyaheiya and it seems that everyone is going to be a thief here in Nyaheiya. While you were here there was theft of cattle only. But now everything is getting stolen. These thieves steal millet from the granaries at night. These thieves come at night with sacks and take the millet from someone's granary. . . . Later they sell the millet—one debe [a 4-gallon kerosene can] [for] Sh 1,500. . . . Other thieves break into people's houses and steal mattresses, blankets, plastic water buckets, cooking pots, etcetera. Other thieves go at night into people's fields and pick all the maize or dig up the sweet potatoes. To live in a place where the thieves are, I feel that I am in a bad situation. . . .

Yours,
Wagesa

CHAPTER 10

Conclusion

Over the course of the past century, as this book has endeavored to demonstrate, Kuria cattle raiding has been transformed by an array of powerful political and economic forces (colonialism, expanding capitalism, and the policies of the postcolonial Tanzanian state) and the behavior of an uncountable number of individuals acting in their own perceived best interest (including cattle buyers, butchers, policemen, soldiers, truckers, public officials, and young Kuria men with poor prospects and few opportunities) from a mechanism of social and cultural integration into an entrepreneurial, organized-crime activity undertaken by small groups of individuals—the cattle raiders—for the purpose of their own enrichment at the expense of the communities where the raiders themselves live.

This is not merely a quantitative change—to be measured by the increased numbers of livestock stolen or casualties inflicted—brought about by improvements in weaponry and/or more effective principles of underworld organization, but rather a qualitative change posing an altogether different theoretical challenge and calling for a new understanding.

A central question raised by this study is the extent to which Kuria cattle raiding, as it is practiced today, represents the residues of colonialism and the disordering of the world system's periphery by capitalism and to what extent it represents the unfolding of an indigenous dynamic. An abiding interest in order and its antithesis has a venerable lineage in anthropology, most particularly with respect to the conundrum of how order is secured in the absence of a state. If, as the British social anthropologists held, order is immanent in social organization, then a new question arises: where does disorder come from? For some, the answer is the contagion unleashed by contact with expanding capitalism.

Writing of the effects of Western contact on the native peoples of Amazonia, but with the explicit intention of applying his theoretical perspective to contacts between states and so-called traditional societies generally, Ferguson maintains that far from suppressing a Hobbesian "war of all against all," the intrusion of the European state fomented warfare:

> Ultimately, wars have ended through pacification or extinction, but prior to that the general effect of contact has been just the opposite: to intensify or engender warfare. For want of a better

word, this process could be called "warrification." (Ferguson 1990:239)

Keeley, on the other hand, while concurring with Ferguson that indigenous warfare patterns must have been *altered* by external contact (Keeley 1996:21), argues that war has been a fact of life over the course of the past 10,000 years in every region of the world that has been subjected to intensive archaeological study: "There is simply no proof," he concludes,

> that warfare in small-scale societies was a rarer or less serious undertaking than among civilized societies. In general, warfare in prestate societies was both frequent and important. If anything, peace was a scarcer commodity for members of bands, tribes, and chiefdoms than for the average citizen of a civilized state. (Keeley 1996:39)

The question of whether Western contact has had the effect of intensifying already existing indigenous warfare patterns has generated similar differences of opinion. Based on an ethnographic comparison of four tribal societies—the Jivaro of the upper Amazon Basin, the Iroquois of the northeastern United States, the Maori of New Zealand, and the Dani of Highland New Guinea—Blick argues that contact with European explorers and colonists brings with it "an escalation in [the] warfare patterns" of tribal societies (1988:654). Warfare in traditional, small-scale societies, he writes,

> is usually of a restricted nature and is often based on a system of blood feuding, called here the revenge complex [which, when] combined with an economic motive, primarily in the form of European-introduced goods such as guns, machetes, horses, etc., expands into a system of genocidal warfare previously unknown in tribal societies. (Blick 1988:654)

Bamforth, however, disputes the notion that Western contact significantly increases the scale and intensity of high-casualty warfare. Drawing on archaeological data from the North American Great Plains, he maintains that high-casualty warfare brought into being by indigenous cultural-ecological processes rooted in unpredictable environmental fluctuations and resource scarcity was endemic in at least parts of the Great Plains for centuries prior to contact (1994:95).

The idea that the periphery of the world system has been cast into disorder by colonialism and capitalism is tightly linked to the Durkheimian formulation that societies constitute moral orders that are inherently inclined toward order and harmony, and its Marxian corollary, by way of Rousseau, that disorder and disharmony, along with alienation and exploitation, are the deformed offspring of capitalism.

For Evans-Pritchard, (intertribal) warfare and (intratribal) feuding among the Nuer functioned as mechanisms of structural maintenance and cohesion. "The structural relations between Nuer tribes and other peoples," he wrote, "and between [Nuer] tribe and [Nuer] tribe are maintained by the institution of warfare[,] and the structural relations between segments of the same tribe are maintained by the institution of the feud" (1940:190). Thus, Nuer warfare against the Dinka—which had, among its main objects, the acquisition of cattle—served to create political order out of conflict/disorder through the bringing into being of larger structures. "[T]hrough war, the memory of war, and the potentiality of war," Evans-Pritchard argued, "the relations between tribes are defined and expressed" (161).

Moreover, "within a tribe fighting always produces feuds, and a relation of feud is characteristic of tribal segments and gives to the tribal structure a movement of expansion and contraction" (Evans-Pritchard 1940:161). Thus, "the blood-feud may be viewed as a structural movement between political segments by which the form of the Nuer political system, as we know it, is maintained" (158).

As is now well-recognized, however, the notion of "traditional" (or "tribal") society, harmoniously organic and homeostatic, is itself an idealized, deeply flawed construction evocative of a past that never really could have been. For Africa, Berman traces its origins to a confluence of sources that included a colonial administrative ideology of "paternalistic authoritarianism grounded in a concept of society as an organic community"; Malinowskian and Radcliffe-Brownian functionalism; and the political self-interest of chiefs and elders who "sought to bolster their legitimacy by accounts that stressed their authoritative role in the maintenance of the order and harmony of pre-colonial society" (Berman 1997 [1991]:657–58). In recent decades, however,

> the dominant image of traditional society as highly integrated, stable, relatively unchanging, and largely free of disruptive internal conflict has been challenged by increasing evidence of the fluidity of political boundaries and ethnic identities and the significant levels of internal conflict revealed in contemporary historical research. (Berman 1997 [1991]:657)

In a famous 1955 BBC radio lecture entitled "The Peace in the Feud," Max Gluckman echoed Evans-Pritchard's view that internal conflict functions as a mechanism of internal cohesion, arguing that disputes arise in society along certain fault lines of allegiance but are prevented from erupting into violence by crosscutting allegiances, with the result that social cohesion is ultimately reestablished (1973 [1956]:2):

> What I am saying is that these conflicting loyalties and divisions of allegiance tend to inhibit the development of open quarrelling, and that the greater the division in one area of society, the greater is likely to be the cohesion in a wider range of relationships—*provided that there is a general need for peace, and recognition of a moral order in which this peace can flourish.* (Gluckman 1973 [1956]:25, my emphasis)

In Tanzania Kurialand today, it is easy to demonstrate "a general need for peace," but increasingly difficult to perceive what Gluckman referred to as the "recognition of a moral order in which this peace can flourish," for what one sees in its place is the increasing triumph of atomization over cohesion. Although Kuria linkages, both direct and indirect, with the world beyond, even far beyond, the local community are indisputably multiplying and expanding at a rapid rate, cohesion within the local community is being severely strained by market-oriented cattle raiding, and perhaps it is even breaking down.

Hendrickson et al. (1996) are guilty of romanticizing "traditional" livestock raiding when, in their zeal to distinguish new forms of livestock raiding among the pastoral Turkana of Kenya from older ones, they employ the term "redistributive raiding" to refer to raiding oriented toward subsistence uses and "predatory raiding" to refer to raiding oriented toward the cash market[1]—because raiding for livestock has always been predatory and, indeed, killing members of the group being raided has often been one of the goals of a raid. When they describe so-called redistributive raids as "internal conflicts, occurring between actors practising the same activity (subsistence pastoralism)," and predatory raiding as "an external activity, occurring between actors who practice different kinds of activities (between pastoralists and 'entrepreneurs' motivated largely by economic gain)," Hendrickson et al. (1996:22) are much more nearly on target—but one ought not lose sight of the fact that, if not among the Turkana then most certainly among the Kuria, young men engaging in

---

1. Spencer more usefully employs the term *predatory* in connection with livestock raiding in distinguishing between what he describes as the "two co-existing modes of production" among pastoralist societies in precolonial times, that is, the "predatory" mode, which "depended heavily on the exploits of young men as successful raiders to augment their herds," and the "pastoralist" mode, which "depended on peaceful husbandry, controlled by the older men as individual stock owners" (1984:68).

subsistence agropastoralism by day not infrequently status-shift into enterprising raiding entrepreneurs at night.

Colonialism introduced and imposed the money economy, established a money market in cattle, and created new links between Kurialand and the world at large. The colonialists suppressed warfare, outlawing indigenous mechanisms of self-help in the process, and opened the door wide to the emergence of the multiclan, multiethnic cattle-raiding gang. By erecting what was to become the Tanzania/Kenya border and dividing the Kuria population in two, colonialism made possible an illicit transnational trade in cattle that the Kuria were enviably situated to profit from. There can be no question that, by radically altering the structure of constraints and opportunities within which Kuria operated, colonialism and capitalism set the stage for the transformation in the nature, conduct, and character of Kuria cattle raiding that has been described in this volume.

But to overlook the reality that many young Kuria men moved with alacrity to avail themselves of the new opportunities, while many other young Kuria men did not, is to deny human agency. Notwithstanding the patronizing talk frequently heard among educated non-Kuria in Tanzania about the Kuria being "backward" and tradition-bound, the fact remains that the Kuria have been in the past, and continue to be in the present, adroit and energetic in seizing the opportunities afforded them by both the actions and inaction of the colonial and postcolonial states. During the colonial period, they joined the police force and army in large numbers, mined for gold in the region's gold mines, and labored for wages on plantations in Kenya. In the aftermath of independence, the Kuria made the Tanzanian military their own.

It was this last accomplishment, of course, expressive not merely of Kuria opportunism but of their core masculine values, that not only enabled many Kuria men to forge valiant army careers, but also made it possible for some unknown number among them to respond decisively and aggressively when, during the 1978–79 war with Uganda, the opportunity to smuggle weapons back into Tanzania for use in cattle raiding knocked.

The decision to become a cattle raider is a matter of personal choice, although, as we have seen, it is, by an overwhelming margin, young men who are culturally and economically disadvantaged—that is, they are sister-poor—who elect to follow this path. Nonetheless, they follow it, notwithstanding the fact that low-technology gold mining is also open to them. Residing in villages that are raided by other gangs as well as by the ones that they themselves belong to, they cannot possibly, as Heald (forthcoming) correctly notes, be unaware of the misery and hardship that raiding inflicts on their neighbors, yet they choose, in spite of this, to carry on with it anyway.

State-sponsored vigilantism, in the form of *Sungusungu,* represents a feeble attempt on the part of the Tanzanian state to stem the violence and disorder wrought by market-oriented cattle theft without expending much in the way of resources to do it. A key incentive for the state in lending either its tacit or overt approval to vigilante efforts is cost (Huggins 1991:12; Bukurura 1996:263). The ratio of police officers to population in Tanzania is said to be 1:10,000 (*Daily News* 30 May 1989 and Nyalali 1990:16, both cited in Bukurura 1996:263), and so, like sheriffs forming posses of citizens to chase down outlaws in America's Old West (Kowalewski 1982:83), the government in effect "deputizes" local people and sets them to work fighting "crime" on the cheap, bypassing the lethargic, corrupt "formal" law-enforcement system.

Sungusungu in its state-sponsored manifestation also provides a number of significant advantages and benefits to local people, enabling them to dispense, for all intents and purposes, with the costly and inefficient, and corrupt services of the police, whom many villagers dismiss as "useless." In their place, it provides them with "law enforcers" who are of the community and accountable to it. It dramatically reduces their own out-of-pocket costs of law enforcement, because the fees paid to *Sungusungu* are lower than the bribes for service habitually demanded by the police, and because all fees and fines collected by *Sungusungu* remain within the community, not only to finance the work of *Sungusungu* but also to carry out other worthy village projects. And, lastly, it enables local people to punish their fellow villagers who have transgressed the law—their friends and neighbors—by administering beatings, levying fines, and exacting compensation, but without handing them over to the formal justice system.

Sungusungu as it functions and operates among the Tanzania Kuria today reflects the deep ambivalence that is felt by many Kuria people, less toward the phenomenon of cattle raiding in general, which they overwhelmingly condemn, than toward how to respond appropriately to the cattle raiders whom they know to be living in their midst. Their ambivalence reflects, in large part, the perceived economic and social costs of actively opposing cattle raiding by fellow villagers who are bound to them by ties of friendship and kinship. Although strong sentiment exists among Kuria people throughout Tarime District in favor of killing invading cattle raiders from outside the village if they are caught in the act, sentiment varies from area to area within the district with regard to how to deal most appropriately with cattle-raiding "insiders." In the villages of the Tarime highlands—that is, those villages most heavily committed to agriculture, particularly cash-crop agriculture, and where formal education and missionization have made the greatest inroads—torching the homes of known or suspected cattle raiders and forcibly expelling them from the village or, albeit much less frequently, lynching them, is the norm, while in Nyaheiya and other lowland villages—that is, those least invested in agriculture, whose populations are less well-educated and Christianized, and where the subsistence cattle economy still thrives—administering whippings to known or suspected resident cattle raiders and admonishing them not to steal again is the preferred form of deterrence. The fact that the Kuria people generally, both in Tanzania and in Kenya (Heald forthcoming), continue to display a measure of tolerance toward the cattle raiders in their midst that has not been characteristic of certain other ethnic groups known to have inflicted much harsher penalties[2] strongly suggests that beyond economics and the diagnostics of "modernization," culturally significant values are also at play here.

The world of the Tanzania Kuria today is not being shaped by government nearly to the extent that officials would like to think. Although the state is striving, lamely, to impose its own brand of order in Nyaheiya and Tarime District's other Kuria villages, the cattle raiders who live in those villages are resisting those efforts, and local people are mediating between them, struggling to find some viable third way. As the area's cattle herd is being relentlessly "raided out," however, and as cattle per capita declines inexorably, the people of Nyaheiya and of other Kuria communities are becoming poorer.

---

2. Heald's (forthcoming) account of a Luo man, in Kenya, who wondered aloud to her why the Kuria have failed to resolve the cattle-theft problem as his community did—by dousing the cattle thieves with kerosene and setting them on fire—is chillingly informative on this score.

A Note on the Study

The field research on which this book is based was carried out in the low-land area of Tarime District, in northern Tanzania, in a Kuria village—pseudonymously renamed Nyaheiya—of the Nyamongo clan during the nineteen-month period from August 1994 to March 1996, followed by a month-long period of archival research in the Tanzania National Archives, in Dar es Salaam. An ensemble of research strategies was employed in the research, including participant observation; a homestead survey; lengthy personal interviews, primarily with active or recently active cattle raiders and their kin; and shorter, generally informal interviews with local officials, policemen, livestock officers, victims of cattle raids, and other relevant parties. Numerous documentary sources were also utilized, including, but by no means limited to, cattle censuses, police reports, agricultural and rainfall statistics, and archival materials. All the Kuria people referred to by name in this volume are identified pseudonymously—the sole exceptions being the especially notorious cattle raiders of the 1980s, referred to in chapter 5—but villages other than Nyaheiya, the primary field site, are identified by their real names with the exception of Ekeng'ooro, a village of the Irege clan, whose real name has also been veiled by a pseudonym. All other place-names in this book are true ones.

The Homestead Survey

Nyaheiya village comprises 350 homesteads, 190 of which were randomly surveyed, this number having been selected for the purpose of ensuring a confidence interval of 5 percent (Bernard 1988:105). In accordance with the sampling procedure outlined by Bernard (1988:107–9), a map of the village was drawn and divided into "random chunks of different sizes" with the aid of a random-numbers table, which was then used to select out 10 of those random chunks for interviewing (Bernard 1988:107); after every homestead in each of those 10 chunks had been identified and assigned a number, a random sample of homesteads to be surveyed was drawn, with an identical number of them drawn from each chunk.

A certain number of minor mistakes was unavoidable owing to the frequent absence of distinguishing landmarks in the grassy village terrain and the crudeness of the hand-drawn map, which sometimes made it a judgment call as to which of two adjoining "wildly uneven spaces" (Bernard 1989:107) on the map represented the proper location of a particular homestead.

At every homestead randomly selected for surveying, a conscientious effort was made to interview the homestead head. Where this was not possible—because the homestead head was either deceased, in jail, or simply unavailable after three unsuccessful attempts to contact him—then another resident of the homestead was asked to stand in for him—that is, either a wife, a widow, a son, or a daughter. Out of the 190 respondents who contributed their time and knowledge to the survey, 58—or 31 percent—of them were stand-ins. Of these 58 stand-ins, 32—or 55 percent—of them were females, and 26—or 45 percent—of them were males.

The survey consists of 117 questions, many of them having multiple parts. For those survey questions that concern the homestead generally (e.g., "Is your land sufficient for supporting your family?" or "How many cattle are in your cattle enclosure?"), statistics derived from the answers to these questions should be validly representative of all of the homesteads in Nyaheiya within a confidence interval of 5 percent.

The survey includes other questions, however, that ask the respondent to provide a personal opinion (e.g., "How would you rate police effectiveness in coping with the cattle-thieving problem in this area?") that may or may not be shared by other members of the homestead and that therefore cannot be taken as representative of the village population at large, numbering an estimated 2,232 people. Wherever answers to a personal-opinion question, such as the one just quoted, are referred to or tabulated in this volume, therefore, the reader should bear in mind that the tabulated answers to a personal-opinion question cannot be regarded as a statistically meaningful reflection of the opinions of the entire population of Nyaheiya. One might ask oneself, however, how many of the purported ethnographic "facts" contained in any ethnography—including this one—came to be accepted by a researcher as factual and published as factual only after having been subjected to the scrutiny of 190 different informants, whatever the manner of their selection may have been.

The police-effectiveness question just referred to is a case in point: asked to select from among four alternatives ranging from "extremely effective" to "ineffective," 93.2 percent of the survey respondents condemned police performance as "ineffective." Let the reader rest assured that even if this question were posed to every adult in Nyaheiya, this overwhelming indictment of police performance would not be meaningfully contradicted.

Foreign-Language Words

With the exception of a very few Nandi and Maasai words employed in chapter 1, all foreign-language words used in this book are either Kuria words or Swahili words, and all are accompanied by their English-language equivalent on every page where they are used. Since the vast majority of these foreign words are Kuria words, the Kuria words have been identified in the text as foreign words only by being italicized, but have not been explicitly identified as Kuria words as such. Swahili words, on the other hand, in addition to being italicized, are all either accompanied by the abbreviation "Swa." or are explicitly identified as Swahili words in the text.

For Kuria orthography and definitions, I have followed Muniko et al. 1996 wherever possible, relying on the "Kuria-English Dictionary" produced by the Maryknoll Language School, in Musoma, Tanzania (Anonymous n.d.), and on information provided by Kuria informants whenever Muniko et al. seemed lacking. There is as yet no standard orthography for Kuria, and, as a consequence, the same Kuria word has often been spelled differently by different writers; even Muniko et al. not infrequently provide alternative spellings.

Kuria is a Bantu language that frequently employs prefixes to alter the meaning of a word. Abakuria (or abaKuria), for example, refers to a plural number of Kuria, or to the entire Kuria people. The singular form, denoting a single Kuria individual, is umuKuria. The area, land, country, or place where the Kuria live is buKuria. Their language is igiKuria.

Similarly, the people of the Nyamongo clan, the Kuria clan with whose people and area this book is largely concerned, are denoted, in the Kuria language, by the plural form, that is, abaNyamongo (or Abanyamongo). An individual member of the abaNyamongo is umuNyamongo. The territory the clan occupies is buNyamongo.

For the purposes of this work, all such words have been anglicized and the distinguishing prefixes omitted: thus, this work makes references to the Kuria people, a Kuria person, Kurialand or Kuria country, and the Kuria language. In those cases where proper nouns like Kuria and Nyamongo are used without a specific, accompanying referent, care has been taken to ensure that the referent is clear from the context in which the word is used.

Cattle Ownership

An important caveat is in order here involving the question of cattle ownership. In 1995—or, to be more accurate, during the two-week period in 1995 when a careful count was undertaken—there were about 5,800 head of cattle in Nyaheiya, divided among the central cattle corrals of some 150 of the village's 350 homesteads, but the Kuria system of stock associate-ship (*ogosagaria*), or "putting out cattle for others to mind," makes it impossible to determine how many cattle any individual man owns or how many of the cattle in his corral are actually his.

Under the *ogosagaria* system, a homestead head routinely lends out some of his animals to other stock owners and/or nonowners, both as a means of spreading the risk of stock losses owing to disease and theft and as a means of fostering ties with others. A cattle owner might, for example, place a total of twenty of his cattle in the enclosures of friends and relatives while at the same time taking into his own corral a larger, smaller, or iden-tical number of cattle belonging to some wholly different, or only partly different, assortment of people.

Generally speaking, a man puts out with others more or less the same number of cattle that others have put out with him, but there is no hard and fast rule. One trusted informant maintained some 120 head of cattle in his own enclosure, including 12 head of cattle that had been put out with him by others, while putting out 32 head with stock associates. This indi-vidual thus owned (120 − 12 + 32 =) 140 head of cattle, but counting the animals in his cattle corral would not have revealed this.

"An old man may have 100 cows in his cattle enclosure," this infor-mant explained. "He may tend them, care for them, and pay taxes on them—yet none of them may be his. Another man may have 5 cows in his cattle enclosure and own them all."

Complicating this matter further is that people living in the more heavily populated, more intensively cultivated highland areas, where pas-tureland for livestock is in short supply, will ofttimes put out entire herds of cattle with stock associates or kin in the lowlands, in villages such as Nyaheiya, where grazing is plentiful, while, at the same time, cattle owners in the lowland villages will often put out some or all of their cattle in other lowland villages that they deem to be better insulated, by virtue of their location, from the threat of cattle raids.

What all this means is that when we speak of the Nyaheiya cattle pop-ulation, we are really referring *not* to the number of cattle that the people of Nyaheiya actually *own,* but simply to the number of cattle residing within Nyaheiya's borders at the time a cattle count was carried out. Sim-ilarly, when we speak of a man as having a certain number of cattle, or as having a certain number of cattle in his homestead's corral, or as having lost a certain number of cattle in a cattle raid, we are really referring to the number of cattle of which that man is (or was) the custodian, and *not,* in all likelihood, to the number of cattle that he himself owns. Throughout this volume, therefore, people who have custody of cattle are termed cattle "holders," *not* cattle "owners."

In discussions of responses to the homestead survey, a distinction is sometimes made between respondents who claimed to have cattle in their own cattle enclosure (or corral) and those who are described as having claimed to "possess" cattle, meaning that they claimed ownership of a cattle herd, of whatever size (i.e., even a "herd" consisting of a single animal), no matter where, or in how many different places, the animals themselves might be located. Since the number of respondents claiming to "possess" cattle (i.e., to have a "herd") includes both those who claimed to have cattle in their own corral *and* those who claimed only to have cattle put out with others, the total number of these so-called possessors is necessarily larger than the number of respondents who claimed only to have cattle put out with others but no cattle whatsoever in their own corral.

Bibliography

Abrahams, Ray
  1987   Sungusungu: Village vigilante groups in Tanzania. *African Affairs*
         86:179–96.
Abuso, Paul Asaka
  1974   The evolution of the Kuria society. Staff seminar paper. Department
         of History, University of Nairobi.
  1980   *A traditional history of the Abakuria c. A.D. 1400–1914.* Nairobi: Kenya
         Literature Bureau.
Almagor, Uri
  1979   Raiders and elders: A confrontation of generations among the Das-
         sanetch. In *Warfare among East African herders,* edited by Katsuyoshi
         Fukui and David Turton, 119–45. Osaka: National Museum of Eth-
         nology.
Anacleti, A. O.
  1979   Historia ya wizi wa ng'ombe Mara Kaskazini 1900–1978. Unpublished
         typescript.
Anderson, David
  1986   Stock theft and moral economy in colonial Kenya. *Africa* 56 (4):
         399–415.
Anonymous
  n.d.   Kuria-English dictionary. Musoma, Tanzania: Maryknoll Language
         School.
Avirgan, Tony, and Martha Honey
  1982   *War in Uganda: The legacy of Idi Amin.* Dar es Salaam: Tanzania Pub-
         lishing House Ltd.
Baker, E. C.
  1935   The Bakuria of North Mara Tarime, Tanganyika Territory. Manu-
         script. Rhodes House Library, Oxford.
Bamforth, Douglas B.
  1994   Indigenous people, indigenous violence: Precontact warfare on the
         North American Great Plains. *Man* 29 (1): 95–115.
Baxter, P. T. W.
  1979   Boran age-sets and warfare. In *Warfare among East African herders,*
         edited by Katsuyoshi Fukui and David Turton, 69–95. Osaka:
         National Museum of Ethnology.
Berman, Bruce J.
  1997   [1991] Nationalism, ethnicity, and modernity: The paradox of Mau
         Mau. In *Perspectives on Africa: A reader in culture, history, and repre-*

sentation, edited by Roy Richard Grinker and Christopher B. Steiner, 653–70. Cambridge, MA: Blackwell.

Bernard, H. Russell
1988 *Research methods in cultural anthropology.* Newbury Park: Sage Publications.

Berntsen, John L.
1979a Maasai age-sets and prophetic leadership: 1850–1910. *Africa* 49 (2): 134–46.
1979b Pastoralism, raiding and prophets: Maasailand in the nineteenth century. Ph.D. dissertation. University of Wisconsin.

Binagi, Lloyd A.
1976 Marriage among the Kuria. *Mila* 5 (1): 13–23.

Blick, Jeffrey B.
1988 Genocidal warfare in tribal societies as a result of European-induced culture conflict. *Man,* n.s., 23:654–70.

Bukurura, Sufian Hemed
1994 The maintenance of order in rural Tanzania: The case of Sungusungu. *Journal of Legal Pluralism and Unofficial Law* 34:1–29.
1996 Combating crime among the Sukuma and Namwezi of west-central Tanzania. *Crime, Law and Social Change* 24:257–66.

Chintowa, Paul
1995 Tanzania-agriculture: Losses mount as cattle disease spreads. Harare: Inter Press Third World News Agency.

Cory, Hans
1945 Kuria law and custom. Manuscript re-edited by E. B. Dobson, 1952. The Cory Collection. University of Dar es Salaam.
1947 Land tenure in Bukuria. *Tanganyika Notes and Records* 23:70–79.

Dyson-Hudson, Neville
1966 *Karimojong politics.* Oxford: Clarendon.

Evangelou, Phylo
1984 *Livestock development in Kenya's Maasailand: Pastoralists' transition to a market economy.* Boulder: Westview.

Evans-Pritchard, E. E.
1940 *The Nuer: A description of the modes of livelihood and political institutions of a Nilotic people.* Oxford: Clarendon.

Ferguson, R. Brian
1990 Blood of the leviathan: Western contact and warfare in Amazonia. *American Ethnologist* 17 (2): 237–57.

Fleisher, Michael L.
1997 Kuria cattle raiding: A case study in the capitalist transformation of an East African sociocultural institution. Ph.D. dissertation. University of Michigan.
1998 Cattle raiding and its correlates: The cultural-ecological consequences of market-oriented cattle raiding among the Kuria of Tanzania. *Human Ecology* 26 (4): 547–72.

Fratkin, Elliot
> 1979 A comparison of the role of prophets in Samburu and Maasai warfare. In *Warfare among East African herders,* edited by Katsuyoshi Fukui and David Turton, 53–67. Osaka: National Museum of Ethnology.

Gluckman, Max
> 1973 [1956] The peace in the feud. In *Custom and conflict in Africa,* by Max Gluckman, 1–26. New York: Harper and Row.

Goldschmidt, Walter
> 1974 The economics of brideprice among the Sebei and in East Africa. *Ethnology* 13:311–31.

Griffiths, J. E. S.
> 1938 Masai cattle auction. *Tanganyika Notes and Records* 6:99–101.

Gulliver, P. H.
> 1955 *The family herds: A study of two pastoral tribes in East Africa, the Jie and Turkana.* London: Routledge and Kegan Paul.

Hathout, S. A.
> 1983 *Soil atlas of Tanzania.* Dar es Salaam: Tanzania Publishing House.

Heald, Suzette
> n.d. Tolerating the intolerable: Cattle raiding among the Kuria of Kenya. In *The meanings of violence,* edited by G. Aijmer and J. Abbink (forthcoming).

Heald, Suzette, ed.
> 1997 *Praise poems of the Kuria.* Nairobi: Phoenix Publishers.

Hendrickson, Dylan, Robin Mearns, and Jeremy Armon
> 1996 Livestock raiding among the pastoral Turkana of Kenya: Redistribution, predation and the links to famine. *IDS Bulletin* 27 (3): 17–30.

Homer-Dixon, Thomas F.
> 1991 On the threshold: Environmental changes as causes of acute conflict. *International Security* 16 (2): 76–116.

Huggins, Martha K.
> 1991 Introduction: Vigilantism and the state—A look south and north. In *Vigilantism and the state in modern Latin America: Essays on extralegal violence,* edited by Martha K. Huggins, 1–18. New York: Praeger.

Huntingford, G. W. B.
> 1953 *The Nandi of Kenya: Tribal control in a pastoral society.* London: Routledge and Kegan Paul.

Iliffe, John
> 1979 *A modern history of Tanganyika.* Cambridge: Cambridge University Press.

Jacobs, Alan H.
> 1975 Maasai pastoralism in historical perspective. In *Pastoralism in tropical Africa,* edited by Theodore Monod, 406–22. London: Oxford University Press.
> 1979 Maasai inter-tribal relations: Belligerent herdsmen or peaceful pastoralists? In *Warfare among East African herders,* edited by Katsuyoshi

Fukui and David Turton, 33–52. Osaka: National Museum of Ethnology.

Kaplan, Robert D.
  1994 The coming anarchy. *Atlantic Monthly* 273 (2): 44–46, 48–49, 52, 54, 58–60, 62–63, 66, 68–70, 72–76.

Keeley, Lawrence
  1996 *War before civilization.* New York: Oxford University Press.

Kelly, Raymond C.
  1985 *The Nuer conquest: The structure and development of an expansionist system.* Ann Arbor: University of Michigan Press.

King, Kenneth
  1996 *Jua kali: Change and development in an informal economy.* London: James Currey.

Kitching, Gavin
  1980 *Class and economic change in Kenya: The making of an African petite bourgeoisie, 1905–1970.* New Haven: Yale University Press.

Kjerland, Kirsten Alsaker
  1995 Cattle breed; shillings don't: The belated incorporation of the abaKuria into modern Kenya. Ph.D. dissertation. University of Bergen.

Kjerland, Kirsten Alsaker, and Ann-Britt Svensson
  1988 *Ibicha Bigikuria gukurua ko mooka go 1904/Kuria pictures from 1904.* South Nyanza: Gosi Cultural Centre/Maranatha Mission of Kenya.

Kowalewski, David
  1982 Establishment vigilantism and political dissent. *Armed Forces and Society* 9 (1): 83–97.

Lancaster, William
  1981 *The Rwala Bedouin today.* Cambridge: Cambridge University Press.

MacGaffey, Janet
  1991 *The real economy of Zaire: The contribution of smuggling and other unofficial activities to national wealth.* Philadelphia: University of Pennsylvania Press.

Macharia, Kinuthia
  1997 *Social and political dynamics of the informal economy in African cities: Nairobi and Harare.* Lanham, MD: University Press of America.

Mair, L.
  1974 *African societies.* Cambridge: Cambridge University Press.

Mesaki, Simeon.
  1994 Witch-killing in Sukumaland. In *Witchcraft in contemporary Tanzania,* edited by Ray Abrahams, 47–60. Cambridge: African Studies Centre, University of Cambridge.

Moffett, J. P.
  1958 *Handbook of Tanganyika.* Dar es Salaam: Government Printer.

Moore, Sally Falk, and Paul Puritt
  1977 *The Chagga and Meru of Tanzania.* London: International African Institute.

Muniko, S. M., B. Muita oMagige, and M. J. Ruel, eds.
  1996   *Kuria-English Dictionary.* London: International African Institute.
Murmann, Carsten
  1974   *Change and development in East African cattle husbandry: A study of four societies during the colonial period.* Copenhagen: Akademisk Forlag.
Prazak, Miroslava
  1992   Cultural expressions of socioeconomic differentiation among the Kuria of Kenya. Ph.D. dissertation. Yale University.
Rigby, Peter
  1985   *Persistent pastoralists: Nomadic societies in transition.* London: Zed Books.
Ruel, Malcolm J.
  1958   Sociological study—Kuria: Notes on cattle and bridewealth amongst the Kuria. Unpublished typescript.
  1959   The social organisation of the Kuria: A field-work report. Unpublished manuscript. Institute of African Studies, University of Nairobi.
  1962   Kuria generation classes. *Africa* 32 (1): 14–37.
  1991   Kuria seers. *Africa* 61 (3): 343–52.
Rwezaura, Barthazar Aloys
  1985   *Traditional family law and change in Tanzania: A study of the Kuria social system.* Baden-Baden: Nomos Verlagsgesellschaft.
Schneider, Harold K.
  1981   *The Africans: An ethnological account.* Englewood Cliffs: Prentice-Hall.
Seba, Magoigo Masubo
  1985   Outlines of the origin and social organisation of Kuria people. Nyanza Province Cultural Festival Symposium paper. Institute of African Studies, University of Nairobi.
Sillery, A.
  n.d.   Working backwards. Unpublished manuscript. Rhodes House Library, Oxford.
Smith, Andrew B.
  1992   *Pastoralism in Africa: Origins and development ecology.* London: Hurst and Company.
Spencer, Paul
  1973   *Nomads in alliance: Symbiosis and growth among the Rendille and Samburu of Kenya.* London: Oxford University Press.
  1984   Pastoralists and the ghost of capitalism. *Production Pastorale et Société* 15:61–76.
Sweet, Louise E.
  1965a   Camel raiding of North Arabian Bedouin: A mechanism of ecological adaptation. *American Anthropologist* 67 (5): 1132–50.
  1965b   Camel pastoralism in North Arabia and the minimal camping unit. In *Man, culture, and animals: The role of animals in human ecological adjustments,* edited by Anthony Leeds and Andrew P. Vayda, 129–52.

Washington, DC: American Association for the Advancement of Science.

Tanner, R. E. S.
1966   Cattle theft in Musoma, 1958–59. *Tanzania Notes and Records* 65:31–42.

Tobisson, Eva
1986   *Family dynamics among the Kuria: Agro-pastoralists in northern Tanzania.* Goteborg, Sweden: Acta Universitatis Gothoburgensis.

Too, Philip, and Benedict Ngetich
1998   10,000 people flee Marakwet. *Daily Nation on the Web* 6 May 1998.

Too, Philip, and George Omonso
1998   Eight feared dead in raid. *Daily Nation on the Web* 2 May 1998.

Turnbull, Colin
1972   *The mountain people.* New York: Simon and Schuster.

Van Creveld, Martin
1991   *The transformation of war.* New York: Free Press.

Vayda, Andrew P.
1968   Hypotheses about functions of war. In *War: The anthropology of armed conflict and aggression,* edited by Morton Fried, Marvin Harris, and Robert Murphy, 85–91. New York: Natural History Press.

Were, Gideon S.
1969   The Western Bantu peoples from A.D. 1300 to 1800. In *Zamani: A survey of East African history,* edited by B. A. Ogot and J. A. Kieran, 177–97. Nairobi: East African Publishing House and Longmans.

Winter, E. H.
1962   Livestock markets among the Iraqw of northern Tanganyika. In *Markets in Africa,* edited by Paul Bohannan and George Dalton, 457–68. Evanston: Northwestern University Press.

World Bank
1995   *World tables 1995.* Baltimore and London: Johns Hopkins University Press.

Tanzania National Archives

TNA 13747 [Secretariat] 7/26/29: Extract from a note taken at a meeting at Arusha between the territorial governor of Tanganyika and the combined Associations of Arusha.

TNA 13747 [Secretariat] 4/8/30: File entry.

TNA 13747 [Secretariat] 5/22/30: Letter, R. B. Jones, District Officer, Musoma, to the Provincial Commissioner, Mwanza.

TNA 13747 [Secretariat] 10/3/31: Letter, Provincial Commissioner, Mwanza and Bukoba, written while "On Safari, North Mara, Musoma," to the Chief Secretary, Dar es Salaam.

TNA 13747 [Secretariat] 9/24/31: Memorandum, "On the administration of Tribes on Kenya-Tanganyika Border (Nyanza-Mwanza)," signed by the Provincial

Commissioner, Mwanza, and the Acting Provincial Commissioner, Nyanza.

TNA 13747 [Secretariat] 10/18/31: Letter, Council of Kuria, Tarime, to the Governor, Dar es Salaam, "through the hand of the District Officer, Musoma."

TNA 13747 [Secretariat] 10/29/31: E. C. Baker, District Officer, Musoma, "Report of Stock Thieving in Bukuria."

TNA 13747 [Secretariat] 11/2/31: Letter, Provincial Commissioner, Mwanza and Bukoba Provinces, to the Chief Secretary, Dar es Salaam.

TNA 13747 [Secretariat] 12/19/31: File entry.

TNA 13747 [Secretariat] 2/26/32: Report, "Stock Theft & Kindred Offences," from McMahon, District Officer, Musoma, to the Provincial Commissioner, Mwanza and Bukoba.

TNA 13747 [Secretariat] 12/22/32 (a): Letter, McMahon, District Officer, Musoma, to the Provincial Commissioner, Lake Province, Mwanza.

TNA 13747 [Secretariat] 12/22/32 (b): Sillery, A., and F. A. Montague, Assistant District Officers, Musoma, "Memorandum on Stock-Theft in North Mara" [attachment to TNA 13747 (Secretariat) 12/2/32 (a), above].

TNA 23426 [Secretariat] 1936: "Note on a Conference held in the Chief Justice's Chambers in Dar es Salaam on the 27th March, 1936, to discuss means of ameliorating the position with regard to stock theft in North Mara."

TNA 23426 [Secretariat] 4/18/36: Letter, McMahon, Acting Provincial Commissioner, Lake Province, to the Chief Secretary, Dar es Salaam.

TNA 23426 [Secretariat] 7/15/36: File entry, A. Sillery, "North Mara: Stock Theft and the Organisation of the Sub-District."

TNA 20/g/11 [Accession 83] 1/14/43: Letter, District Commissioner, Musoma, to the Provincial Commissioner, Lake Province, Mwanza, with "Musoma District: Annual Report, 1942," attached.

TNA 20/g/11 [Accession 83] 12/21/43: Letter, Assistant District Officer, North Mara, to the District Commissioner, Musoma, with "Notes for Annual Report 1943" attached.

TNA 20/g/11 [Accession 83] n.d.: District Officer, North Mara, "Annual Report on North Mara for the Year 1944."

TNA 20/g/11 [Accession 83] 1/2/46: District Officer, North Mara, "Notes for Annual Report, 1945—North Mara."

TNA 20/g/11 [Accession 83] 12/28/46: G. Winnington-Ingram, Assistant District Officer, North Mara, "North Mara Division Annual Report for 1946."

TNA 36704 [Secretariat] 9/18/47: Letter, N. R. Reid, Acting Director of Veterinary Services, Department of Veterinary Science and Animal Husbandry, Mpwapwa, to the Chief Secretary to the Government, Dar es Salaam.

TNA 36704 [Secretariat] 11/26/47: Letter, under the heading "Meat Supply to Troops in East Africa," signed Lt. Col. T. Spinks (for Major-General, Director of Supplies and Transport), the War Office, Northumberland Avenue, London, to the Under Secretary of State, the Colonial Office, Downing Street, London, with "Extract from Colonial Primary Products Committee Interim Report" attached.

TNA 36704 [Secretariat] 1/16/48: Letter, N. R. Reid, Director of Veterinary Services, Department of Veterinary Science and Animal Husbandry, Mpwapwa, to the Member for Agricultural and Natural Resources, the Secretariat, Dar es Salaam, with "Notes on the Problem of Slaughter Stock Supplies" attached.

TNA 36704 [Secretariat] 2/10/48: "[E]xtract from the minutes of the Provincial Commissioners' Conference held at Tabora in January 1948."

TNA 36704 [Secretariat] 2/16/48: Extract from minutes.

TNA 36704 [Secretariat] 3/17/48: R. W. R. Miller, Member for Agriculture and Natural Resources, "Memorandum No. 26 for Executive Council: Meat Supplies."

TNA 39092 [Secretariat] 7/14/49: Letter, Directory of Veterinary Services, Department of Veterinary Science and Animal Husbandry, Mpwapwa, to the Member for Agriculture and Natural Resources, the Secretariat, Dar es Salaam.

TNA 6/46 [Accession 83] 2/18/50: Memorandum, Assistant Superintendant of Police, Tarime, North Mara, to the District Commissioner, Tarime, North Mara.

TNA 1/65 [Accession 83] 1/9/51: Letter, District Commissioner, North Mara, to the Provincial Commissioner, Lake Province, Mwanza, with amended "Crime" graph for the years 1940–1950, for inclusion in "Annual Report 1950," attached.

TNA 41672 [Secretariat] 4/3/51: Letter, R. de Z. Hall, Member for Local Government, to the Provincial Commssioner, Lake Province, Mwanza.

TNA 6/46 [Accession 83] 2/5/53: Letter, under the heading "Subj: Cattle Raiding," District Commissioner, Musoma, to the District Commissioner, North Mara.

TNA 6/46 [Accession 83] 7/5/53: Telegram, under the heading "Compensation for Raid on Masai: February 24th/25th," District Commissioner, Narok, Masai District, Kenya, to the District Commissioner, Tarime, Tanganyika Territory.

Index